UNIVERSITY OF CALIFORNIA
BIBLIOGRAPHIC GUIDES

UNIVERSITY OF CALIFORNIA BIBLIOGRAPHIC GUIDES

J. Richard Blanchard and Harald Ostvold: *Literature of Agricultural Research*

Ann Phillips Basart: *Serial Music: A Classified Bibliography of Writings on Twelve-Tone and Electronic Music*

Claire John Eschelbach and Joyce Lee Shober: *Aldous Huxley: A Bibliography 1916–1959*

SOURCES OF

BUSINESS INFORMATION

by Edwin T. Coman, Jr.

REVISED EDITION

UNIVERSITY OF CALIFORNIA PRESS

BERKELEY AND LOS ANGELES 1964

University of California Press
Berkeley and Los Angeles, California

Cambridge University Press
London, England

To My Wife

PREFACE TO
THE SECOND EDITION

Business has always been subject to uncertainties and change. It is affected by the elements, by wars, by mass movements, by changes in the wants and desires of consumers, and by governmental regulation. Above all, competition tends continually to modify the business structure. New methods, new products, and new processes introduce new elements that undermine the supremacy of one industry or firm or even a whole system of doing business. And the trend toward increasing regulation of business by governmental bodies here and abroad must not be ignored. In short, one generalization that truly applies to all business is: Change is continuous and inevitable.

The competitive struggle extends to individuals, too; no business can rise higher than its leaders. Individuals who are actively engaged in business and who aspire either to improve their own concerns or to assume a position on the policymaking level in another organization must be aware of current trends and developments. The author has observed how costly the trial-and-error method can be to business. The writings on business, however, have grown to such proportions within the past twenty years that the businessman with a basic knowledge of where and how to search for information can draw on the accumulated experience and research of thousands of firms and individuals.

The purpose of this book is to provide him with the means both of locating that elusive statistic or essential bit of information to answer a specific problem, and of gaining a broad picture of the business situation that will enable him to evaluate his own position. Furthermore, he is given the key to many storehouses of information—public libraries, special libraries, and the reference sources presented in yearbooks and handbooks. A second aim is to enable the ambitious young person to locate sources of knowledge that will help him in preparing for a more responsible job.

The works cited may be termed *basic*. By no means do they exhaust all publications that deal with each phase of business activity, but it is felt that a carefully selected set of working tools will be more helpful to the reader than an enormous mass of references without critical comments. The author also presents simple research methods and points out how resources such as libraries, trade associations, and the chamber of commerce in a locality can be used for securing needed data.

The arrangement of the material in this book is itself an aid to the user. Bibliographies to consult in locating information on each topic are presented at the beginning of each chapter. They are followed by works that contain the largest amount of data in one volume. Certain authoritative handbooks that compress a large number of facts in one volume are included because they do not become out of date as rapidly as more specialized works. Yearbooks and annual summary numbers of periodicals are stressed, since they are frequently the best sources of current business information. Trade magazines, supplementary bulletins, and other publications that keep these annual volumes current are next in order, followed by books and magazines that treat the topic from the broad, general viewpoint. Finally, the rather specialized phases of a given business activity are presented and sources of information on them provided.

The user of this book probably will not become an accomplished research worker, but by thoughtfully observing the suggestions and comments made he should be able to work through his problems in the field of business publications with a minimum of wasted effort and time.

Within the past fourteen years since this book was first published, there has been a tremendous increase in the number of business publications. So many of these works are of such high quality as to make selection difficult; one is tempted to list too many titles. But then this book would become a checklist, and would be thereby less helpful to the user.

The activities of many capable librarians in schools of business and in special libraries have resulted in a marked increase in the number of excellent bibliographies and checklists. Many of these have been published by the Special Libraries Association and have made the literature of business much easier to locate and to utilize than formerly.

Another development of the last decade is the publishing of bibliographies, indexes, and abstracts as a commercial enterprise. These range from those devoted to a particular field of business to those covering all aspects of business activity. Most of these publications operate on a current basis and, therefore, make the locating and evaluating of material much quicker and easier.

The revision of this book was simplified by the help and suggestions of my fellow librarians. I am indebted to Mr. Donald T. Clark (formerly librarian of the Harvard Graduate School of Business Administration, now University librarian, University of California, Santa Cruz) for the opportunity to utilize the splendid resources of the Harvard library. Mrs. Lorna M. Daniells, reference librarian, was of immense help in bringing important current material to my attention and suggesting methods of locating items. The friendly and expert assistance of the other members of the library staff is much appreciated.

Much of the final checking of sources was done in the Graduate School of Business Library, University of California, Los Angeles. I am grateful to Miss Charlotte Georgi, librarian, for her suggestions and help in locating books and other publications. Miss Isabella M. Frost, manager of the Library Department, Safeway Stores, Inc., suggested a number of important indexes and bibliographies which I might otherwise have overlooked. In addition to these librarians already mentioned, the staff of the University of California, Riverside, particularly Miss Dorothea Berry, reference librarian, has been on the alert to call references to my attention and has sent for items not in the library.

Finally, I wish to acknowledge how much I owe to my wife, Evelyn Brownell Coman, for reading and correcting the entire manuscript and for her encouragement while I was writing this book.

EDWIN T. COMAN, JR.

CONTENTS

1

METHODS OF LOCATING FACTS

If information is to be located quickly and with a minimum of effort, the exact definition of the problem is a most important preliminary step. What facts are needed, and what type of information is desired? It is part of wisdom to decide whether one isolated fact, a detailed historical account, a comparative presentation, a series of index numbers, or a long series of actual data will provide the answer. Often, an examination of the problem develops the desirability of gathering additional facts in order that the entire situation may be analyzed in proper perspective.

After the type and scope of the desired information is clearly visualized, the next step is to locate the data. We go to the bank for aid and advice, and to the grocery store for food. The natural place to turn for facts is to the library, where large collections of books, pamphlets, and magazines are assembled, systematically arranged, and handled by librarians who are experts in locating information and who possess a wide knowledge of business subjects. Public libraries have greatly expanded their service to business and, by 1960, there were sixty-seven American and five Canadian public libraries which provided services tailored to the needs of businessmen. These are well-distributed from coast to coast in cities of 100,000 population or larger. However, the basic business reference works are usually found in the library of any city which has extensive manufacturing or commercial activities. In some instances all works on business and technology are housed in branch libraries easily accessible to the business district. Excellent resources in the fields of business and technology are available in the Cleveland, Los Angeles, Newark, and San Francisco public libraries.

During the latter part of the nineteenth century many institutes were formed to enable mechanics and clerks to improve themselves through courses of study and reading. A number of these institutes have built up extensive collections of business publications and have now become specialized libraries. Their earlier educational function has dwindled in significance as trade and technical schools increased. Although they are open to members only, the membership is usually nominal.

Business education on the collegiate level has become widespread, and many colleges and universities, particularly those having schools of business, maintain excellent business libraries. These collections are usually larger and contain more scholarly, theoretical, and historical material than do the public libraries. While these institutions are largely concerned with their own students and scholars who are doing research, they are usually ready to assist any businessman in locating information if his request is a legitimate one. However, the resources of the public library should be exhausted before it becomes necessary to turn to the colleges and universities. The leading libraries in this category are those at the Graduate School of Business Administration, Harvard, the Stanford University Graduate School of Business, the Wharton School of Finance and Commerce, University of Pennsylvania, Dartmouth College, Amos Tuck School of Administration and Finance and those at the University of California (Berkeley and Los Angeles), Columbia University, University of Chicago, University of Illinois, University of Michigan, and New York University. Many other educational institutions have accumulated special collections of published and unpublished material in a specific field, such as accounting, or material of local or regional interest which is useful to the businessman.

The larger and more progressive business firms have established libraries to serve their own organizations. Such collections are usually rigidly specialized in the literature dealing with a particular business activity, although they may include some general business information as well. It is in these libraries that one can often find the most complete and up-to-date information on a particular phase of an industry or business activity.

An aid to the location of special libraries is a publication of the Special

Libraries Association—*Special Library Resources,* Rose M. Vormelker, editor, New York, The Association, 1941–1947. Volume I lists 765 research library collections in special libraries and special collections in public and university libraries in the United States and Canada. Volumes II and III contain information on holdings of 1659 libraries not included in Volume I. The location, extent of the library and the subject in which it is strong are all indicated in these volumes. Libraries are grouped under their geographical locations—a most helpful arrangement for anyone desiring to locate material in his own locality. The special collection, personnel, and subject indexes in each volume and cumulated in Volume IV provide for every conceivable need of the user. The rapid expansion of special libraries and changes in personnel in the past fifteen years have reduced the usefulness of these volumes. Later sources are Special Libraries Association, *Special Libraries Directory,* New York, The Association, 1953, which lists 2,000 special libraries, and Lee Ash, comp., *Subject Collections: A Guide to Special Book Collections and Subject Emphasis Reported by University, College, Public, and Special Libraries in the United States and Canada,* 2d ed., New York, R. R. Bowker Co., 1961. Current information on special libraries may be obtained from the Special Libraries Association, 31 East 10th Street, New York 3, New York.

Many technical and professional societies and business associations maintain excellent libraries. Use of these facilities is limited, generally, to their research staffs and members, but the librarians are usually willing to answer legitimate inquiries. The National Industrial Conference Board, The National Association of Cost Accountants, and the American Engineering Societies all have fine library facilities. Unfortunately for the rest of the country, the headquarters of these organizations are located along the eastern seaboard.

The United States Department of Commerce maintains regional offices in the principal cities. Files of the publications of the department are available for consultation as is a small stock of current issues for purchase.

Local trade associations and chambers of commerce often have valuable data on local business conditions, exports and imports peculiar to the area, the condition of agriculture in the surrounding territory, the labor market, real estate valuations, and the local tax situation. These organizations often publish valuable local statistics and trade journals of the locality.

State Planning Boards publish much useful information on the economic resources and development and population trends in their particular localities.

With his problem clearly in mind and with the library as the place to which to turn for the necessary books, the businessman must then locate the information. The utilization of works which bring together large bodies of facts in one publication is a real time and effort saver. These compilations, though seldom original sources, very often supply the requisite information without further search. It is always wise to consult one of these broad sources first to gain a general background of the subject, and one may find additional clues to further information.

Dictionaries, almanacs, yearbooks, and encyclopedias are all packed with general information. They also contain much statistical data. The format of dictionaries makes them very easy to use. In addition to the brief definitions and terse statement of facts, dictionaries contain much biographical information throughout the text and particularly in the special biographical section. The dates of birth and death and some indication of the fields of activity and achievements of the individuals recorded are noted. The gazetteer of geographical place names is another time-saving feature. Very often the dictionary can supply all the necessary information. In any case, it should be consulted to clarify the meaning of unfamiliar words.

The most easily accessible reference works are *The World Almanac* and the *Information Please Almanac*. Their value is based on the tremendous amount of factual, statistical, and general information brought together annually within the covers of one publication: isolated facts, such as the names of government officials; dates of events; accounts of business, cultural, and political activities; commercial, manufacturing, and vital statistics; and much miscellaneous information on all phases of human endeavors. The *Information Please Almanac* interprets the political, cultural, and other important events of the year in a series of articles before it embarks on the more factual and statistical sections. *The World Almanac* is entirely factual in its approach.

New York World-Telegram. *The World Almanac and Book of Facts.* New York, New York World-Telegram. Annually since 1885.

The sections which are most useful to the businessman are Government Agencies, Population, Trade and Transportation, Agriculture, and Manufactures.

Information Please Almanac, Atlas and Yearbook. New York, Simon and Schuster. Annually since 1947.

    After a running commentary on the events of the year, there are a series of reviews of drama, literature, music, medicine, science, and, the space age. These are followed by a series of simple maps showing the location of political events and new developments. The remainder of the book is given over to the presentation of statistics.

Whitaker's Almanac. London, Joseph Whitaker. Annually since 1868.

    This publication provides the same kind of information for the British Commonwealth that the World Almanac supplies for the United States. It is especially helpful in providing data on organizations in the United Kingdom.

Yearbooks differ from almanacs in that fuller information is supplied and very frequently an attempt is made to interpret the recorded facts. These publications, with the exception of *The Statesman's Year-Book* and *The Yearbook of World Affairs,* are published on a regional basis which permits a more detailed treatment than in the more general works. The rise of many new countries since World War II has brought forth a number of yearbooks which are often the most current sources of information on these areas. Yearbooks are published annually or biennially and are often the official publications of the countries described. They usually contain information as to recent laws affecting commercial transactions within the country and give some indication as to customs dues and regulations.

The Statesman's Year-Book. Edited by M. Epstein. London, Macmillan and Co., Limited. Annually since 1863.

    The brief tables at the beginning of each volume are useful as a résumé of world production of eight selected commodities. Each country is briefly described as to type of government, area and population, religion, education, justice, defense, commerce and industry, and finance. The account includes information on weights and measures, coinage, names of British diplomatic representatives within the country and the country's representatives in Great Britain. A very helpful feature is the list of "Books of Reference" which concludes each account. The British point of view and the expression of monetary values in British units detracts from its usefulness to Americans.

Political events are having an increasing influence on business activities and *The Yearbook of World Affairs* interprets these happenings.

The Yearbook of World Affairs. New York, Frederick A. Praeger. Annually since 1947.

    Political developments and happenings of international significance are analyzed. A most helpful section is that of reviews and digests of important books dealing with broad and vital areas of world affairs.

Yearbooks of individual countries all follow much the same pattern. They contain a brief history of the country, a description of its area and topography, an account of the prevailing form of government, and the names of its more important officials. Information on the legal and social institutions is usually included, followed by a detailed discussion of commercial, manufacturing, and financial activities. These accounts are supported by statistical tables. Often they include digests in English of laws affecting trade. Many include a "Who's Who" section, which is often the only source of information on local industrialists and business leaders. Statistics from countries less highly developed commercially should be used with discretion, as they are apt to be based on estimates and usually tend to overstate the situation.

The Canada Yearbook is perhaps the best example of a regional yearbook. It is an official government publication and supplies a large amount of statistical information on Canadian trade and industry and is the best source for information on that country. A companion volume, which supplements *The Canada Yearbook,* is the *Canadian Almanac & Directory.* Two other works that tend to be more guidebooks than yearbooks are *The Year Book and Guide to Southern Africa* and *The Year Book and Guide to East Africa.*

Canada. Dominion Bureau of Statistics. *The Canada Yearbook.* Ottawa, Edmund Cloutier, Queen's Printer, 1944–.

    The short, well-written accounts of Canadian activities are packed with facts and statistics. The history of the country is briefly reviewed, and the names of all elected and appointed officials are listed. Vital statistics and the record of governmental activities come next, followed by sections dealing with production, agriculture, forestry, mines and minerals, fisheries, furs, manufactures, construction, internal and external trade, and, finally, transportation and communications.

Canadian Almanac & Directory. Edited by Beatrice Logan. Toronto, The Copp Clark Publishing Company, 1847–.

    The almanac section is largely confined to a detailed description of customs duties and tariff regulations with some data on imports and exports. The very detailed directory, which extends to the smallest towns, is most helpful. Persons included are national, provincial, city, and village officials. Local managers of banks and insurance companies are listed under the town in which they are located as well as the national officers of these firms. Other information covers postmasters, local school boards, and educators; newspapers with their editors, book publishers, and educational institutions.

The Year Book and Guide to Southern Africa. London, S. Low Marston, 1893–.
    A brief history of the area covered is followed by data on industry, mining, and crops. The remaining information supplied is on travel routes, hotels, and points of interest. Steamship and railroad lines are indicated.

The Year Book and Guide to East Africa. London, R. Hale, 1950–.
    After a terse description of the history of each country, there follows an account of the economic development and industrial facilities, farm and mines production, and major exports. Roads, rail and steamship lines, and hotels are described.

On occasion the businessman needs certain facts dealing with industries, events, places, and processes. These are seldom covered satisfactorily by almanacs, yearbooks, or handbooks. If data are included in these works, the discussion is usually very sketchy and limited to happenings during the interval covered by that particular volume. Encyclopedias fill the need for authoritative information that is presented in a concise manner and easy to locate. There are numerous encyclopedias on the market, but the leading publications of this type are the *Encyclopedia Americana,* the *Encyclopaedia Britannica,* and *Collier's Encyclopedia.* Each of these works has distinctive features, and the use of one should not exclude reference to the others. All are kept up-to-date through continuous revision and the annual publication of yearbooks that chronicle the events, new developments, and discoveries of the year. The yearbooks also contain a necrology: brief information on prominent persons who have died during the year. Another very valuable feature in both the regular edition and the yearbook supplements is the list of authoritative books which follows each article. These bibliographies enable the reader to pursue the subject more exhaustively and offer a good opportunity to keep abreast of new books on a particular topic.

Encyclopaedia Britannica. Chicago, Encyclopaedia Britannica, Inc. First published in 1768 and, at present, continuously revised.
    Articles are, in the main, scholarly, detailed, and well-illustrated. They are particularly good for authoritative accounts of subjects that include the history and background. It is a splendid source of general information on the arts, science, technology, and the political and economic developments of European countries and cities. However, American cities are not as fully treated as are their European counterparts. Another strong feature which contributes to the ease of locating material is the excellent, detailed, alphabetical index. Annual

yearbooks are also published to describe the developments of the year and to
provide a chronology of important events.

Encyclopedia Americana. New York, Americana Corporation. First published in
1904 and now continuously revised.

The accounts of scientific and technological developments are generally
complete and up to date. The descriptions of American cities are particularly
good. They give an historical account of their founding, statistics of commerce
and manufacturing, and some indication of the cultural and educational advantages available. Each account is followed by a current and carefully collected
bibliography. The yearbooks contain descriptions of important events of the
year; list a necrology of important individuals, including a brief statement of
the fields in which they were prominent; and keep statistical data current.

Collier's Encyclopedia. New York. P. F. Collier and Son Corporation. First published in 1952 and subject to continuous revision.

Since this encyclopedia was an entirely new publication produced in 1952,
there is a minimum of obsolete material presented. Important subjects are
treated at considerable length. There are also many topics covered by short
articles. This work is profusely illustrated with up-to-date photographs and
diagrams. The lack of bibliographies at the end of the longer articles is a weakness of this publication. Yearbooks provide current data.

The Encyclopedia Americana is probably the encyclopedia best suited
to the needs of the businessman. The information is current, the treatment
authoritative and thorough, and the recommended references are carefully
chosen. The businessman should turn to this work first and utilize the
others only if the *Americana* cannot supply the information which he desires. The *Americana* is found in all the larger libraries.

A number of encyclopedias are available on specific subjects, but most
of them are of such a technical nature that they are generally of little interest to the businessman. One most useful work in this field should be
noted, however—the *Encyclopedia of the Social Sciences.*

Encyclopedia of the Social Sciences. Edwin E. A. Seligman, editor-in-chief. New
York, Macmillan, 1935. New edition in process.

This publication deals entirely with the fields of economics, history, political and social science, sociology, law, statistics, and education. Articles on individual types of business include a short summary of the background of the
business; offer some indication of its importance, labor and technological requirements, and operating rates; and there is a reading list of the leading publications on the subjects published prior to 1935. The encyclopedia is very valuable
for descriptions of broad phases of economic and social life, such as mercan-
tilism, the labor movement, and so forth. Excellent biographies of leaders in
the social sciences are included.

CHECKLIST OF GENERAL SOURCES

ALMANACS

Information Please Almanac, Atlas and Yearbook. New York, Simon and Schuster, 1947–.
New York World-Telegram. *The World Almanac and Book of Facts.* New York, New York World-Telegram, 1885–.
Whitaker's Almanac. London, Joseph Whitaker, 1868–.

ENCYCLOPEDIAS

Collier's Encyclopedia. New York, P. F. Collier & Son, 1952–.
Encyclopaedia Britannica. Chicago, Encyclopaedia Britannica, Inc., 1786–.
Encyclopedia Americana. New York, Americana Corporation, 1918–.
Encyclopedia of the Social Sciences. New York, Macmillan, 1935. New edition in process.

YEARBOOKS

Canada. Dominion Bureau of Statistics. *The Canada Yearbook.* Ottawa, Edmund Cloutier, Queen's Printer, 1944–.
Canadian Almanac & Directory. Edited by Beatrice Logan. Toronto, The Copp Clark Publishing Co., 1847–.
The Statesman's Yearbook. Edited by M. Epstein. London, Macmillan and Company, Limited, 1863–.
The Year Book and Guide to East Africa. London, R. Hale, 1950–.
The Year Book and Guide to Southern Africa. London, S. Low Marston, 1893–.
The Yearbook of World Affairs. New York, Frederick A. Praeger, 1947–.

The above list of yearbooks includes the best known standard works. Readers interested in a particular area should of course locate one of the many other regional and national yearbooks that have been published.

2

BASIC TIME-SAVING SOURCES

There are increasing numbers of aids for locating material useful to the businessman. These are in the form of books on how to use and locate business publications, bibliographies, services and indexes. Some of these are broad in their treatment and cover all phases of business, but there are many more confined to specific types of business activity, such as accounting, marketing, and so forth.

Books on how to locate and use sources of business information plus certain basic reference works, will provide the keys to unlock a large proportion of the information needed by the businessman. Familiarity with these sources and efficient ways of using them will greatly speed up the location of needed data.

The *Business Executive's Handbook* contains a wealth of concrete, up-to-date information on business practices.

Brown, Stanley M. and Doris, Lillian, eds. *Business Executive's Handbook*. 4th rev. ed. Englewood Cliffs, N.J., Prentice-Hall, 1953.
    Written clearly and with a minimum of technical detail, this handbook provides the answers to many perplexing questions which arise in the day-to-day conduct of a business. The information supplied is explicit, and the methods of applying it are well illustrated. Especially good material on correspondence and sales letters can be found in this work.

Numerous other handbooks of a more specialized nature are published that are useful chiefly to one seeking a particular kind of information.

Many trade associations, professional societies, chambers of commerce, and government organizations assemble large bodies of facts and statistics and make the information available to their publications. These organizations are usually glad to furnish additional data to persons doing serious research.

There are two books which give much sound advice as to how to use a business library and what sources are most important. *Business Information—How to Find and Use It* written by Marian C. Manley, for many years head of the Business Branch of the Newark N.J. Public Library, carries the wealth of her experience and knowledge to the searcher of information. H. W. Johnson and S. W. McFarland have worked out a guide to the use of a business library and a bibliography of sources in their *How to Use a Business Library with Sources of Business Information.*

Manley, Marian C. *Business Information—How to Find and Use It.* New York, Harper, 1955.

> Nine short chapters clearly and tersely describe methods of locating information and basic sources of data in the first part. Part II, "Information Sources for Special Subjects," is an annotated bibliography of books, periodicals, and bibliographies in broad business subject fields. This book is most useful when it is used in conjunction with the publication of the Newark Public Library, *Business Literature.*

Johnson, H. W. and McFarland, S. W. *How to Use a Business Library with Sources of Business Information.* 2d ed. Cincinnati, South-Western Publishing Co., 1957.

> This work is an excellent brief introduction to the literature of business. The first portion is given over to a rather detailed discussion of the mechanics of locating material such as the card catalog, bibliographies, and indexes. After these instructions as to how to locate books and use the library, the authors provide a discussion of source materials, which includes handbooks and yearbooks, periodicals, reports and pamphlets, directories, services, government publications, publications of research foundations, trade, industrial and commercial organizations, encyclopedias, dictionaries, and almanacs. The sections on government publications and trade and commercial organizations are very good. A helpful guide to anyone who uses business sources.

BIBLIOGRAPHIES

In recent years there have been an increasing number of bibliographies published by a large number of organizations. A useful and quick way in which to gain knowledge of the literature is by referring to the many check-

lists and bibliographies which have been published by the Special Libraries
Association, the Business Branch of the Newark, New Jersey Public Library, the Business and Technology Department of the Cleveland Public
Library, and by various associations and collegiate schools of business.
Their published lists are selections of the better works published on business and usually indicate the approach and particularly valuable features
of the titles and works mentioned. The majority deal with one special field,
such as accounting, management, retailing, and so forth, although some
bibliographies cover the broad field of business in a generalized way. All
of these bibliographies and checklists either are arranged by subjects or
have a good subject index. A good selection would include:

Baker Library. Graduate School of Business Administration. Harvard University.
    Reference Lists.
        Frequently revised and highly selective, these lists are most helpful in
    keeping the businessman up to date. Although the majority of these publica-
    tions deal with particular business topics, the following is an excellent general
    bibliography;
—— *Business Literature: A Reading List for Students and Businessmen.* Com-
    piled by Harriette L. Williams. (Reference List No. 17, Rev. ed.) 1959. A
    new edition is in progress in 1962.
        Broad subjects are broken down into smaller groupings of selected books
    and periodicals. The material is well-selected and up to date. Appendix A,
    "Reference Books and Periodicals," and Appendix C, "Publishers," are very
    helpful features.
Dartmouth College. Amos Tuck School of Administration and Finance. *A Reading
    List on Business Administration.* 8th revision. Hanover, N.H., Dartmouth
    College, 1962.
        This list represents an attempt to select the leading works in each subject
    field of business. The arrangement is a grouping under subjects with a brief
    annotation and includes both magazines and books.
UNESCO. *International Bibliography of Economics.* Paris, UNESCO. Annually since
    1952.
        A world-wide bibliography of books, periodicals, government reports
    (printed and mimeographed), periodical articles and pamphlets published dur-
    ing the year. Much of the material is concerned with economic theory and
    methodology, but it also covers many topics of interest to the businessman. It
    is most useful in locating statistical data and information on current conditions
    in areas outside the United States, particularly in Asia, Africa, South America,
    and the USSR. There are very detailed author and subject indexes. This is a
    valuable source.
Association of University Bureaus of Business and Economic Research. *Index of*

Publications of Bureaus of Business and Economic Research, 1950–1956. Eugene, Ore., Bureau of Business Research, University of Oregon, 1957. Supplement 1957–1958.

A checklist of the publications of these research organizations.

Pittsburgh University. Bureau of Business Research. *Small Business Bibliography.* 2d ed. Pittsburgh, Pa., Pittsburgh University, Bureau of Business Research, 1958.

An attempt has been made in this bibliography to provide a complete list of the publications dealing with small businesses except for the enormous literature on retail stores. Literature cited includes books, pamphlets, government documents, and periodical articles. Under broad captions of "Establishing a Small Business," "Management and Operation of a Small Business," "Economic Aspects of Small Business," "Government and Small Business," and, "Chain Stores in Relation to Small Business," a large number of references are listed. These include material on location, organization and management, financing, and competition. A very helpful and complete unannotated bibliography.

U.S. Small Business Administration. *Basic Library Reference Sources for Business Use.* (Small Business Bulletin 18.) Washington, D.C., Small Business Administration, 1959.

A useful guide to the first steps in locating business information. The concentration on the basic sources and the clear and simple descriptions of materials make this publication a worthwhile tool in the beginning of a search for data. Periodic revisions keep it up to date.

A number of other bibliographies and checklists deal with business literature, but because most of these concentrate on some particular phase or business activity such as accounting, management, marketing, and so forth, they will be discussed later on.

Any bibliography or checklist begins to become obsolete the moment it is completed. Although certain books do become fundamental or "standard" texts on a given subject, business is changing so rapidly and is affected by so many technological changes that businessmen must constantly have the very latest information to enable them to operate successfully. Furthermore, as more and more graduates of business schools move into key positions, they demand more and better data. Two types of publications have been developed to serve this need. The current annotated bibliography or simple checklist of the more important publications put out during a given period and abstracts of books and articles that have significance to the businessman. Three current listings of business material are *Business Methods Index* published by the Keith Business Library, *Business Literature* of the Newark, New Jersey, Public Library and *Business and Technology Sources* put out by the Cleveland Public Library. Both of these latter magazines devote each issue to a single topic of current interest to the businessman, for example, Latin American Markets, Automation, or Business Magazines.

Business Methods Index. Ottawa, Box 453, Canada, Keith Business Library. Monthly except July.

The new business and technical books, pamphlets, magazine articles, films, maps, and government publications of interest to business and civic managers are indexed. All American, Canadian and British publishing sources are covered including the book trade, government, academic, association, research, corporation, and the leading 300 business magazines and journals. The material is grouped under twenty-five broad headings and published in fourteen editions to meet the needs of particular users. Source and price of books and pamphlets are given. There are quarterly cumulated indexes. An attempt to give complete coverage of the most important business publications in English on a current basis.

Business Literature. Newark, N.J., Newark Public Library. Monthly except July and August.

The suggestions as to how to locate and utilize material are excellent. References include books, magazine articles, government publications, and pamphlets—a well-chosen selection of current references which are described in pithy annotations.

Business and Technology Sources. Cleveland, O., Business and Technology Department, Cleveland Public Library. Four to six issues a year.

The larger number of references and the longer annotations compensate for the less frequent publication. Each issue, or two issues, is concerned with a broad topic of immediate interest and brings together books, magazine articles, and pamphlets on the subject. The issue "Business Books" is a highly selected list of the most important business books published during the year.

Abstracting services attempt to give the reading public some idea of the content, approach of the author, and the importance of the material abstracted. Two publications perform this service currently.

The Executive. Monthly. Boston, Mass., The Executive.

This publication is designed to bring significant books, pamphlets, and periodical articles to the attention of busy executives. The selection and the summarizing of this material by a staff based on the Baker Library of the Harvard Graduate School of Business Administration assures excellence.

Economic Abstracts. A Semi-monthly Review of Abstracts on Economics, Finance, Trade and Industry, Management and Labour. The Hague, Martinus Nijhoff, 1954–.

The broad coverage includes abstracts of books, periodical articles, reports of governments and international organizations. It is largely confined to publications issued in Europe, North America, and Great Britain. This timely résumé of current economic material is somewhat less useful to the American reader because the abstracts are in the language of the original. The classified arrangement with an adequate subject index, makes this publication easy to use. The list of periodicals from which articles are abstracted is also helpful.

INDEXES TO PERIODICALS

Although all of the sources listed in this chapter include magazine articles, the businessman needs a quick method of locating such material. Because business is constantly changing and new processes, products, and developments appear daily, the businessman must refer constantly to the very latest publications containing information on his problems. Such data are usually published first in newspapers, magazines, and pamphlets. Trade and technical journals run into the hundreds, and pamphlets into the thousands. The average businessman, though aware of the literature in his own field, is usually unacquainted with publications in other lines which might provide just the bit of information he needs to solve his particular problem. The beginner in business, or an experienced one doing research in a strange field may be bewildered by the variety of publications and may be at a loss as to where to turn to locate the needed data.

He wants to know what magazines are published in his field of industry and where to find articles on specific topics. Information on what magazines are published on various business subjects has been assembled in Harvard University, Graduate School of Business Administration, Baker Library, Reference List 3, *Magazines for the Business Executive,* May, 1948. Periodic revisions of the Reference List, *Business Literature: A Reading List for Students and Businessmen* (See page 12.) bring this partially up to date.

The indexes to magazine articles are indispensable to anyone searching for information in this type of publication. Although *The Engineering Index, The Education Index,* and *Chemical Abstracts,* are too highly specialized to be of much assistance to the average businessman, four others cover the most important business magazines. These are: *The Readers' Guide to Periodical Literature, Business Periodicals Index, Applied Science and Technology Index,* and *Public Affairs Information Service Bulletin. The Readers' Guide* indexes magazines of general interest and those dealing with the broader aspects of business, commercial, and political life. The

Business Periodicals Index and *Applied Science and Technology Index* represent a split up in 1958 of the periodicals indexed in the *Industrial Arts Index,* and this latter title should be used to find articles prior to that date. The *Business Periodicals Index* covers business policies, management activities, accounting, marketing, and so forth. The factory operation, product and process development, and technology are the magazines and other publications indexed in the *Applied Science and Technology Index.* In addition to business and technical magazines, the publications of a number of technical societies and associations in the United States, Canada, France, Great Britain, and Germany, as well as the publications of the U.S. Bureau of Foreign and Domestic Commerce, are indexed in these two indexes. The arrangement of these indexes by broad subjects sometimes requires a bit of ingenuity on the part of the user to discover the subject under which his topic is classified.

The preceding indexes do not cover pamphlets and government publications very completely, but the *Public Affairs Information Service Bulletin* supplies this lack. Although the emphasis is on political science, it also lists and analyzes many magazines, pamphlets, and governmental publications of interest to businessmen. It is also a good source for the factual publications of international congresses and conventions that are difficult to locate elsewhere.

All of these indexes are published monthly with quarterly, semiannual, and annual cumulations. They make available promptly the keys which unlock the wealth of current information contained in magazines and, to a lesser extent, that in pamphlets and governmental publications.

A recent publication, *Current Contents,* attempts to assist economists and businessmen to decide what periodical articles are of interest to them and another, *Index of Economic Journals,* 1886–1959, opens the way to retrospective use of periodicals.

Current Contents. Philadelphia 3, 33 South Seventh Street, The Institute for Scientific Information. Bi-weekly.
>   Thirty-nine tables of contents of periodicals in the social sciences are published bi-weekly. These include articles on management, accounting, marketing, and labor relations, as well as those on theoretical economics. The publication provides a quick method of scanning some of the literature of business.

American Economic Association. *Index of Economic Journals,* 1886–1959. Homewood, Ill., Irwin, 1961–. 5 vols.

Indexes eighty-two economic periodicals for articles in English which cover material of interest to teachers and researchers in economics. The material covered includes articles, comments, rejoinders, papers from meetings of professional organizations, reports of symposia, meetings and roundtables, editorials, obituaries containing biographical or bibliographical information, and subject bibliographies. A most useful section is the author index wherein all the articles, by an individual, for the period covered, are brought together. The main body of the index is under a classified subject arrangement.

The other major source of current information is the daily newspaper. There are three indexes to newspapers, the *New York Times Index,* the *Wall Street Journal Index,* and the *Official Index of the London Times.* The coverage of these papers is so complete that they can be relied upon to supply information on national and international affairs in addition to a large amount of business and financial news. Most metropolitan newspapers maintain extensive libraries and their files, called "morgues," contain practically all the local news items published in their own papers. However, because the libraries are not equipped to give reference service to the general public they should be consulted only as a last resort. If a businessman has a serious and long-continued interest in some particular topic, he should employ a clipping bureau to supply him with the newspaper articles on his subject.

GOVERNMENT PUBLICATIONS

Considered from the point of view of quantity, the publications of governmental bodies probably rank first. They are published in a variety of formats and series by a great number of departments, bureaus, sub-bureaus and independent agencies, but the fact that writing and research programs are shifted from one bureau or department to another, or consolidated, makes it difficult to locate these publications. Much information in these publications is of vital importance to the businessman. Besides, government agencies have become the only organizations that can afford to compile and publish the tremendous mass of statistical information needed by both business and the general public. However, the most useful information to the businessman is concentrated in a few departments, such as Commerce, Labor, Agriculture, and the Board of Governors of the Federal Reserve System. There are also a number of independent regulatory agencies whose decisions vitally affect business; the more important of these are Federal Trade Commission, Securities and Exchange Commission, Federal Reserve Board, and the National Labor Relations Board.

Although the mass of material published by the federal and state governments appears formidable, it is well indexed in readily available publications. In recent years certain publications that have appeared in mimeographed form have not been included in the governmental indexes. Locating such bulletins becomes a matter of patient search.

The titles of catalogs and lists which are most useful for locating material published by the federal government are given here; how to use them will be explained later.

If an individual in search of information desires to locate all the material published by the federal government on a specific topic, he should consult the *Catalog of the Public Documents . . . of the Government of the United States* for publications prior to December 31, 1940. Since that date federal documents can be found listed in the *United States Government Publications Monthly Catalog,* which is within three months of being current and has a cumulative annual index. The semimonthly *List of Selected United States Government Publications* brings federal government publications about as up to date as possible. *The Public Affairs Information Service* is also a useful source of information on government documents. The *Price Lists* issued annually by the U.S. Superintendent of Documents bring together under broad subjects all the publications which are in stock dealing with a given topic, regardless of the issuing agency. *Commerce and Manufactures; Finance; Foreign Relations of the United States; Forestry, Lumber, and Timber; Interstate Commerce; Irrigation, Drainage and Water Power; Labor; Laws; Mines; Pacific States; Political Science;* and *Tariff and Taxation* are, for the businessman, the most important *Price Lists.*

If the information is of a kind usually supplied by one department, the various departmental indexes provide the most direct method of approach. One of the best is *United States Department of Commerce Publications,* which was published in 1952 and is kept current by annual supplements and the weekly *Business Service Checklist.*

INDEXES TO THE PUBLICATIONS OF THE
UNITED STATES GOVERNMENT

U.S. Superintendent of Documents. *Catalog of the Public Documents of Congress and of all the Departments of the United States for the period March 4, 1893— December 31, 1940.* Washington, D.C., Government Printing Office, 1945. 25 vols.

To find material in this catalog, the user must know the Congress within which the document was published if he is searching for a specific item. The arrangement is by author and subject with numerous cross references. Other volumes cover earlier Congresses from 1893. For later documents see next reference.

U.S. Superintendent of Documents. *United States Government Publications Monthly Catalog.* Washington, D.C., Government Printing Office. Monthly since 1895.

Publications are grouped under the issuing department and are further subdivided by Bureaus and Divisions. The detailed subject index and the annual author, title, subject index published in recent years make it easy to locate publications. The lag of two or three months between publications of a document and its listing in the catalog detracts somewhat from the latter's usefulness.

U.S. Superintendent of Documents. *List of Selected United States Government Publications.* Washington, D.C., Government Printing Office. Semimonthly. (Formerly *Weekly List of Selected United States Documents* and now appearing semimonthly.)

This leaflet now appearing semimonthly lists the more important government publications under the proper subject headings. It is most valuable for its timeliness.

U.S. Superintendent of Documents. *Price Lists of Government Publications.* Washington, D.C., Government Printing Office. 1898–.

Out of the seventy-five *Price Lists* which have been published, only forty-six have been maintained. These have been kept up and are revised at least annually. These lists, which represent the publications in stock, are a most valuable compilation of the bulk of the government publications on a given topic. Publications are grouped under subject headings which largely obviate the need of an index.

U.S. Commerce Department. *United States Department of Commerce Publications.* Washington, D.C., Government Printing Office, 1952, with annual supplements.

The increase both in number and frequency of departmental indexes has made their publications much easier to locate. Publications are listed according to the bureau which prepares and issues them and are grouped according to series.

U.S. Commerce Department. *Business Service Checklist.* Washington, D.C., Government Printing Office. Weekly.

This checklist records the printed material made available by the department each week. It is the most current source of information on Commerce publications.

U.S. Census Bureau. *Catalog of the United States Census Publications* 1790–1945. Washington, D.C., Government Printing Office, 1950.

A complete catalog of all the publications of the Bureau since its inception.

U.S. Census Bureau. *Census Publications, Catalog and Subject Guide,* 1945–1951. Washington, D.C., Government Printing Office, 1951.

Supplements the previous reference.

U.S. Census Bureau. *Catalog of United States Census Publications,* 1951–. Washington, D.C., Government Printing Office. Quarterly with annual cumulations.

This is a cumulative guide to all publications issued by the U.S. Census Bureau each quarter since 1951. Publications are grouped under appropriate subjects. It provides a key to the largest amount of current statistical information published by the Bureau.

U.S. Bureau of Foreign Commerce. *Checklist of BFC Publications.* Washington, D.C., U.S. Bureau of Foreign Commerce. Irregular.

The most current listing of the Bureau's publications. The more important titles are annotated.

U.S. Labor Department. *Publications of the United States Labor Department, Subject Listing, 1948–57.* Washington, D.C., Government Printing Office, 1957. Supplements 1958 and 1959.

The subject grouping of publications makes this index very useful.

Much data compiled by the federal government appears in mimeographed or in some form of photo-reproduction. Some of these items appear in the Superintendent of Documents or departmental checklists. Helpful information on locating this material can be found in Schmeckebier and Eastin, *Government Publications and Their Use.*

Those persons who do not have the time to go through the Congressional Record will find the *Congressional Quarterly, News Features* a handy digest of the activities of Congress.

Congressional Quarterly. News Features. Washington 6, D.C., 1159 19th St., Congressional Quarterly. Quarterly.

The information provided covers the legislative and political activities of Congress and congressmen including voting records, bills introduced and acted upon, and lobbies and lobbyists.

There have been several publications issued to assist people in locating and using government documents and the following titles contain many helpful hints as to location and use and much valuable information on documents.

Boyd, Anne M. *United States Government Publications: Sources of Information for Libraries.* 3d ed. revised by Rae Elizabeth Rips. New York, H. W. Wilson, 1949.

> Current publications are described and listed, and, in addition, there is a compilation of the publications of terminated government agencies.

Hirshberg, Albert S. and Melinat, Carl H. *Subject Guide to United States Government Publications.* Chicago, American Library Association, 1947.

> Although this work is obsolescent, its subject arrangement still makes it a useful source for locating publications.

Leidy, W. Philip. *A Popular Guide to Government Publications.* New York, Columbia University Press, 1953.

> References are to specific publications of the United States government of a nontechnical nature and popular appeal.

Schmeckebier, L. F. and Eastin, R. B. *Government Publications and Their Use.* Rev. ed. Washington, D.C., The Brookings Institution, 1961.

> Here is a most welcome revision of this excellent guide to United States government documents. Bibliographies, departmental, independent office and congressional publications are described in detail. The arrangement of this book and the descriptions as to how to locate material make it a handy reference. Two new chapters on government periodicals and facsimile reproductions supply current information in an area of increasing importance.

Brown, Everett S. *Manual of Government Publications; United States and Foreign.* New York, Appleton-Century-Crofts, 1950.

> This is the only one of these manuals which deals with foreign government documents. Brief information is supplied on the more important publications of the United States, Canada and other members of the British Commonwealth, major European governments, Latin American countries and international organizations. Many bibliographies of government documents are listed.

Individuals who are searching for a few guideposts to direct them through the maze of government departments, bureaus, sub-bureaus, and independent agencies will find that the *United States Government Organization Manual,* published by the Federal Register Division, Federal Archives, is very helpful. This work, published annually, describes the purpose, functions, and operation of each government agency and lists the personnel from those in top executive positions down to the names and addresses of field representatives.

The federal government also publishes a wide variety of periodicals which contain much statistical and other information of vital importance to the businessman. In addition to the chapter on government periodicals in Schmeckebier and Eastin, *Government Publications and Their Use,* the following pamphlet is useful:

U.S. Superintendent of Documents. *Price List 36—Government Periodicals.* Washington, D.C., Government Printing Office. Irregular.

> Government periodicals are arranged by title and some suggestion is given
> of the contents of the more important items.

Publications of the various states are harder to locate than those of the
federal government. The *Monthly Checklist of State Publications* prepared
by the United States Library of Congress and published by the Government Printing Office from 1910 on provides the most up-to-date listings.
Though it is admittedly incomplete, it does list the more important documents. State libraries and the larger public and university libraries usually
index the publications of their home states.

The rapid growth of communications and a closer interrelationship
between countries has made a knowledge of foreign government publications useful. Those of the English speaking countries are both the most
numerous and valuable and they can be located though the following
bibliographies:

Great Britain. Her Majesty's Stationery Office. *Consolidated List of Government
Publications.* London, H.M. Stationery Office. Annually.

> A compilation of all documents published during the year and includes both
> parliamentary and nonparliamentary documents.

Great Britain. Her Majesty's Stationery Office. *Government Publications Monthly
List.* London, H.M. Stationery Office. Monthly.

Canada. *Consolidated Annual Catalogue of Canadian Government Publications.*
Ottawa, Queen's Printer. Annually.

> This is the annual cumulation of all the nonconfidential publications to
> the previous year.

Canada. *Canadian Government Publications Monthly Catalogue.* Ottawa, Queen's
Printer. Monthly.

One other index of value is that of the United Nations:

United Nations. *United Nations Documents Index: United Nations Specialized
Documents and Publications.* N.Y., United Nations. Monthly with annual
cumulative index.

> References are arranged by numbers assigned to issuing bodies and can
> be located through the subject and author index. Each February issue has a
> list of periodicals published by the United Nations. Current and past issues of
> the bibliographical series are indicated.

LOOSE-LEAF SERVICES

The trend toward an increasing regulation of business by the federal and state governments that has been evident during the past twenty years has made it imperative for the businessman to keep abreast of changes in laws and regulations. He needs specific and authoritative data on his particular problem. The information he needs can be located by using the indexes discussed in this chapter. Sometimes, however, the desired facts are buried in a mass of detail and hard to find. Fortunately, all the material bearing on a topic is brought together, discussed and interpreted in various loose-leaf services that are constantly revised and thoroughly indexed. Since loose-leaf services play such an important part in the day-to-day conduct of a business, especially for businessmen, accountants, and lawyers, their contents and how they can be most effectively used are described on the following pages.

The loose-leaf services have two basic characteristics not found in other types of publications: First, the loose-leaf format permits the user of the service to remove obsolete pages and insert new pages in their place, thus keeping the information continuously up to date; second, consolidation of all available information on a subject in a given service enormously reduces research time.

The tremendous growth of administrative law has made loose-leaf services a necessity to lawyers and businessmen. In many fields today—taxation, labor, government regulation of business—a person's or firm's rights depend not only upon statutes and cases, but also upon administrative regulations, rulings, and decisions.

DEVELOPMENT OF LOOSE-LEAF SERVICES

With the federal income tax law of 1918 came the first loose-leaf services. The interest of accountants and lawyers in this law was, of course, intense. But the rapidity with which regulations were issued and amended, the rulings and court decisions handed down, made it apparent that the only satisfactory way to keep track of subsequent developments was in specialized loose-leaf form. Loose-leaf services spread rapidly. They were published first as "Reports" on the then new Federal Trade Commission; they extended to the field of state taxation, corporation law, and other fields. Under the impetus of New Deal legislation and the ever-increasing scope of federal and state taxation, loose-leaf services grew to their present status as an invaluable tool to all affected by the laws. In this growth, the leading services changed from "Reports" to "Services." Instead of merely reporting developments, the mass of official information was scientifically organized by service editors who are trained technicians in their particular field—and its significance and application were explained editorially to the user.

From the late 1930's on, loose-leaf services have covered fully the various fields of administrative law and have met every important test of usability by professional people and business executives. The idea of reporting, in a single service, a specific statute and its interpretation by court decisions and administrative rulings and regulations, is today a highly perfected field in itself.

GENERAL SCOPE OF LOOSE-LEAF SERVICES

It is evident that the special fields for loose-leaf services are those in which change is continuous, and the nature of those changes is such that immediate information is imperative. Almost without exception services consist of basic material, used with a continuing flow of new developments. Current reports made by leading services publishers consist of revisions of this basic material, the addition of new laws, rulings, and decisions, plus complete editorial analysis of these developments. These are printed on separate drilled pages for insertion in a binder. The user then has in one place the most recent developments in the particular field and, most important of all, coordination of older and newer data by the use of special indexes. (See the explanation of the loose-leaf services index systems on page 26.)

ORGANIZATION BY SUBJECT

Each loose-leaf service is a highly specialized unit, devoted exclusively to one topic or group of very closely related topics. For example, in a loose-leaf service on Labor Law and Relations all laws (both federal and state), parts of laws, regulations, rulings, and decisions on the subject, including labor relations, wages and hours, child labor, labor injunctions, arbitration and mediation, and many others are assembled for easy reference.

The specialization even includes coördination of all types of legal authority and other pertinent information on a given topic or subtopic as a single unit of research. This approach is a great contribution, especially in legal research, because existing legal research tools are not well adapted to locating administrative decisions, regulations, and rulings.

The publishers of loose-leaf services have endeavored to make their publications as useful for businessmen as they are for lawyers and other specialists, by avoiding in their explanations all legal terminology, by pointing out the problems created by the laws, and by offering practical guidance in solving these problems. They have made use of simple examples, outlines, suggestions, warnings, and other techniques in converting a mass of official matter into simple explanations.

How to Use a Loose-Leaf Service—General Aids

Most loose-leaf services are similar in arrangement. The binders allow sufficient space for inserting the current supplements, but the arrangement of material will of course vary depending on the subject matter. Contents of a typical service, however, would be organized like this; (1) The text of the statute; (2) the basic text or "compilation," based on the law, regulations, decisions, and other authorities; (3) a section on forms; (4) a cross-reference table or index for locating current developments (see The Index System, page 26); (5) the current matter section; and (6) the index.

Services have certain general aids, described below to assist the user. Familiarity with them is important if the service is to be used effectively.

DESCRIPTIVE INTRODUCTIONS

The introductory page which explains the scope and setup of the service and instructs subscribers on its use should be read carefully. All special features of the service are explained, and a hypothetical problem is usually posed and "tracked down" or solved as an example of how to use the service.

TAB CARDS

The constantly expanding information in a service binder is separated by guides or tab cards. These signal the topical breakdown and organization of the contents, and enable the user to locate quickly a particular section. Numbers on the tabs indicate the sequence of paragraph numbers, and a few key words indicate the content of the material tabbed. For example, a tab card with this legend "10,000—Federal Wage and Hour Law —Explanation" indicates that the material tabbed is the text or compilation on the Fair Labor Standards Act, starting at #10,000. Indexes, and other aids in locating information, explained below, are also tabbed.

TABLES OF CONTENTS

A table of contents immediately following each tab card provides a skeleton outline of the contents of that part of the service. Use of contrasting type sizes for headings and subheadings in many services assists the user in his search.

UNIFORM OUTLINE SYSTEMS

Services reporting state laws are frequently organized on a uniform basis; i.e., each topic in each state section has an identical paragraph number. For example, in a State Labor Law Service, the different types of laws for each state would be listed and described under a uniformly numbered heading. Thus, a single index entry indicates that night work laws for women are to be found at #46,713, and the user then locates the requirements for any state by looking at #46,713 under the appropriate state name.

THE INDEX SYSTEM OF LOOSE-LEAF SERVICES

Loose-leaf services can be used effectively only if the difference between them and traditional legal working tools is recognized. Locating information in the text or compilation of a service follows traditional methods—an index is used. However, locating data on current developments is a specialized technique. A simple three-step procedure to locate both the basic information and all current developments has been worked out:

STEP 1. THE INDEX ITSELF. The user must first go to the index to locate material on his problem. The index will refer him to a paragraph number or series of paragraph numbers in the basic text or compilation in which his problem is discussed.

There are certain features of service indexes which should be kept in mind. Many services have two types of index: a master index for the entire field of the service, such as federal taxes, plus a unit or divisional index for logical divisions of the subject, such as estate taxes, and so on. Furthermore, the organization of service information by numbered paragraphs permits a very detailed index. For example, material on "medical expenses" would be indexed under "Expenses," "Deductions," and "Medical Expenses." The user should look under "Medical Expenses" for the quickest references, because this is the most precise characterization of his general problems.

STEP 2. THE TEXT OR COMPILATION. By turning to the paragraphs indicated in the index, the user will get the complete information on his subject. All that remains is to make sure he has missed no new developments.

STEP 3. THE CROSS-REFERENCE TABLE. To locate current developments, he next turns to the device called a cross-reference table, cumulative index, or some similar term. The approach to these devices is strictly by number. The user looks up on this table, usually in a left-hand column of figures, the numbers he has been reading in the text. Opposite them will appear the number of all new items on his specific problem, plus a descriptive headnote to tell him what each new item is about.

The use of cross-reference tables or indexes is simple; it is strictly a mechanical function, virtually foolproof. All the user needs to know is the number of the text paragraphs he is reading. The user who fails or forgets to use the cross-reference table or index loses a great part of his service's value—namely, up-to-date information coördinated with the existing official and editorial material.

OTHER AIDS FOR LOCATING INFORMATION

In addition to the basic methods of locating information, explained above, loose-leaf services provide other aids designed for quick location of specific types of information:

1. CASE TABLES. Case tables, which are standard equipment in most services, refer to the paragraph where the case is reported or digested. If decisions of administrative boards, i.e., the National Labor Relations Board, are also reported, these are reported in the same table. Some services provide a special table for cases appearing in the new developments section.

2. CITATOR TABLES. The Citator, used with some services on federal

taxation, is an invaluable tool to the tax practitioner. The Citator lists alphabetically all cases it has on federal taxation; for each of these it indicates all the other cases in which it has been cited. A code system tells the user at once whether the case has been affirmed, reversed, followed, distinguished, discussed, overruled, or otherwise acted upon in each instance where it has been cited, "Precedent value" of each case is easily determined by using the Citator table.

3. FINDING LISTS. The finding list, a type of parallel table, is used in many services to locate special types of information. For example, if regulations have certain code numbers for part of a regulation, the finding list will be arranged according to these numbers. Opposite the code numbers appears a brief description of what that particular part of the regulation covers, and the paragraph number in the service where it is located. Finding lists can be organized numerically or alphabetically for the location of almost any type of information: statute sections, regulations, rulings, releases, forms, contract clauses, administrative orders, exemption orders, and so on.

4. ANALYTICAL TABLES. Much litigation between the government and private individuals and companies results from failure of the individual or company to analyze properly all the facts which might bear on his problems. Obviously, the time to figure the effect of a course of action is before it is taken. Some services use analytical tables to do this. On any given subject, the analytical table states the general proposition, and points out all possible factors affecting it, with references to service paragraph numbers where these factors are discussed and explained.

5. PILOT DEVICES. Some services use the Pilot Chart, or Pilot Paragraph, immediately preceding information on a given topic. This device outlines the entire scope of the subject, and indicates key paragraph references where particular phases of the problem are discussed in detail.

6. PENDING LEGISLATION. Most services carry sections reporting developments of legislation pending in federal and state legislatures. Proposed laws are described briefly and action on them noted. Supplementary sheets are provided with each service report, and a large black dot, star, or other device indicates the most recent action.

7. DIRECTORIES. Directories listing the officials in government administrative agencies are included in many services and kept up to date by replacing pages.

A number of publishers are engaged in reporting by the loose-leaf method. Some of the services published are competitive; others are unchallenged. Although their contents vary, services in general are of three types: (1) The editorial type explains problems in the field editorially with reference only to key cases; (2) the reporter type presents all official information with little consolidation or coördination; and (3) the combination editor-reporter type presents all available information, coördinates it in a single column, and "ties it together" editorially. Throughout this book references are made to loose-leaf publications that deal with the subjects in each chapter.

SUMMARY OF GENERAL TECHNIQUES

To summarize the general technique of locating business information two outlines are provided: (1) *The Complete Technique* for the individual who is commencing a search for complete information on a subject of which he is ignorant; and (2) *The Short Method,* for persons searching for facts to supplement their knowledge.

THE COMPLETE TECHNIQUE

1. The problem must be defined accurately. Be sure that the type of information required is clearly understood, and use the dictionary to clarify the meanings of unfamiliar words.

2. The next step is to go to the library where the greatest accumulation of pertinent material is available. If the public library has a business branch, and the topic being researched is a business one, the search is made that much easier. However, if the business firm conducting research has its own library, the latter is the first place to start.

3. The general background of the subject is acquired by consulting the *Encyclopedia Americana, Encyclopaedia Britannica, Collier's Encyclopedia,* and the *Encyclopedia of the Social Sciences.* The annual yearbook volumes should be examined too, and references at the end of each article should be noted.

4. Examine the almanacs and yearbooks, such as *The World Almanac,* the *Information Please Almanac, The Statesman's Year-Book,*

and the various regional yearbooks if the topic is within the limits of their subjects.

5. The next step is to consult the subject index of the card catalog to locate books containing the needed information. Various selective reading lists all emphasize the better books—such as the Baker Library, Harvard Graduate School of Business Administration, *Business Literature: A Reading List for Students and Businessmen* and *A Reading List on Business Administration* by Dartmouth College, Amos Tuck School of Administration and Finance, and the previously mentioned publications of the Business Branch of the Newark, New Jersey Public Library, the Business and Technology Department of the Cleveland Public Library, and Special Libraries Association.

6. Locate the pertinent government publications by consulting the *United States Public Documents Monthly Catalog* and the semimonthly *List of Selected United States Government Publications*. If the subject is included in one of the United States Superintendent of Documents *Price Lists,* this source can be a real time-saver.

7. An even more direct method for locating exact information on laws and regulations is to utilize the appropriate loose-leaf service which presents the desired information directly to the reader without further research on his part.

8. The most recent data on the topic should then be secured from magazines, pamphlets and newspapers, especially the *New York Times* and the *Wall Street Journal.* Consult the *Business Periodicals Index, Applied Science and Technology Index, Readers' Guide to Periodical Literature, Public Affairs Information Service,* the *New York Times Index,* and the *Wall Street Journal Index.*

9. If the preceding steps do not unearth the information desired, visit or write trade associations, technical societies and Chambers of Commerce for help. It is quite possible that they will have unpublished information which will solve your problem.

SHORT METHOD

It is assumed that the individual is well acquainted with his subject and needs only one or two facts to complete the picture. At times, however, the assumption on the part of the researcher that he has all the facts can lead to trouble if conclusions are based on incomplete or erroneous information.

1. Consult the library card catalog.

2. Examine various almanacs and yearbooks.

3. Review briefly various government document catalogs.

4. Complete the job by checking the periodical indexes which were mentioned in the first list of suggestions.

This chapter has been concerned with suggestions for the general sources of information that aid in location of both material and facts. Succeeding chapters will follow the same general outline, but will deal with the sources of information for one field of business.

CHECKLIST OF BASIC TIME-SAVING SOURCES

BIBLIOGRAPHIES

Association of University Bureaus of Business and Economic Research. *Index of Publications of Bureaus of Business and Economic Research.* Eugene, Oregon. Bureau of Business Research, University of Oregon, 1957. Supplement 1957–1958.

Baker Library. Graduate School of Business Administration, Harvard University. Business Literature: *A Reading List for Students and Businessmen.* Compiled by Harriette L. Williams (Reference List No. 17, Rev. ed.), 1959.

Dartmouth College. Amos Tuck School of Administration and Finance. *A Reading List on Business Administration.* 8th revision. Hanover, N.H., Dartmouth College, 1962.

Pittsburgh University. Bureau of Business Research. *Small Business Bibliography.* 2d ed. Pittsburgh, Pa., Pittsburgh University, Bureau of Business Research, 1958.

UNESCO. *International Bibliography of Economics.* Paris, UNESCO. Annually.

U.S. Small Business Administration. *Basic Library References for Business Use* (Small Business Bulletin 18), Washington, D.C. Small Business Administration, 1959.

GOVERNMENT DOCUMENTS

Boyd, Anne M. *United States Government Publications. Sources of Information for Libraries.* 3d ed. revised by Rae Elizabeth Rips, New York, H. W. Wilson, 1949.

Brown, Everett S. *Manual of Government Publications. United States and Foreign.* N.Y., Appleton-Century-Crofts, 1950.

Hirshberg, Albert S. & Melinat, Carl H. *Subject Guide to United States Government Publications.* Chicago, American Library Association, 1947.

Leidy W. Philip. *A Popular Guide to Government Publications.* New York, Columbia University Press, 1950.

Schmeckebier, L. F. and Eastin, R. B. *Government Publications and Their Use.* Rev. ed. Washington, The Brookings Institution, 1961.

HANDBOOK

Brown, Stanley M. and Doris, Lillian, eds. *Business Executives Handbook.* 4th rev. ed. Englewood Cliffs, N.J., Prentice-Hall, 1953.

HOW TO LOCATE INFORMATION

Johnson, H. W. and McFarland, S. W. *How to Use a Business Library with Sources of Business Information,* 2d ed. Cincinnati, South-Western Publishing Co., 1957.

Manley, Marian C. *Business Information—How to Find and Use it.* New York, Harper, 1955.

INDEXES TO PERIODICALS

Applied Science and Technology Index. Monthly with quarterly, semiannual and annual cumulations. New York, H. W. Wilson Company.

American Economic Association. *Index of Economic Journals, 1886–1859.* Chicago, Erwin, 1961. 5 vols.

Business Periodicals Index. Monthly with quarterly, semiannual and annual cumulations. New York, H. W. Wilson Company.

Current Contents. A biweekly. Philadelphia 3, 33 South Seventh Street, The Institute for Scientific Information.

New York Times Index. Monthly with annual cumulations. New York, New York Times.

Official Index of the London Times. Bimonthly. London, London Times.

Public Affairs Information Service Bulletin. Weekly with quarterly, semiannual and annual cumulations. New York. Public Affairs Information Service.

Readers Guide to Periodical Literature. Monthly with quarterly, semiannual and annual cumulations. New York, H. W. Wilson Company.

U.S. Superintendent of Documents. *Price List 36—Department Periodicals.* Washington, D.C., Government Printing Office.

Wall Street Journal Index. Monthly with annual cumulations. New York, Dow Jones Company.

INDEXES TO FOREIGN GOVERNMENT PUBLICATIONS

Canada. *Canadian Government Publications Monthly Catalogue.* Ottawa, Queen's Printer.

Canada. *Consolidated Annual Catalogue of Canadian Government Publications.* Ottawa, Queen's Printer.

Great Britain. Her Majesty's Stationery Office. *Consolidated List of Government Publications*. London, Her Majesty's Stationery Office. Annually.

Great Britain. Her Majesty's Stationery Office. *Government Publications Monthly List*. London, Her Majesty's Stationery Office.

United Nations. United Nations Documents Index: *United Nations Specialized Documents and Publications*. Monthly with annual cumulative index. New York, United Nations.

INDEXES TO PUBLICATIONS OF THE UNITED STATES

GOVERNMENT

U.S. Census Bureau. *Catalog of the United States Census Publications, 1790–1945*. Washington, D.C., Government Printing Office, 1950.

—— *Catalog of United States Census Publications*. Quarterly with annual cumulations. Washington, D.C., Government Printing Office, 1951–.

—— *Census Publications. Catalog and Subject Guide, 1945–1951*. Washington, D.C., Government Printing Office, 1951.

U.S. Bureau of Foreign Commerce. *Checklist of BFC Publications*. Irregular. Washington, D.C., U.S. Bureau of Foreign Commerce.

U.S. Commerce Department. *United States Department of Commerce Publications*. Washington, D.C., Government Printing Office, 1952 with annual supplements.

U.S. Labor Department. *Publications of the United States Labor Department, Subject Listing, 1948–1957*. Washington, D.C., Government Printing Office, 1957. Supplements 1958 and 1959.

U.S. Superintendent of Documents. *Catalog of the Public Documents of the 76th Congress and of all the Departments of the United States for the period June 1, 1939—December 31, 1940*. Washington, D.C., Government Printing Office, 1945.

—— *List of Selected United States Government Publications*. Semimonthly. Washington, D.C., Government Printing Office. (Formerly Weekly Selected United States Documents.)

—— *Price Lists of Government Publications*. Washington, D.C., Government Printing Office, 1898–.

—— *United States Government Publications Monthly Catalog*. Washington, D.C., Government Printing Office, 1895–.

PERIODICALS

Business and Technology Sources. Four to six issues per year. Cleveland, O., Business and Technology Department, Cleveland Public Library.

Business Literature. Monthly except July and August. Newark, N.J., Newark Public Library.

Business Method: Index. Monthly except July. Ottawa, Box 453, Keith Business
    Library.
Congressional Quarterly, News Features. Washington 6, D.C., 1156 19th St., Con-
    gressional Quarterly.
Economic Abstracts. *A Semi-monthly Review of Abstracts on Economics, Finance,
    Trade and Industry, Management and Labor.* The Hague, Martinus Nijhoff,
    1954-.
The Executive. Monthly. Boston, Mass., The Executive.

3

LOCATING INFORMATION
ON FIRMS AND INDIVIDUALS

The need for answering the question Who? What? and Where? confronts the businessman every day in the operation of his business. He wants to know who manufactures needed machines and materials and where they are located. Or he may want to verify the spelling of an individual's name or address. His sales department wants all the information possible regarding the background, affiliations and tastes of prospective customers. Perhaps he needs to locate research specialists in certain fields or organizations which can supply essential information.

The items most frequently desired are the name and address, the business connections, and the individual's position in the firm. Facts on the achievements and activities of the individual are often helpful too. These can be secured from the professional organization, lodge, or club to which he belongs. Books and articles he has published and positions he has held in civic and governmental agencies throw further light on an individual's abilities and position in the community. The sports and hobbies in which he is interested aid in rounding out the picture.

DIRECTORIES

General information on business firms is usually limited to the name and address, products produced or services rendered, including brand names and trademarks and the names of the principal officers. In some cases branches and the names of branch managers are listed. Certain specialized directories give information on the financial setup of the larger firms. For smaller firms and individuals, Dun & Bradstreet's *Reference Book* supplies credit information, the address, a statement as to type of business, and a credit rating. Other credit rating agencies publish credit rating books on particular industries. These, as well as the Dun & Bradstreet *Reference Book,* are available to subscribers only.

There are several publications which are helpful in locating directories. These are:

Association of North American Directory Publishers. *Catalog of City, County and State Directories.* New York, the Association, 1961.

    Issued periodically by the Association, this catalog indicates the type of information contained in the directory, date of publication and publisher. In the alphabetical listing of towns by states, all the towns included in a particular directory are listed. Canadian towns and cities are also covered.

Chamber of Commerce of the United States. *Guide to Listings of Manufacturers.* Washington, D.C., Chamber of Commerce of the United States, 1961.

    This publication is both a listing of directories and a suggested method of locating firms. In addition to the commercial directories and those dealing with specific industries, government and annual directories published by periodicals are covered. This is a good basic list.

Metropolitan Research Company. *Association Index. A Source List of Directories and Other Publications.* Los Angeles, 55, P.O. Box 5345 Metropolitan Station, 1958.

    One thousand and eighty-three publications are listed by title in the first section. Information provided is frequency of publication, cost, and address of the publisher. The coverage and type of information supplied by each publication is noted. The second part is a finding list where author, title, and subject are combined into one alphabet. This is a good source in which to locate directories of special groups.

Chamber of Commerce of the United States. State Chamber of Commerce Service Department. *Sources of State Information and State Industrial Directories.* Washington, D.C., Chamber of Commerce of the United States, 1958.

    The more difficult to locate sources of information on states are indicated along with the names and addresses of public and private organizations which can supply it. A list of available directories is in one section of this publication.

Sales Management. *State Industrial Directories.* New York, 630 Third Avenue, Sales Management, July 10, 1959.

    Directories for all states are included.

Foreign directories may be found through the use of:

United States Bureau of Foreign Commerce. *A Guide to Foreign Business Directories.* Washington, D.C., Government Printing Office, 1955.

> A descriptive list of directories arranged by country. The cross references
> as to where data on smaller areas or dependencies can be found in larger
> works are helpful. A products directory adds to the usefulness of this work.
> Information is supplied on directories of exporters, suppliers, business and pro-
> fessional men, and government officials.

The telephone directory is usually sufficient for securing names and
addresses. The classified section groups firms and individuals in the same
line of business and is a handy means of locating suppliers or manufacturers of a given product in the locality. The offices of the Telephone
Company, the larger pay stations, and metropolitan public libraries have
reference copies on each of the surrounding towns and larger cities. The
compilation of directories is an expensive task. Many are issued annually;
however, it has become prohibitively costly to prepare a directory of the
largest cities such as New York, Chicago, and Los Angeles and none have
been prepared for these cities since World War II. As a result the telephone directory is the best available source of current information.

Next in availability are the city directories which are published by
various commercial firms, of which the R. L. Polk Company is perhaps
the best known. These directories differ in the amount of information
supplied, although the following basic information is contained in each
of them: the name, occupation, and home address of each inhabitant.
Sometimes the firm of employment and the position occupied in the
organization is included, particularly if it is of a supervisory nature. The
directories include the names and titles of state and county officials living
in the city and the members of the municipal government. The classified
section follows the alphabetical listing groups, the names of firms, organizations, and individuals under the appropriate product, service, or
activity. The street guide is an aid to the quick location of addresses. The
very sketchy statistical review of the cities concerned is of only the most
general value.

The financial services may also be utilized as directories. The home
office address is given; the names of the directors and principal officers are
listed under each company. *Moody's Manuals of Investments (American*

and Foreign) and *Standard Corporation Records* are the best publications for this purpose and the most widely available.

DIRECTORIES OF MANUFACTURERS

If it is necessary to locate firms manufacturing machinery, equipment, and the raw materials needed for a business, or to find out the producers of various types of products—for example, when planning a sales campaign or establishing a sales agency—a comprehensive directory of manufacturers should be consulted.

Dun & Bradstreet Million Dollar Directory. Annual with monthly supplements. New York, Dun & Bradstreet.

> All firms with a net worth of a million dollars are listed. The directory is in three sections: the first is an alphabetical arrangement by company; the second, by geographical location, and type of industry: and, the third a compilation of the top officials of the firm. Subsidiaries are in a separate section with cross references to the parent company. The information supplied is the name and address of the company, annual sales, number of employees, names of executives, type of business, and names of major divisions. Codes give an exact description of the type of business amplifying the more general written terms.

Thomas' Register of American Manufacturers. Annually. N.Y., Thomas Publishing Company, 1910–.

> More than 70,000 products are listed. Under the name of each product are arranged the firms which manufacture it, listed by state and city location. From this book the businessman can learn who makes what, the address, and, in many instances, the names of the principal officers and an indication of the capital invested in the business. Subsidiaries and merged firms are shown. Separate sections list the commercial associations (largely Chambers of Commerce), banks, and trade papers. The compilation of trade names and trademarks into one list provides an indispensable source of information for locating the manufacturers of widely advertised products.

MacRae's Blue Book. Annually. Chicago, MacRae's Blue Book Co., 1895–.

> The information in this directory is less detailed than that in *Thomas' Register,* although the "Address and Local Distributors" section is somewhat more complete for branch offices. It includes a classified materials section and lists trade names. The format makes this publication slightly easier to use, but it lacks the completeness of the preceding directory.

Kelly's Directory of Merchants, Manufacturers and Shippers. Annually. London, Kelly's Directories, Ltd., 1889–.

> The British Isles are covered comprehensively in four sections. These are

followed by a section on British Commonwealth Overseas and a final section or supplement on the other countries of the world. The information supplied is name, type of business, and address. Indexes to towns and countries, trades, exporters, and importers make it easy to locate a product or a manufacturer or dealer. The fore-edge breakdown of the book into sections makes for quick references.

Somewhat narrower in scope than the preceding four directories is:

Plant Purchasing Directory. Biennially. Chicago, Conover-Mast Publications.
    This is a buyers' guide especially designed to meet the needs of plant managers, superintendents, maintenance men, and purchasing agents.

Frequently trade publications issue directories of firms supplying the trade which they cover. *The Chemical Buyers' Guide,* published annually by the magazine *Chemical Markets* is a particularly good directory of this kind.

Additional directories that deal with specific types of business will be found in the chapters on foreign trade, on transportation, and on basic industries.

In many cities the local Chambers of Commerce compile directories of manufacturers and associations in their locality. Newcomers to the area and persons starting a new business will find these lists of value.

Much useful information can be obtained from trade associations and research organizations. A goodly portion of their investigations (if published) can be located by referring first to the periodical indexes. However, it is advisable for the businessman to be acquainted with the activities of trade and research organizations in and outside his own field. He may contact them direct for unpublished material and thus become acquainted with the experience and findings of the businessmen who belong to the association.

There are two up-to-date lists of trade and professional associations which are helpful to the businessman. The first mentioned is the most inclusive in that it attempts to cover all associations of whatever nature.

Gale Research Co. *Encyclopedia of Associations.* Detroit 26, Mich. 2200 Book Tower, Gale Research Co. Two volumes of an eventual five volumes published in 1961.
    All types of national organizations appear in these volumes and they are agricultural, business, cultural, educational, fraternal, governmental, Greek letter, labor, medical, national and ethnic, professional, public affairs, religious, social welfare, technical, and veterans. The information provided is the name

and address of the organization, name of secretary or other officer, date of founding, number of members and staff, description of activities, publications, and date of annual meeting. Excellent subject and alphabetical indexes make this information easily available. Volume I covers national associations and Volume II is a geographical and executive index. Projected volumes are: *State and Local Associations of the Mid-East; State and Local Associations of the U.S.—West;* and, *National Organizations of Canada.*

A directory more specifically dealing with business associations is:

U.S. Business and Defense Services Administration. Office of Technical Services. *Directory of National Associations of Businessmen.*
> Compiled by C. J. Judkins. Washington, D.C. Office of Technical Services, 1961. (A new basic directory is in process.) Data is supplied on over 2,000 organizations operating nationally. Approximately half of the Associations are related to manufacturing, the remainder are concerned with construction, finance, retail trade, and so forth. The name of the organization, address, name of secretary or manager, total membership, and type of membership comprises the information contained in this work.

Two publications of the National Research Council provide directories of research organizations. The first of these treats activities carried on outside business itself, whereas the second deals with research conducted within industry.

National Research Council. *Scientific and Technical Societies in the United States and Canada.* 7th ed. Washington, D.C., National Research Council, 1961.
> Part I is for societies in the United States, and Part II is the Canadian section. Date of founding, history, membership (both number of members and qualifications for membership), research conducted and fields of research, publications issued, and research organizations financed by industry constitute the information given in this publication. It is the directory to which the businessman may turn with assurance to get help in the solution of some techncial difficulty beyond the abilities of his own organization.

National Research Council. *Industrial Research Laboratories of the United States Including Consulting Research Laboratories.* 11th ed. Washington, D.C., National Research Council, 1960.
> The kinds of research activities and those responsible for research activities and those responsible for research in industry along with the names of the organizations concerned are listed.

BIOGRAPHIES

The pioneer biographical works are *Who's Who* and *Who's Who in America.* The general method of presentation is the same. *Who's Who,* a British publication, is world-wide in its coverage. Consequently, the number of Americans listed is less extensive than in the American publication. *Who's Who* is an excellent source of information for both prominent individuals in the British Empire and the most distinguished Europeans and Americans. To the American businessman, however, *Who's Who in America* is considerably more helpful. Similar biographical works are available on the leading citizens of other countries. Very often yearbooks of a country have a biographical section. A large number of these compendiums are published in English. A very helpful publication, *Who's Who in Latin America,* contains biographical information on the leading individuals in all countries south of the Rio Grande.

Frequently, an individual who is prominent in local affairs is not sufficiently distinguished to appear in national collections. Data on him may be found in one of the state or regional works, such as *Who's Who in the West, Moore's Who's Who in California,* and the like. The more localized works generally have irregular publication and revision dates which cause them to lack the up-to-dateness and completeness of the larger publications.

The presentation of data is quite similar in all these biographical compilations both local and national. After the listing of the individual's name and such vital statistics as date of birth, marital status and children, and education, the body of the account records the achievements of the person. Positions held, both in business and other organizations, are set forth in chronological order from the earliest to the present. Directorships held in corporations and other organizations are noted, followed by the titles of publications, sports, hobbies, the individual's home address and, usually, the business address.

These brief sketches do give a fairly good outline of a person's interests, connections, and activities, thus enabling the reader to gain a very general impression. The various who's who publications, however, have three defects from the businessman's point of view. Of necessity it must be selective, which naturally limits the number of persons included. Information about some specialist in a certain phase of business activity or technology may be extremely valuable to the businessman, but the individual in question may be comparatively unknown outside his own group and therefore not included in the general biographical work. Also, the young men who are beginning to emerge as leaders are seldom listed. Secondly, the very general nature of the information given often leaves unanswered the specific questions the businessman asks. Probably no one book can do this; but by consulting a variety of sources, much useful information can be acquired. Finally, there is the time lag between volumes which ranges from one to several years. This requires an additional search for current sources of information.

SPECIALIZED BIOGRAPHIES

The search for biographical data can be expedited by using publications confined to special groups or particular fields of activity. More individuals, prominent in fields too specialized to fall within the scope of the general biographical publications are listed in these specialized biographies.

World Who's Who in Commerce and Industry has the broadest coverage of these more specialized biographies. It supplies the usual basic information plus many more details on the individual's business activities. The positions a person has held and the firms he has worked for are listed, together with any directorships helds in other corporations. This *Who's Who* gives more information on less prominent businessmen as well as useful details of a more general nature than appear in works restricted to one field of business activity. The directory of corporations in the second section is useful in locating the top-level officers of a company.

A handy source for the location of longer biographies of businessmen and histories of business firms is *Studies in Enterprise* by Lorna M. Daniells. This well-selected list by industry, is most helpful in relating individuals to *their industry*. Both book and periodical biographies are included.

The most detailed biographical information on the personnel of the federal government can be found in the *Congressional Directory,* published semiannually. It supplies biographies of members of Congress, lists the membership of all committees, and gives the names of top-ranking personnel of executive departments and independent offices. State *Bluebooks* and directories provide similar information on state officials.

There are three publications of the federal government which can be used to locate individuals in government service. The *United States Government Organization Manual* supplies list of officials in all branches of the government each year. This includes all divisional department and bureau chiefs. The *Federal Register,* published annually with a weekly supplement, notes changes in personnel along with changes in laws and regulations. A listing for state officials, but not so inclusive, is performed biennially by the Council of State Governments in its *Book of the States.*

It is common practice to get the most successful men or those with large financial interests to serve on boards of directors. Published lists of directors indicate what men are active and influential and are responsible for the policy-making activities of a firm. This information is of value to the businessman if he is incorporating a new company, is desirous of interesting some other firm in buying his products, or is seeking a business connection.

Poor's Register of Directors and Executives, published annually with three supplements a year, is the most comprehensive of these directories. Executives and directors of corporations in the United States and Canada are listed in this volume. In the first section the companies are grouped according to the type of business in which they are engaged. The main office address is given, and the major officers and the purchasing agent are named. Usually each individual's address is given, too. The names of directors and major officers are arranged alphabetically in the second part, where all the directorships and offices held by each person are listed. The date and place of a man's birth, his college, and year of graduation, are also given. A separate volume arranged on a state and city basis and entitled *Poor's Register of Directors and Executives, Geographical Section,* is a handy index to the main volume.

Directories of directors compiled on a regional or state basis are useful to the businessman because they list the officials of smaller or more closely held firms who do not appear in the national directories. *Walker's Directory of California Directors and Corporations* is a good example of a comprehensive local list.

For British companies or those with British affiliations or branches *The Directory of Directors* published by Thomas Skinner & Co., London, gives the names of some 32,000 directors of companies whose securities are listed on the stock exchanges of the United Kingdom. Each man's name, address, and the companies of which he is a director is supplied; no corporation section is included in this work.

The *Rand McNally Bankers Directory* is a source of information for the names of directors of all banks in the United States and abroad.

A number of biographical directories have been published on individuals active in certain fields of business, or the professions, or research. *Who's Who in Public Relations* is a typical biography of men engaged in a specific business activity. *Who's Who in Engineering* and two works edited by Jacques Cattell—*American Men of Science–Physical and Biological* and a second volume *Social and Behavioral Sciences* and *Directory of American Scholars*—briefly describe the type of research and activities of individuals in these fields. From time to time various scientific and professional associations also issued biographical directories that are useful to the businessman who is seeking information on certain persons.

All biographies tend to become obsolete as soon as they are published. The A. N. Marquis Company, publishers of *Who's Who in America,* attempted to remedy this situation in 1938 by publishing the *Monthly Current Biographical Reference Service.* This brings up to date the biographies of persons already in *Who's Who in America,* includes new biographies which will appear in the next volume, and brief sketches of persons in the news. The H. W. Wilson Company has been issuing a very similar publication since 1941 in its *Current Biography, Who's Who in the News and Why.* This publication supplies brief biographies of individuals who have been currently in the news. Each biography has a list of recent news articles for those who desire to pursue the subject further. The bulk of the persons whose biographies are included are prominent in politics and government, the military, and the arts. However, the businessman may find what he needs in the sections on business, finance, aviation, radio, and technology.

A most troublesome problem is that of locating information on department heads below the rank of vice president and branch managers; no one publication gives very much data on them. Their names sometimes may be found in the annual reports of companies. Biographical data may appear in "write-ups" in the publications of professional and trade associations or of Junior Chambers of Commerce. The library of the local newspaper (the morgue) can probably supply some information, although this source should only be utilized as a last resort under exceptional circumstances because the newspaper is not equipped to handle inquiries from the general public. Information on persons who belong in the middle-management category is usually secured only after consulting a variety of sources.

A summary of information sources on firms and individuals would include:

1. Name and address—telephone and city directories.

2. Personal data—*Who's Who in America. World Who's Who in Commerce and Industry, Current Biography, Poor's Register of Directors and Securities,* and biographical works dealing with special groups.

3. Location of firms—*Thomas Register of Manufacturers;* special directories issued by trade magazines.

4. Trade and professional associations—United States Business and Defense Services Administration, Office of Technical Services. *Directory of National Associations of Businessmen;* Gale Research Co; *Encyclopedia of American Associations;* National Research Council, *Scientific and Technical Societies in the United States and Canada;* local lists published by Chambers of Commerce.

CHECKLIST FOR LOCATING PEOPLE AND FIRMS

Bibliographies of Directories

Association of North American Directory Publishers. *Catalog of City, County and State Directories.* New York, The Association, 1961.

Chamber of Commerce of the United States. *Guide to Listings of Manufacturers.* Washington, D.C., Chamber of Commerce of the United States.

Chamber of Commerce of the United States, State Chamber of Commerce Service Department. *Source of State Information and State Industrial Directories.* Washington, D.C., Chamber of Commerce of the United States, 1958.

Metropolitan Research Company. *Association Index. A Source List of Directories and Other Publications Listing Associations.* Los Angeles 55, Box 5345 Metropolitan Station, Metropolitan Research Company, 1958.

Sales Management. *State Industrial Directories.* New York, 630 Third Ave.; Sales Management, July 10, 1959.

U.S. Bureau of Foreign Commerce. *A Guide to Foreign Business Directories.* Washington D.C., Government Printing Office, 1955.

Biography—Current

Current Biography, Who's Who in the News and Why. New York, H. W. Wilson Company, 1941–.

Monthly Current Biographical Reference Service. Chicago, A. N. Marquis Co., 1939–.

BIOGRAPHY—GENERAL

Who's Who. New York, Macmillan. Annually.
Who's Who in America. Chicago, A. N. Marquis Co. Biennially.
Moore's Who's Who in California. Los Angeles, John M. Moore, 1959.
Who's Who in Latin America. 3d ed. Chicago, A. N. Marquis Co., 1945–1951.
Who's Who in the West. 7th ed. Chicago, A. N. Marquis Co., 1960.

BIOGRAPHY—SPECIALIZED

Cattell, Jacques, ed. *American Men of Science–Physical and Biological Sciences.* 10th ed. Tempe, Ariz., Jacques Cattell Press Inc., 1960.
Cattell, Jacques, ed. *American Men of Science–Social and Behavioral Sciences.* 9th ed. New York, R. R. Bowker, 1956.
Cattell, Jacques, ed. *Directory of American Scholars.* 3d ed. New York, R. R. Bowker, 1957.
Congressional Directory. Washington, D.C., Government Printing Office, semi-annually.
Daniells, Lorna M. *Studies in Enterprise.* Boston, Baker Library, Harvard University, Graduate School of Business Administration, 1957.
Council of State Governments. *Book of the States.* Chicago, Council of State Governments. Biennially.
Who's Who in Engineering. New York, Lewis Historical Publications, Inc., 1960.
World Who's Who in Commerce and Industry. 7th ed. Chicago, A. N. Marquis Co., 1959.

DIRECTORIES—FIRMS

The Chemical Buyers' Guide. New York, Chemical Markets Magazine. Annually.
Dun & Bradstreet. *Million Dollar Directory.* New York, Dun & Bradstreet. Annually with monthly supplements.
Kelly's Directory of Merchants, Manufacturers and Shippers. London, Kelly's Directory, Ltd. Annually.
MacRae's Blue Book. Chicago, MacRae's Blue Book Co. Annually.
Plant Purchasing Directory. Chicago, Conover-Mast Publications. Biennially.
Thomas' Register of American Manufacturers. New York, Thomas Publishing Co. Annually.

DIRECTORIES—ORGANIZATIONS

Gale Research Co. *Encyclopedia of Organizations.* Detroit 26, Mich. 2200 Book Tower, Gale Research Co., 1961.
National Research Council. *Scientific and Technical Organizations of the United States and Canada.* 7th ed. Washington, D.C., National Research Council, 1961.

—— *Industrial Research Laboratories of the United States Including Consulting Research Laboratories.* 11th ed. Washington, D.C., National Research Council, 1960.

U.S. Business and Defense Services Administration. Office of Technical Services. *Directory of National Associations of Businessmen,* 1961. Compiled by C. J. Judkins, Washington, D.C., Office of Technical Services, 1961 (A new basic directory is in process).

DIRECTORIES—PERSONS

Directory of Directors (British). London, Thomas Skinner & Co. Annually.

Moody's Manual of Investments, American and Foreign. New York, Moody's Investors Service. Annually with continuous revisions.

Poor's Register of Directors and Executives. New York, Standard and Poor's Publishing Company. Annually.

Poor's Register of Directors and Executives. Geographical Section. N.Y., Standard and Poor's Publishing Company. Annually.

Rand McNally Bankers Directory. Chicago, Rand McNally & Co. Semiannually.

Standard Corporation Records. New York, Standard and Poor's Corp. Continuously revised.

Telephone Directory

U.S. Federal Archives. Federal Register Division. *Federal Register.* Washington, D.C., Government Printing Office. Annually with weekly supplements.

U.S. Federal Archives. Federal Register Division. *United States Government Organization Manual.* Washington, D.C., Federal Register Division. Annually.

Walker's Directory of California Directors and Corporations, 1940–1941. San Francisco, Walker's Manual, Inc., 1941.

DIRECTORY—FINANCIAL RATINGS

Dun & Bradstreet Reference Book. Bimonthly. New York, Dun & Bradstreet, Inc.

4

THE BUSINESS SCENE

Business activity, so significant a part of human life today, is itself affected by varied influences, man-made and otherwise. The increasing importance of foreign trade, both as a source of raw materials and an outlet for his products, makes it essential that the businessman be alert to changes all over the world. In spite of the advances in scientific development, the weather is still a factor in business planning. Adequate advance weather reports can save transportation and utility systems from damage, forecast shortages or abundance of raw materials, and indicate an expanding or declining market. The weather is reported in the daily papers, the *Daily Weather Reports of the United States Weather Bureau,* and from special reports made by several weather forecasting services. Sometimes by predicting conditions as much as thirty days in advance with a high degree of accuracy these services have saved movie producers and contractors, for example, from heavy losses.

The rise of many new countries with varied social and political developments plus the rapid increase in population makes it necessary for the businessman to consider these trends in his attempts to plan business operations. He may find restrictions on his freedom of action, or on the other hand, new programs may create a new demand for goods and services. As an example: He will want to know how his business will be affected by the uptrend in both the older age groups and those of school age in the population. He must be able to anticipate the changes in the defense program. Changes in the governments of foreign countries may affect drastically his foreign sales or branch factories abroad. The development of the European Common Market may have far-reaching effects on his export business.

Newspapers supply the day-to-day accounts of happenings that touch on business. Although they all report the more important events, they vary greatly in completeness of coverage and in the slant given to the news.

The *New York Times* can be found in the libraries of all the large and medium sized cities in the United States. Its availability, plus its broad coverage, detailed reporting, and the fact that practically every item can be located in an index make the *Times* a splendid source of current information. Dow, Jones and Co. Inc., has recently started publishing the *National Observer*. Factual articles on world affairs, economic and political developments and news of individuals are featured along with the general news. The *Christian Science Monitor* is also well known for its sober factual treatment of national and foreign affairs.

The weekly magazines *Newsweek* and *Time* and the monthly *Changing Times* review briefly the political trends in this country and abroad, furnish a résumé of business activities, and present new developments in science, medicine, religion, and the arts. Regular reading of these magazines enables the businessman to keep abreast of current events with a minimum expenditure of hours and effort. Activities highlighted in these magazines may develop leads for further investigation.

The businessman should be aware of the thinking and plans of groups other than his own occupational and social circles. For example, various political and socio-economic organizations have been highly successful in influencing both government policy and private industry. *The Nation, New Republic,* and *New Outlook* discuss various current social problems that often have far-reaching effects.

The mass of conflicting statements which appear in the news each day makes it difficult for the reader to evaluate significant factors and to detect trends in national and international affairs. A variety of publications and services attempt to present an analysis of the current situation. The general news magazines, and the trade magazines as well, have sections on the political scene. However, *The United States News and World Report* has more detailed news on trends in certain sections of direct interest to the businessman.

The United States News and World Report. Weekly. Washington, D.C., United
States News Publishing Corp.

The brief, two-page feature article "Tomorrow" gives a concise summary
of economic, social, and political trends that is a timesaver for busy people.
The "News You Can Use" answers some of the definite questions of businessmen. The "National Week" analyzes national and international situations. Each
issue features a special report on some economic problem. "Trends of Business"
(U.S.) gives some indication of the direction in which business is moving.
This magazine also publishes the official texts of important speeches and government reports.

Another source is:

Dun's Review and Modern Industry. Monthly. New York, Dun & Bradstreet Publishing Company.

"The Washington Desk," "Trend of Business," and "Business Failures"
supply capsule reports on business in general. Excellent longer articles on the
general situation in business, new methods, business firms, employee relations,
and articles on foreign developments provide a wealth of information on
business and industry. Indexes on retail and wholesale trade, failure data, and
"Dun & Bradstreet's Fourteen Financial Ratios" also appear in the publication.

A number of services provide information on the general political and
economic situation, national and international.

Kiplinger Agricultural Letter. Biweekly. Washington, D.C., Kiplinger Washington
Agency.

Prices, trends, production forecasts, and notices of governmental action
appear in this publication.

Kiplinger Washington Letter. Weekly. Washington, D.C., Kiplinger Washington
Agency.

A roundup of opinion in and out of Washington is presented in brief
accounts of trends in politics, business, and industry.

Whaley-Eaton American Letter. Weekly. Washington, D.C., Whaley-Eaton Service.
This service discusses and forecasts politics and economic developments in
Washington.

Whaley-Eaton Foreign Letter. Weekly. Washington, D.C., Whaley-Eaton Service.
Presents an analysis of the foreign political and economic situation.

Report on the Business Outlook. Daily. Washington, D.C., Bureau of National
Affairs, Inc.

The activities of the federal government that affect business are reported
to the businessman the following day by airmail. The report is in two parts:
Part I—"Forecast," Part II—"Background and Analysis." In addition, information is supplied on the availability and prices of industrial and agricultural
commodities, loan policies, foreign trade controls, and wage and salary levels.

What's Happening in Taxation and Government Regulation. Weekly. New York, Prentice-Hall Inc.

Important current happenings in federal and state taxation, social security, labor laws, wage-hour laws, price-fixing laws and other regulatory activities are reported, digested and explained. Concise suggestions are made as to what to do about each new development.

Many a businessman becomes so engrossed in his own particular field of activity that he overlooks trends and developments outside his own interests—even developments that may affect him drastically. Because his contacts are with his own group, he is apt to accept its thinking as representative of all groups. Any such assumptions are likely to becloud his judgment. Therefore, it is wise for him to check his own conclusions against information divorced from the business viewpoint.

Fortune is a magazine whose editorial policy is between that of the general news publications and those concerned strictly with the problems of business. Each monthly issue usually includes one or two articles on foreign affairs, a description of some new product or an industry, and almost always the story of some company or businessman. Very frequently an whole issue will be given over to a socio-economic study of an entire region, a foreign country, or an industry. These articles, colorfully written, throw much light on the development, trends and interrelationships of industry. They are not overburdened with statistical tables. The accounts of businessmen's activities are often fuller than those obtainable elsewhere. *Fortune* also attempts to trace political, social, economic, and cultural trends through surveys and full-length articles. The business and industrial biographies and the regional and foreign surveys are probably the most useful sections of this publication. Much of this material is of a background nature and will not supply all the detailed facts needed for a serious study of a subject.

Time and *Newsweek* have been previously mentioned as periodicals of a general nature, with reports and interpretations of the news.

The magazines that discuss business in general and trends from the businessman's point of view are best represented by *Business Week* and *Nation's Business.* Almost all trade publications cover some general business news, and a certain amount of information on trends and governmental activities. However, the above-mentioned two have the broadest and most detailed coverage. The content is presented in a clear, informative style (complicated statistical tables are omitted) and is highly useful when used with straight statistical data obtained elsewhere.

Business Week, published by the McGraw-Hill Publishing Company, has the most complete coverage of these two general business magazines. Short, chatty articles deal largely with new products and trends in business, business personalities, and the effect of activities of the federal government. The competitive, labor, and political trends are noted. One of the most valuable features is the brief account of new products, new firms, and new activities of old firms. The "Reports to Executives" section provides a concise, detailed study of some subject that is of immediate interest to the businessman. This magazine probably gives the best current over-all picture of business.

Nation's Business is the official publication of the Chamber of Commerce of the United States. At times this fact has colored its reporting of labor and governmental activities. A series of vignettes on world affairs, activities in Washington, and the highlights of business present a government résumé of activities in these fields for the month past. Well-written news articles on local developments, foreign affairs or governmental activity, and the experiences or practices of some one firm comprise the remainder of this periodical. It is more informative on general policies and broad trends than for any great body of factual material.

The National Industrial Conference Board publishes a number of very valuable magazines and pamphlets. As most of them are on specific phases of business, they will be mentioned under their proper subject. The *Conference Board Business Record* presents the businessman with an excellent survey of business trends each month. From month to month it records changes in inventories, costs of living, and wages. Its "Selected Business Indicators" give indexes of production, distribution, commodity prices, securities, and finances that enable the businessman to tell at a glance the direction in which business is moving. Other articles survey business practices and developments in industry as a whole. A handy index to major current events is provided in the "Chronicle of Business." "Tax Briefs" summarizes recent court decisions and treasury rulings that are of interest to the businessman.

The National Industrial Conference Board also publishes *Studies in Business Economics,* which appear irregularly and are concerned with fundamental economic factors which affect business.

The publication *Survey of Current Business* discusses the general trend of business. This monthly periodical of the United States Office of Economics has two main sections. The first section is concerned with the business situation in general and in addition, includes discussions of the immediate prospects of particular industries or such broad topics as prices, earnings, or the causes of business mortality. The opening article of each issue, "The Business Situation," briefs the reader on business activity of the past month, ventures forecasts as to the probable volume and trends of business, and points out underlying factors of business strength and weakness. This study is replete with charts and tables. The remainder of the first section is composed of one or two articles on broad business subjects or studies of industries. The treatment is largely factual and statements are supported by tables and charts. The second, and larger, portion of *Survey of Current Business* is given over to an extremely valuable cumulation of statistics that is a tremendous timesaver. This second section will be discussed in detail in Chapter 5, Statistical Sources.

The publications mentioned thus far deal largely with business trends and activities on a national or international basis. A number of regional, state, and city studies on these subjects are also published by trade associations, Chambers of Commerce, banks, and university research bureaus. The alert businessman should be thoroughly acquainted with these local sources of information because local conditions will affect him more quickly and directly than national trends. But he will have to steer his course, based on data from both sources; to ignore either will be to invite trouble.

Although the publications mentioned above carry a certain amount of news on foreign business and firms, the coverage on them is far less extensive than for domestic reporting. The *Economist* gives a weekly review of British trade and industry. The general state of business is discussed and the impact of various government regulations is analyzed. Commercial activities in various countries and regions abroad are then reviewed. The quarterly *Economic Journal,* a publication of the Royal Economic Society, combines articles on economic theory with a discussion of British and Dominion economics and activities of business firms. Another publication by the Society is *London and Cambridge Economic Services Report on Current Economic Conditions.* The general economic situation is analyzed quarterly in this periodical. A fourth source of foreign business information is the *Times Review of Industry* published as a separate publication each month by the *London Times*. British industry is surveyed in detail in the first portion and this is followed by sections on business all over the world, technical articles, book reviews, and personal data on businessmen and industrialists. It is helpful to an American businessman to understand the British evaluation of conditions in this country and to compare their views with those he obtains from domestic sources.

All the publications referred to in this chapter attempt to keep the businessman informed on current trends and the day-to-day happenings of business. But analytical studies which cover a longer period and supply answers on the significance of trends and on the value and effect of various business and governmental practices are also needed. These are supplied by the various collegiate schools of business where individuals have the training, time, and facilities to do scholarly work. The results of such studies are made available to the businessman in magazines, monographs, and books written by recognized authorities in their fields.

For individuals who desire to obtain basic information on economics, one of the following named works should prove helpful:

Bye, R. T. and Hewett, W. W. *Applied Economics*. 5th ed. New York, Crofts, 1960.
Gemmill, P. F. *Fundamentals of Economics*. 6th ed. New York, Harper, 1960.
Ise, John. *Economics*. Rev. ed. New York, Harper, 1950.
Samuelson, P. A. *Economics*. 5th ed. New York, McGraw-Hill, 1961.

The businessman is constantly on the horns of a dilemma. Not only must he meet the numberless daily problems of his business but he must also endeavor to forecast those trends and developments which will affect his own business and business as a whole and organize a suitable course of action. He must anticipate and prepare for business cycles of varying severities and length. The effects of obsolescence, competition, changes in supply sources, costs, and types of raw materials are vital factors also. To achieve any degree of success in forecasting the future state of business requires long and painstaking analysis of a tremendous mass of statistical material.

The Baker Library *Reference List No. 20 Business Forecasting for the 1960's. A Selected, Annotated Bibliography,* compiled by Lorna M. Daniells, provides a current listing of material in this field. The rapid increase of population has become a factor in economics planning. The *Population Index* supplies a very complete quarterly bibliography of books, articles and studies of all phases of population throughout the world.

The literature of forecasting has been growing rapidly. These publications range from abstract mathematical treatises to glib accounts that are little more than shrewd guesses. The works which follow will provide useful information on the basic factors that should be considered when analyzing business trends for forecasting purposes:

Abramson, A. G. and Mack, R. H., editors. *Business Forecasting in Practice: Principles and Cases.* New York, Wiley, 1956.
American Management Association. *Evaluating and Using Business Indicators, With Special Reference to the Current Economic Outlook.* (AMA Management Report, No. 25.) New York, The American Management Association, 1959.
Bassie, V. L. *Economic Forecasting.* New York, McGraw-Hill, 1958.
Biggs, R. M. *National Income Analysis and Forecasting.* New York, Norton, 1956.
Bratt, E. C. *Business Cycles and Forecasting.* 5th ed. Chicago, Irwin, 1961.
Dauten, C. A. *Business Fluctuations and Forecasting.* Chicago, South-Western Publishing Co., 1954.
Estey, J. A. *Business Cycles: Their Nature, Cause and Control.* 3d ed. Englewood Cliffs, N.J., Prentice-Hall, 1956.
Maisel, S. J. *Fluctuations, Growth and Forecasting: the Principles of Dynamic Business Economics.* New York, Wiley, 1957.
Ruggles, R. and Ruggles, N. D. *National Income Accounts and Income Analysis.* 2d. ed. New York, McGraw-Hill, 1956.

These books do not, of course, exhaust the number of excellent works on the subject of business trends and forecasting. However, their very broad treatment of the subject will provide the businessman with basic information. Anyone desiring to pursue the topic more intensively may refer to the very complete bibliographies contained in these works.

Current studies of business trends, forecasts and developments in business and industry in general are treated quite fully in specialized business magazines such as the *Harvard Business Review, Business Topics* of Michigan State University, *The Quarterly Review of Economics and Business* issued by the University of Illinois, *Journal of Business of the University of Chicago* and, the *Michigan Business Review.*

The *Harvard Business Review,* issued quarterly, contains scholarly articles of considerable length on various phases of management, government and business, labor relations, specific industries, and problems of supply. The editorial approach is that of the research worker; it tends to give greater breadth and a more dispassionate analysis than is usually provided by writers who are concerned more directly with business operations.

The results of research in all phases of business and economic activities that affect business are published in the *Business Research Studies* issued by the Harvard Graduate School of Business Administration. In a sense, these studies supplement the *Harvard Business Review* through more detailed and complete analysis of specific problems. Of particular value are certain studies that are brought up to date and are published annually. The wealth of facts provided is of tremendous assistance for comparative studies.

The *Journal of Business of the University of Chicago* (also published quarterly) covers somewhat the same ground as the *Harvard Business Review*. Each issue treats four or five subjects but emphasis is on a statistical rather than an expository approach. The majority of the studies are closely allied to the business life of the Middle West.

It is advisable for the businessman to be aware of bias (including his own) when reading business literature, particularly that dealing with trends and forecasts. It is most difficult for human beings to be completely objective either in their writing for publications or their reading of them and prejudice may have serious consequences if it warps the judgment of others. Such consequences are more likely today, probably, than at any other time because of the growing number of pressure groups that are, naturally, trying to substantiate their particular programs at every opportunity. An individual's best safeguard is to obtain information from a a number of sources of divergent viewpoints that will tend to counteract each other. This information can then be sifted and evaluated in line with the individual's own common sense, experience, and training, and should enable him to reach a fairly acceptable base for making a decision. It is certainly unwise to follow any suggestions that may result in the making of long-term policies without first assembling as many facts as possible and thoroughly testing them.

The bare minimum program for becoming familiar with the trends of business would be:

1. A knowledge of the principles and criteria set up in the books mentioned on business cycles and forecasting.

2. A regular and thoughtful reading of *United States News and World Report, Business Week, Survey of Current Business,* and the *Harvard Business Review.*

3. The reading of a daily newspaper, bearing in mind the interpretations of the news presented by the publications above.

For other than current events and more complete news coverage the *New York Times* and the *Wall Street Journal* should be consulted. The desired items can be easily located through the indexes to these newspapers.

Perhaps this is a rather formidable assignment to one who is already hard pressed for time. These publications, however, contain the gist of the world's happenings and present a tremendous amount of factual and interpretative material in a comparatively small compass. Their contents are of such vital importance to the businessman that he cannot afford to be oblivious to what is going on.

CHECKLIST OF GENERAL BUSINESS SOURCES

Bye, R. T. and Hewett, W. W. *Applied Economics.* 5th ed. New York, Crofts, 1960.
Gemmill, P. F. *Fundamentals of Economics.* 6th ed. New York, Harper, 1960.
Ise, John. *Economics.* Rev. ed. New York, Harper, 1950.
Samuelson, P. A. *Economics.* 5th ed. New York, McGraw-Hill, 1961.

FORECASTING

Abramson, A. G. and Mack, R. H., eds. *Business Forecasting in Practice: Principles and Cases,* New York, Wiley, 1956.
American Management Association. *Evaluating and Using Business Indicators With Special Reference to the Current Economic Outlook.* New York, American Management Association, 1959.
Bassie, V. L. *Economic Forecasting.* New York, McGraw-Hill, 1958.
Biggs, R. M. *National Income Analysis and Forecasting.* New York, Norton, 1956.
Bratt, E. C. *Business Cycles and Forecasting.* 5th ed. Chicago, Irwin, 1961.
Dauten, C. A. *Business Fluctuations and Forecasting.* Chicago, South-Western Publishing Co., 1954.
Estey, J. A. *Business Cycles: Their Nature, Cause and Control.* 3d ed. Englewood Cliffs, N.J., Prentice-Hall, 1956.

Maisel, S. J. *Fluctuations, Growth and Forecasting: the Principles of Dynamic Business Economics.* New York, Wiley, 1957.
Ruggles, R. and Ruggles, N. D. *National Income Accounts and Income Analysis.* New York, McGraw-Hill, 1956.

FORECASTING—BIBLIOGRAPHY

Baker Library. *Business Forecasting for the 1960s. A Selected Annotated Bibliography.* Compiled by Lorna M. Daniells. (Reference List No. 20.) Boston, Baker Library, Graduate School of Business Administration, Harvard University, 1960.

INDEX—POPULATION

Population Index. Quarterly. Princeton, N.J., Office of Population Research, Princeton University.

PERIODICALS

Business Topics. Quarterly. East Lansing, Mich., Graduate School of Business Administration, Michigan State University.
Business Week. Weekly. New York, McGraw-Hill.
Changing Times. Monthly. Washington, D.C., Kiplinger Washington Agency.
The Conference Board Business Record. Monthly. New York, National Industrial Conference Board.
Dun's Review and Modern Industry. Monthly. New York, Dun & Bradstreet.
Economic Journal. Quarterly. London, Royal Economic Society.
Economist. Weekly. London, Economist Newspaper Ltd.
Fortune. Monthly. New York, Time and Life Publications.
Harvard Business Review. Quarterly. Boston, Mass., Harvard Graduate School of Business Administration.
Journal of Business of the University of Chicago. Quarterly. Chicago, University of Chicago.
London and Cambridge Economic Services Report on Current Economic Conditions. Quarterly. London, London and Cambridge Economic Service.
Michigan Business Review. Bimonthly. Ann Arbor, Mich., School of Business Administration, University of Michigan.
Nation's Business. Monthly. Washington, D.C., Chamber of Commerce of the United States.
Newsweek. Weekly. New York, Newsweek, Inc.
Quarterly Review of Economics and Business. Quarterly. Champaign, Ill., Quarterly Review of Economics and Business.
Survey of Current Business. Monthly. Washington, D.C., United States Office of Economics.
Times Review of Industry. Monthly. London, The Times.

The United States News and World Report. Weekly. Washington, D.C., United States News Publishing Co.

RESEARCH STUDIES

Business Research Studies. Boston, Mass., Harvard Graduate School of Business Administration.
Studies in Business Economics. New York, National Industrial Conference Board.

SERVICES

Kiplinger Agricultural Letter. Biweekly. Washington, D.C., Kiplinger Washington Agency.
Kiplinger Washington Letter. Weekly. Washington, D.C., Kiplinger Washington Agency.
Report on the Business Outlook. Daily. Washington, D.C., Bureau of National Affairs, Inc.
Whaley-Eaton American Letter. Weekly. Washington, D.C., Whaley-Eaton Service.
Whaley-Eaton Foreign Letter. Weekly. Washington, D.C., Whaley-Eaton Service.
What's Happening in Taxation and Government Regulation. Weekly. New York, Prentice-Hall.

5

STATISTICAL SOURCES

Business is so interrelated with and vitally affected by political, social, and economic developments that some measure of business activities and indication of trends is necessary. To present this information so that it can be grasped easily and compared, if necessary, is desirable. If data is discussed solely in narrative form, the reader may easily lose the connection between the facts as given and the making of comparisons becomes almost impossible. The use of statistics in well-organized tables, charts, and graphs reduces the tremendous mass of statistical material to manageable proportions. Such devices make similarities and differences in trends stand out more clearly.

The businessman needs two types of statistical information. He desires to know the actual figures for a given period; for example, the number of shoes produced, net sales, profits of particular types of businesses, security and commodity prices, and other exact information. These data are vital to the day-to-day operation of his business. Secondly, he needs this same information brought together and condensed in some form that will indicate trends for business as a whole and for his own business. The various indexes arrived at mathematically are indicators of business activity as a whole and of special segments of business, such as retail sales, building, heavy industry, and credit conditions.

A study of the general indexes may enable the businessman to plan more effectively the course of his own business. Obviously, he would be foolish to expand his inventories in the face of falling prices in a period which gave every appearance of a cyclical downswing. However, a temporary dip in prices might well provide a profitable opportunity to increase his supplies in anticipation of a rising market. Frequently, statistical sources provide clues to unusual sales opportunities that might otherwise escape notice. They also show what industries are expanding and what ones are declining—facts of vital importance to the investor or anyone planning to make a new business connection.

The actual figures and indexes for his own industry provide a yardstick whereby the businessman can measure the progress of his own firm against that of the industry at large. If his inventories are above or below the average, or the turnover is slower, he should regard these as warnings calling for investigation of his business methods and operations. Comparison of his working capital, ratio of gross to net profit, and return on his investment with the average of these items for his industry enable the businessman to check periodically on the relative efficiency of his business and the soundness of his policies as indicated by the results.

To control his own business properly, the businessman must have the facts on the operations of the various departments. He must know production, costs, and sales figures. But raw figures mean little unless they are organized to make comparison with past results easy.

The use of statistics, particularly indexes, is not without its dangers. The statement "Figures do not lie but liars figure" has a substantial element of truth. If indexes are to be employed as the major basis of policymaking decisions, it is most advisable for the businessman to know something of the sources used and the method of compilation.

In the compilation of an index care must be taken that the statistical data used are related to a collection of homogeneous objects; that is, objects of the same kind or nature or consisting of elements of a like nature. Obviously, bushels of wheat cannot be added to yards of cloth in the construction of an index.

The source of the figures should be known. Has the maker of the index, or chart, or graph collected the information first-hand through questionnaires, extensive sampling, and personal observation, or has he utilized the figures from some other source which has made the actual collection of statistics? Although there are opportunities for error in the collection and compilation of the basic figures, there is a basis for comparison between two indexes which have been independently constructed. Lack of agreement between two similar but independently prepared indexes should make the businessman pause for further thought and investigation. He should also realize that much statistical information is drawn from secondary sources, and, if an error has crept into the primary figures, it will be perpetuated.

The base year is always indicated in a graph or index and should be considered in the light of its effect on the figures. An attempt is usually made to select a relatively stable period for a base; otherwise, serious distortions can arise and wholly erroneous conclusions can be drawn from the data. As an example, if 1932 or 1944 was used as the base year for steel production, the index in each case would show radically different conditions. The year 1944 was one of peak production, therefore, the subnormal rate of operations in the 1930's would be exaggerated, whereas if 1932 was used as a base year, the uptrend would be unduly emphasized. In either instance the index would be an unreliable basis for long-term planning.

For various reasons base years are sometimes changed, or the weighting of various components is changed after an index has been compiled according to a certain pattern for a number of years. This modification may change the effectiveness of the index as a reflection of current conditions. Unless the earlier tabulations are adjusted to the revised data, comparison between the two periods becomes exceedingly difficult. The businessman must watch for these changes and recognize the fact that they may affect his own statistical compilations and planning.

If many assorted tabulations are used which reflect business or commercial activities in a number of fields it is customary to give greatest weight to certain figures than to others. This weighting is usually based on how large the activity represented by the figures bulks in the economy and on the extent of the use of its products. In a cost-of-living index the price of bread would naturally be more heavily weighted than the price of truffles, because every person eats bread, but truffles are a luxury item purchased by few people. Weighting has its pitfalls, as conditions may change which throw the weighting out of balance, and the index will present a false picture of the situation. Before revision of the Dow-Jones Averages, railroad stocks were heavily represented, as were the stocks of textile companies. With the difficulties faced by railroads during a period between 1910 and 1940, and the rapid growth of public utilities and strong industrial companies, this index became meaningless as an indicator of stock price trends. The user of statistical information must always be alert to changing conditions which may affect the validity of his sources.

Likewise, the value of indexes and statistical series is apt to improve with age. A larger body of information tends to reduce the possibility of error in deduction, and the longer period covered tends to smooth out short-term and minor fluctuations. It also is helpful in providing a more accurate basis for comparison when the past can be utilized as the basis for future planning. It must always be borne in mind that change may seriously alter the practical value of statistics. Many businessmen have gotten into difficulty by using too short a period for the basis of their calculations and assuming that either it is a normal condition or that it indicates a trend which will continue for some time.

It is a human failing to generalize from the particular. One sees several drunken soldiers and he may very likely, but falsely, assume that all soldiers are drunkards. Many businessmen have fallen into this same error and have undertaken costly changes in methods and products or embarked on extensive sales campaigns, all of which were planned on the basis of inadequate statistical information. Unusual circumstances may tend to increase or decrease costs unduly. A new product may be accepted readily by one locality and yet not sell on a national basis. Test checks or sampling should extend over a large enough area and a long enough period of time to minimize any special conditions which would influence the results.

Bias is present in all human thinking, and it is certainly not absent in statistical compilations. The results are often consciously or unconsciously influenced by the bias of the compiling agency. Both business and governmental agencies seek to prove various contentions through the use of statistics. Sometimes the case is bolstered through a selection of figures and weighting but more often the difference arises from a variance in interpretation. It is unfortunately true that diametrically opposite conclusions can often be deduced from the same set of statistics. About the only course the businessmen can follow is to get both sides and attempt to make his plans in the light of his own best judgment and the conditions peculiar to his own business.

Since statistics have become a necessary adjunct to business, the businessman will find them an invaluable tool of management provided that he uses them with a full knowledge of their limitations. If he utilizes them with the awareness of the factors which influence their accuracy and with some insight into the methods of their compilation, he will not be led astray.

The following books give some insight into statistical methods and the value and use of various indexes:

Croxton, F. E. and Cowden, D. J. *Practical Business Statistics*. Englewood Cliffs, N.J., Prentice-Hall, 1960.

    The authors have brought the earlier material up to date through reference to current statistical series. However, they place more emphasis on statistical methods than on the various kinds of business statistics. This book is a good source as to how indexes, charts, and graphs are compiled. It also illustrates the common errors that creep into the compilation of statistics. Furthermore, the nontechnical presentation makes the subject matter intelligible to the amateur statistician.

Spurr, W. A. and others. *Business and Economic Statistics*. 2d ed. Homewood, Ill., Irwin, 1960.

    One of the most valuable features of this text is that explanations of statistical methods are all based on examples drawn from business. Various types of business indexes are discussed and evaluated. The subject treatment is on a very practical basis with a minimum of theory. The authors stress how the statistics are to be interpreted after they have been collected and the reader has been thoroughly grounded in basic statistical theory.

Since World War II, the collection and publication of statistics has increased manyfold. National and international organizations have expanded and improved their statistical techniques. Although statistics published by the newer countries and those behind the iron curtain are open to questions as to their accuracy, they do give some indication trends of development.

The bibliographical keys to statistical material have become far more extensive and much more comprehensive. Probably the most thorough and scholarly bibliography is:

Cole, Arthur H. *Measures of Business Change: A Baker Library Index*. Chicago, Irwin, 1952.

    This very thorough study of statistical sources lists indexes by topic or activity covered along with the compiling agency. This section is by a "Reference List of Basic Sources" followed by a directory of the names and addresses of compilers. The subject coverage, title, compiler, and frequency of publication are then given for each index. The location of current and historical data and the period covered follows. Each index is described fully as to its base period and components. This book should be at the right hand of every statistician.

Another very inclusive bibliography of statistical material:

Kendall, M. G. and Doig, A. G. *Bibliography of Statistical Literature.* 1950–1958. Edinburgh and London, Oliver and Boyd, 1962.

  The first of a projected three volume work covering the literature of statistics from the sixteenth century. The 9,000 entries are arranged by author. Titles in the non-roman alphabet are given in English. The material cited is that which the compilers believe will be most useful to researchers and historians. In addition to periodicals, this bibliography covers international conferences and national meetings. Twelve statistical journals are indexed almost completely and forty-three others analyzed for relevant articles. Coverage is world-wide but the bulk of the citations are from American, British, and Russian publications. This work should be of great assistance to professional statisticians.

Three publications serve as aids to the location of current statistics which appear in trade magazines as well as those which are published in government publications.

Wasserman, P., Allen, E., Kruzco, A. and Georgi, C., eds. *Statistics Sources.* Detroit, 26, Mich., 2200 Book Tower, Gale Research Company, 1963.

  This alphabetical subject arrangement of primary sources of statistical data covers American publications and organizations national in scope. A brief indication of the type and period covered in addition to frequency of publication. The very detailed subject listing covers products, foreign countries, trade, and population among other subjects.

Statistical Sources Review. Monthly. Detroit 26, Mich., 2200 Book Tower, Gale Research Company.

  Statistical sources in periodicals, yearbooks, books, pamphlets, and special reports by government and private agencies are reviewed. The subject and title index is cumulated quarterly.

Special Libraries Association. *Guide to Special Issues and Indexes of Periodicals.* New York, Special Libraries Association, 1962.

  This work is designed to facilitate the location of specialized data and statistics in trade, technical, and consumer journals. The 799 periodicals analyzed are listed alphabetically and information supplied is a description of the supplements, indexes, annual issues with month of release, frequency, form and type of indexes, and title, subject, and release date of special issues. A detailed subject index makes the material most usable.

Government agencies are the largest producers of statistics. This is inevitable because they have the facilities and funds to carry on this costly collection and analysis of statistics. Guides to U. S. Government statistics:

Andriot, John L. *Guide to U.S. Government Statistics.* 3d ed. Arlington 10, Mass., Documents Index, 1961.

This is a biennial publication of very great usefulness. All publications containing statistical data are fully listed under department and issuing bureau with a description of the publication, type of statistics, and frequency of publication. Independent agencies, the judiciary, executive and legislative branches are also included. A coded subject index indicates the type of statistics in each item cited.

Hauser, Philip M. and Leonard, William R., editors. *Government Statistics for Business Use.* 2d ed. New York, Wiley, 1956.

This complete revision of the earlier edition brings up to date governmental statistics since World War II. Excellent descriptions of statistical series, usually with indications as to their composition, how to locate them, how these statistics are useful to businessmen, and suggestions as to other sources and series of statistics are presented in this book.

A very helpful publication for the location of statistical information on smaller than national units is:

U.S. Bureau of Foreign and Domestic Commerce. *Sources of Regional and Local Business Statistics,* compiled by Elma S. Moulton (Domestic Commerce Series, No. 115). Washington, D.C., Government Printing Office, 1940.

The content consists of information that is generally available on a daily, weekly, or monthly basis by region, state or city. No mention is made of any publication other than the one in which the statistics are originally published. The content is extremely valuable to the businessman because (a) it presents statistical information of immediate value to his business and (b) it is compiled on an area basis.

U.S. Office of Statistical Standards. *Statistical Services of the United States Government.* Washington, D.C., Office of Statistical Standards, 1959.

This publication describes the programs and statistical activities of the federal government. A bibliography of publications in which data are available to the public is a second section.

A directory of persons doing statistical work in the United States Government is:

U.S. Office of Statistical Standards. *Federal Statistical Directory.* Washington, D.C., Office of Statistical Standards, 1960.

A directory of personnel involved in statistical activities of federal agencies concerned with the collection of data, research, and planning in the social sciences which lists individuals by departments, offices, and bureaus. The name index makes for easy location of persons within their organization.

The bibliographies on statistics which have been mentioned thus far are largely concerned with statistics of the United States.

Bibliographies of a broader nature are the next to be presented.

U.S. Library of Congress. *Statistical Yearbooks, An Annotated Bibliography of General Statistical Yearbooks of Major Political Subdivisions of the World.* Washington, D.C., U.S. Library of Congress, 1953.

The history and content of the latest issue of a statistical yearbook is described for each country, colony, and territory.

Inter-American Statistical Institute *Bibliography of Selected Statistical Sources of Income and Wealth.* Cambridge, Mass., International Association for Research on Income and Wealth, 1937–1957.

An annotated bibliography of statistical and other sources supplying information on the wealth and income of over fifty countries. Topics treated are components of national income, its distribution and utilization, labor force, and economic analysis. This is an excellent source for locating data, both factual and theoretical, on countries outside the United States.

Inter-American Statistical Institute *Bibliography of Selected Statistical Sources of the American Nations.* Washington, D.C., Inter-American Statistical Institute, 1947.

The coverage is 2,500 titles including books, periodicals, and articles in the major statistical sources in twenty-two American nations. The first part is an alphabetical author list, the second by country, and the third by subject.

The time consumed in the location and utilization of statistical sources can be reduced substantially if the businessman will consult publications that bring together a large amount of statistical information within the covers of one work. As the collection and compilation of statistics is a costly process, it is only natural that the bulk of this work is done by national government agencies. In the United States, the Census Bureau is responsible for bringing together and consolidating in one publication much of the statistical work done by other agencies. This information has been published annually for the past sixty-five years, interrupted only by World War II, in the following named volume.

U.S. Bureau of the Census. *Statistical Abstract of the United States.* Washington, D.C., Government Printing Office, 1878–.

This keeps current (on annual basis) much of the information which appears in the decennial censuses. Not only are all the important governmental statistical agencies represented, but many of the commonly used private agencies' statistics are included. Many of the series run back for a number of years and make comparative studies easy. All sources are given and any changes in method of calculation or base years are indicated at the foot of each table. The "Bibliography of Sources of Statistical Data" is an almost complete list of statistics-collecting agencies. One drawback to the use of this publication is the lag between the end of the year and its availablity, which is usually about three months.

Another publication which draws together statistics of direct interest to businessmen is:

U.S. Bureau of Foreign and Domestic Commerce. *Business Statistics*. Washington, D.C., Government Printing Office. Biennially.

This work provides a large number of statistical series on a wide range of business indicators carried back to 1929. This has replaced the *Statistical Supplement of the Survey of Current Business*.

A publication of the U. S. Census Bureau which is most helpful in forecasting business trends is:

U.S. Bureau of the Census. *Business Cycle Developments*. Monthly. Washington, D.C., U.S. Census Bureau.

Seventy different kinds of indicators of business activity are covered. These are grouped under "leading indicators" or those that run ahead of business trends; "coincident indicators" that more or less run with the business cycle; and "lagging indicators" that run behind general business trends. The charts and tables are inclusive and graphic illustrations of business trends. This publication and the *Survey of Current Business* should be in every business library.

Similar data plus forecasts of the economic situation can be found in:

U.S. President's Council of Economic Advisors. *Economic Indicators*. Monthly. Washington, D.C., Government Printing Office.

The *Midyear Economic Review* and *Annual Economic Review*, by this same body cumulates and amplifies the material in *Economic Indicators*. These reports describe the state and outlook for the economy and gives some indication of actions of the federal government.

The United States Congress, Joint Committee on the Economic Report in its annual *Report to Congress* covers the same ground as does *Economic Indicators*.

Another compilation of statistics of a current nature which is very inclusive is:

Economic Statistics Bureau. *The Handbook of Basic Economic Statistics*. Monthly
    with quarterly and annual cumulations. Washington, D.C., Economic Statistics
    Bureau.
        Each issue contains more than 1,800 series relative to different aspects of
    the national economy and assembled from both governmental and private
    sources. Annual data are carried back to 1913 or the earliest year available
    thereafter. Monthly or quarterly figures are supplied for the past four years.
    National product and income, general business indicators, production, labor
    productivity and prices, are the sections of the greatest interest to the business-
    man. This service provides a cumulation of statistics from a wide variety of
    sources in addition to its own research on a current basis. It saves both time
    and trouble in locating the more important statistical series.

The *Federal Reserve Chart Book on Financial and Business Statistics*
published monthly with an annual *Historical Supplement* by the Federal
Reserve Systems carries a large body of statistics. Although the emphasis
is on financial statistics, it is useful for the Federal Reserve Board Index
of Business and statistics on consumer buying.

Two private organizations also assemble statistics in quantity.

National Industrial Conference Board. *The Economic Almanac*. New York, News-
    week, Inc. 1939–.
        It is the aim of The Conference Board to provide statistical information
    of practical interest to business and the general public. The data are current,
    and, in most instances, those presented have been tested by this organization
    as to their validity. Many of the statistics are the result of studies undertaken
    by the research staff of the Conference Board and they provide a check on
    statistics from other sources. The "Glossary of Selected Terms" defines in a
    strictly business sense many of the terms ordinarily found in business reports.
Standard and Poor's Corporation. *Trade and Securities Statistics*. New York,
    Standard and Poor's Corporation, 1928–.
        This service brings together a tremendous mass of statistical information.
    Most of the leading indexes are reproduced in addition to many original com-
    pilations of indexes of security prices and yields. While the heaviest emphasis
    is on financial data, there is a large amount of statistical material on general
    business conditions, cost of living, and prices. The coverage of the available
    series and the monthly supplements which keep the figures current, makes the
    Trade and Securities Statistics one of the first statistical sources to which a
    businessman should turn. The more important Canadian statistics are also
    included.

One of the important factors in the American economy is the expansion of plant and other capital equipment. Each year McGraw-Hill

Publishing Company circulates a questionnaire to business firms as to the intended capital expenditures for the next year. These are published in:

McGraw-Hill Publishing Company. *Business Plans for New Plants and Equipment.* New York, McGraw-Hill. Annually.

> This report is based on replies to questionnaires sent manufacturers and companies in all industries. The information supplied indicates both the amount and kind of investment in plant and equipment, also the sales expectations and the projected expenditures on research.

A number of statistical publications prepared by the federal government and issued by its Department of Agriculture, Bureau of Foreign Commerce, and other bureaus and offices are also useful to the businessman. These deal largely with specific industries or particular phases of business activity. Several trade associations publish statistics on a single industry or business activity. One of the more inclusive of these is the biweekly *National Fact Book* published by the National Association of Manufacturers which presents statistics from governmental and other sources. Many banks and even some individual firms publish statistics as well as trade journals. Many of these indexes and statistical series are included in the works mentioned in this chapter.

Aside from the decennial censuses there is not too much data available on American cities. The International City Managers' Association does supply this lack in:

International City Managers' Association. *Municipal Year Book.* Chicago, International City Managers' Association. Annually.

> Information on population and economic data is supplied on American cities. A number of statistical charts portray municipal activities, finances, and so forth. A directory of city officials is also part of this publication.

The publications which have been mentioned are chiefly concerned with statistics on activities in the United States. *The Economic Almanac* of the National Industrial Conference Board and the *World Almanac* carry some statistics on foreign countries, but neither publication makes any pretense of supplying complete figures. The United Nations and its various allied organizations have supplied statistics on an international basis since 1948. Prior to that date, the League of Nations made this data available in two publications; League of Nations, Economic Intelligence Service, *Statistical Yearbook of the League of Nations,* Geneva, League of Nations, 1927–1945, and, League of Nations, Economics, Financial and Transit Department, *World Economic Survey,* Geneva, League of Nations, 1933–1945. The United Nations publication which continues this is:

United Nations. *Statistical Yearbook.* New York, United Nations, 1948–.

This publication has a world-wide coverage of statistics on population, over-all production, agriculture, forestry, fisheries, mining and quarrying, manufacturing, construction, electricity and gas output, consumption, transport, communications, internal and external trade, balance of payments, wages and prices, finance, education and culture, and housing. Subject and country indexes make the data easy to locate. This work supplies a basis of comparison between countries outside the United States because the United Nations has attempted to make the figures comparable.

In the publication of statistical work, a certain time lag is inevitable. The operation of a business requires statistical information to be as current as possible. Services, magazines and the newspapers supply the up-to-date data.

The following directory of organizations that supply statistical and other information of value to the businessman has been published by the Special Libraries Association:

Special Libraries Association. *Directory of Business and Financial Services.* New York, Special Libraries Association, 1963.

This expanded and current edition of two previous issues makes this publication available again. This is a selective list of newsletters, bulletins, reports, and other published services covering business economics and finance. The names and addresses of five hundred publishers is supplied along with the title and content of the service, frequency of publication and cost. One thousand and fifty services are listed.

The magazines cited below all carry statistical material. In addition, this material is often interpreted in the light of business trends and forecasts.

Survey of Current Business. Monthly. Washington, D.C., U.S. Office of Business Economics.

The bulk of this magazine is comprised of statistical data. Indexes of the major fields of business activity are carried on for the current month and the preceding twelve. Prices, construction, domestic trade, employment and payrolls, finance and production, and stocks of various commodities are a portion of the statistical information presented in indexes and tables. Each monthly

issue analyzes the current business situation and forecast trends. Usually there
are other articles on some new developments affecting business. The February
issue contains statistics for the past year.

Survey of Current Business, Weekly Supplement. Washington, D.C., U.S. Office
of Business Economics.

The indexes of production and general business activity which appear in
the *Survey of Current Business* are kept current in this leaflet.

Federal Reserve Bulletin. Monthly. Washington, D.C., U.S. Board of Governors
of the Federal Reserve System.

The majority of statistics presented are related to finance but the indexes
of industrial production, employment, construction, cost of living, retail sales,
and "Consumers' Buying Preferences" are of general interest. The industrial
production index is one of the most widely used indexes.

The Conference Board Business Record. Monthly. New York, N.Y., National Industrial Conference Board.

The discussion and analysis of current statistics assist the businessman in
interpreting the tabulated data. "Selected Business Indicators" brings this information in the *Economic Almanac* up to date each month. Special business
conditions are analyzed each month.

Weekly Chart Service. Weekly. New York, National Industrial Conference Board.

These charts show at a glance various aspects of the business and economic
scene, usually over a ten year period.

Weekly Desk Sheet of Business Indicators. Weekly. New York, National Industrial
Conference Board.

One page of the more important indexes of business activity with brief
comments. Its timeliness is its most useful feature.

Current Statistics. Monthly. New York, Standard & Poor's Corporation.

Indexes of activity in basic industries and production as a whole are
furnished each month. Figures on stocks and prices of commodities are also
included. This keeps the *Basic Statistics* section of *Trade and Securities Statistics*
up to date.

Dun's Review and Modern Industry. Monthly. New York, Dun & Bradstreet, Inc.

Statistical material on general business conditions and indexes on retail
and wholesale trade, business failures, and "Dun & Bradstreet's Fourteen Financial Ratios" comprise the statistical content of this publication. Some, but not
all of the statistics which appeared in *Dun's Statistical Review* are included.

Business in Brief. Quarterly. New York, Chase Manhattan Bank.

This publication contains a number of graphs on business trends, gross
national product, investment prices and other data on the state of the economy.
Chase Manhattan Bank also publishes a bulletin on European markets.

Cleveland Trust Company Business Bulletin. Monthly. Cleveland, Ohio, Cleveland
Trust Company.

The general discussion of business conditions is often critical of other evaluations of the situation, thereby providing the reader with another point of view for comparison. Each monthly issue contains statistics on some business activities. No large body of statistics is published regularly.

Economic Outlook. Monthly. New York, Labor Board Association.

Digests of data from a wide variety of sources on the state of the economy, employment, social welfare and other related topics useful to Labor Unions make up this publication.

Economic Trends and Outlook. Monthly. Washington, D.C., AFL-CIO Economic Policy Committee.

In short articles this publication comments on the business scene as it affects labor and from the union viewpoint.

The Review of Economics and Statistics. Quarterly. Cambridge, Mass., Harvard University.

Statistics are analyzed for long-range trends, methods of statistical analysis are discussed and evaluated, and the validity of forecasts are assessed. Contributors present forecasts of trends. The statistical data are not cumulated nor do comparable figures appear in each issue. The primary value of this publication is its comments on current economic and statistical developments.

Journal of American Statistical Association. Quarterly. Washington, D.C., American Statistical Association.

Methods of preparation of statistical material and the evaluation of statistical theories and series are featured in this periodical. It is more useful to the professional statistician than to the average businessman.

American Statistician. Five times a year. Washington, D.C., American Statistical Association.

There has been an increasing recognition of the importance of statistics since World War II on the part of national and international bodies. The United Nations has actively gathered and published statistics.

United Nations Monthly Bulletin of Statistics. Monthly. New York, United Nations.

This publication supplies current statistics between issues of the *Statistical Yearbook.*

United Nations Economic Bulletin for Asia and the Far East. Quarterly with March issue including the "Survey." New York, United Nations.

Articles are published on the economic activities and problems of the area plus statistics on production, consumption, exports, prices, cost of living, among others. March issue cumulates information and data for the year.

United Nations Economic Bulletin for Europe. Quarterly. New York, United Nations. March issue is entitled "Economic Survey."

The trends and developments of the area are discussed along with a statistical section covering all facets of European economic activity.

Organization for European Economic Coöperation, General Statistics. Annually with monthly supplements. Paris, France. Organization for European Coöperation.

Complete data are published on all activities of a financial and commercial nature, national finances, agricultural production, industrial production, balance of payments and man power of the Organization. This publication provides the statistical background of the Common Market.

Many countries outside the United States publish statistics prepared by Central statistical bureaus or, in the case of most of the South American republics, by the central banks which are governmental agencies. The following titles are a representative list of such publications, but do not exhaust the field.

Boletim Estatistico. Bimonthly. Rio de Janeiro, Instituto Braseileiro de Geogrefia e Estatistico.

This work covers all phases of Brazilian activities.

Canadian Statistical Review. Monthly with weekly and biennial supplements. Ottawa, Dominion Bureau of Statistics.

A compilation comparable in quality and coverage to the U.S. *Survey of Current Business.*

Economic Trends. Monthly. London, Great Britain, Central Statistical Office.

Presents selected indicators which portray trends in the British economy.

Monthly Abstract of Statistics. Monthly with weekly supplement. New Delhi, India, Central Statistical Organization.

This publication provides a very complete coverage through statistical tables and charts of all phases of Indian economic life and economic indicators, employment, fuel and power production and consumption, industrial production, transport, foreign trade, consumption and stocks, banking and currency, joint stock companies, finance, population, and vital statistics.

Monthly Digest of Statistics. Monthly. London, Great Britain, Central Statistical Office.

This work is a most thorough compilation of statistics on all phases of economic activity, population and other vital statistics, and even the weather.

Three central bank publications that are representative of publications of these organizations are:

Statistical Surveys. Monthly. Ottawa, Bank of Canada Research Department.

Economic Statistics. Monthly. Tokyo, Bank of Japan.

Revista del Banco Central de Venezuela. Bimonthly. Caracas, Banco Central de Venezuela.

Not only does this publication supply detailed statistics on all phases of the economy but it also gives digests of recent legislation and detailed information on the petroleum industry.

Two reviews of the economic situation abroad published by an American and a British Bank are: *The Fortnightly Review* by the Bank of London and South America; and *The Situation* in Argentina, a monthly by the First National Bank of Boston.

Three publications of a nongovernmental nature carry a large body of statistical data and comment on an area or world-wide basis.

Oriental Economist. Monthly. Tokyo, The Oriental Economist.

    The statistics for the Japanese economy are very complete as are the articles on Japanese business. Each issue carries articles on the economics of Japan, the Malay States, and Hong Kong.

The Economist. Weekly. London, Economist Newspaper, Ltd.

    Most of the statistical information presented is of a financial nature. Statistics on commodity production and prices on the leading commodity exchanges are published each week. The analysis of the political and economic situation in Great Britain and elsewhere abroad is of value to American businessmen.

Statist. Weekly. London, Statist.

    A statistical section and index of business activity is a regular feature of each issue. Cost of living, prices, and investment data are also included. The discussion of trends in finance, industry, and foreign trade is naturally from the British point of view.

Every trade journal and most general business magazines carry some statistics of business and forecasts of trends. These figures in trade journals are generally closely related to the industries concerned or are those that have already appeared in a general statistical publication. This is particularly true of the financial publications that include business forecasts in addition to purely financial data.

The businessman frequently needs statistical information on his own state or city. The monthly reviews of the twelve Federal Reserve banks furnish data on business activities of each of the Reserve Districts. State and local Chambers of Commerce, the research departments of the larger banks, and certain schools of commerce and business frequently publish local and regional statistics. This type of information is usually quite valuable to the businessman because it is so closely related to his own activities. A list of such sources would include:

1. On a national basis: *Economic Indicators, the Survey of Current Business* with its *Weekly Supplement* and February *Annual Review; Business Cycle Develop-*

ments; The Federal Reserve Bulletin; The National Industrial Conference Board's *Economic Almanac* supplemented by the monthly *Business Record* and the *Weekly Desk Sheet of Business Indicators;* and, finally, Standard and Poor's *Trade and Securities Statistics* and the monthly *Current Statistics* issue by the same firm.

2. On a local or regional basis: *The Monthly Review* of whichever Federal Reserve bank operates in the section for which information was desired; publications of state and local Chambers of Commerce; local bank reviews of the economic situation; and publications of the business research bureaus of schools of commerce and business.

3. International statistics: United Nations' *Statistical Yearbook* which is kept current by the *Monthly Bulletin of Statistics,* and its *Economic Bulletin for Europe,* and *Economic Bulletin for Asia and the Far East;* the *Oriental Economist,* the *Statist;* the *Economist;* and the publications of government statistical bureaus and those of various foreign central banks.

CHECKLIST OF STATISTICAL SOURCES

CUMULATIONS OF STATISTICS

International City Managers' Association. *Municipal Yearbook.* Chicago, International City Managers' Association. Annually.

League of Nations Economic, Financial and Transit Department. *World Economic Survey.* Geneva, League of Nations, 1933–1945.

—————— Economic Intelligence Service. *Statistical Yearbook of the League of Nations.* Geneva, League of Nations, 1927–1945.

National Association of Manufacturers. *Fact Book.* Washington, D.C., National Association of Manufacturers. Annually.

National Industrial Conference Board. *The Economic Almanac.* New York, Newsweek, Inc., 1939–.

Standard and Poor's Corporation. *Trade and Securities Statistics.* New York, Standard and Poor's Corporation, 1928–.

United Nations. *Statistical Yearbook.* New York, United Nations, 1948–.

U.S. Board of Governors Federal Reserve System. *Chartbook on Financial and Business Statistics. Historical Supplement.* Washington, D.C., U.S. Board of Governors Federal Reserve System. Annually.

U.S. Bureau of Foreign and Domestic Commerce. *Business Statistics.* Washington, D.C., Government Printing Office. Biennially.

U.S. Bureau of the Census. *Statistical Abstract of the United States.* Washington, D.C., Government Printing Office, 1878–.

U.S. Economic Statistics Bureau. *The Handbook of Basic Economic Statistics.* Washington, D.C., U.S. Economic Statistics Bureau, 1947–.

CURRENT FOREIGN STATISTICS

[In language of the country where published (unless otherwise specified).]

Boletim Estastistico. Bimonthly. Rio de Janeiro, Instituto de Geographical Estastistico. (Portuguese and English.)

Canadian Statistical Review. Monthly with weekly and biennial supplements. Ottawa, Dominion Bureau of Statistics.

Economy Review. Monthly. Buenos Aires, Bank of the Argentine Nation.

Economic Statistics. Monthly. Tokyo, Bank of Japan. (English and Japanese.)

Economic Trends. Monthly. London, Great Britain, Central Statistical Office.

The Economist. Weekly. London, Economist Newspaper Ltd.

Fortnightly Review. Semimonthly. Buenos Aires, Bank of London and South America.

Monthly Abstract of Statistics. Monthly with weekly supplements. Delhi, India, Central Statistical Organization.

Monthly Digest of Statistics. Monthly. London, Great Britain Central Statistical Office.

Organization for European Economic Coöperation. General Statistics. Monthly supplements to annual issue. Paris, Organization for European Coöperation.

Oriental Economist. Monthly. Tokyo, The Oriental Economist (English).

Revista del Banco Central de Venezuela. Bimonthly. Caracas, Banco Central de Venezuela.

The Situation in Argentine. Monthly. Boston, First National Bank of Boston.

The Statist. Weekly. London, The Statist.

United Nations Economic Bulletin for Asia and the Far East. Quarterly with March issue including the "Survey." New York, United Nations.

United Nations Economic Bulletin for Europe. Quarterly with March issue entitled "Economic Survey." New York, United Nations.

United Nations Monthly Bulletin of Statistics. Monthly. New York, United Nations.

CURRENT STATISTICS

Business Cycle Developments. Monthly. Washington, D.C., U.S. Census Bureau.

Business in Brief. Quarterly. New York, Chase Manhattan Bank.

Cleveland Trust Company Business Bulletin. Monthly. Cleveland, O., Cleveland Trust Company.

The Conference Board Business Record. Monthly. New York, National Industrial Conference Board.

Current Statistics. Monthly. New York, Standard and Poor's Corporation.

Dun's Review and Modern Industry. Monthly. New York, Dun & Bradstreet, Inc.

Economic Indicators. Monthly. Washington, D.C., Government Printing Office.

Economic Outlook. Monthly. New York, Labor Research Association.

Economic Trends and Outlook. Monthly. Washington, D.C., AFL-CIO Economic Policy Committee.

Federal Reserve Bulletin. Monthly. Washington, D.C., U.S. Board of Governors of the Federal Reserve System.

Federal Reserve Chartbook on Financial and Business Statistics. Monthly. Washington, D.C., U.S. Board of Governors of the Federal Reserve System.

Handbook of Basic Economic Statistics. Monthly. Washington, D.C., Economic Statistics Bureau.

Survey of Current Business. Monthly. Washington, D.C., U.S. Office of Economics.

Survey of Current Business. Weekly Supplement. Weekly. Washington, D.C., U.S. Office of Economics.

Weekly Chart Service. Weekly. New York, National Industrial Conference Board.

Weekly Desk Sheet of Business Indicators. Weekly. New York, National Industrial Conference Boards.

DIRECTORY OF STATISTICIANS

U.S. Office of Statistical Standards. *Federal Statistical Directory.* Washington, D.C., Office of Statistical Standards, 1960.

LOCATION OF STATISTICS

Cole, Arthur H. *Measures of Business Change: A Baker Library Index.* Chicago, Irwin, 1952.

Inter-American Statistical Institute. *Bibliography of Selected Statistical Sources of the American Nations.* Washington, D.C., Inter-American Statistical Institute, 1947.

Kendall, M. G. and Doig, A. G. *Bibliography of Statistical Literature, 1950–1958.* Edinburgh and London, Oliver and Boyd, 1962.

Special Libraries Association. *Directory of Business and Financial Services.* New York, Special Libraries Association, 1963.

Special Libraries Association. *Guide to Special Issues and Indexes of Periodicals.* New York, Special Libraries Association, 1962.

Statistical Sources Review. Monthly. Detroit 26, 2200 Book Tower, Gale Research Co.

U.S. Bureau of Foreign and Domestic Commerce. *Sources of Regional and Local Business Statistics.* (Domestic Commerce Series, No. 115.) Washington, D.C., Government Printing Office, 1940.

U.S. Library of Congress. *Statistical Yearbook: An Annotated Bibliography of General Statistics, Yearbooks of Major Political Sub-divisions of the World.* Washington, D.C., U.S. Library of Congress, 1953.

U.S. Office of Statistical Standards. *Statistical Services of the United States Government.* Washington, D.C., Office of Statistical Standards, 1959.

Wasserman, P., Allen, E., Kruzco, A. and Georgi, C. *Statistics Sources.* Detroit, Gale Research Company, 1962.

Periodicals on Statistics

The American Statistician. Five issues a year. Washington, D.C., American Statistical Association.

Journal of the American Statistical Association. Quarterly. Washington, D.C., American Statistical Association.

The Review of Economics and Statistics. Quarterly. Cambridge, Mass., Harvard University.

Statistical Methods

Croxton, F. E. and Cowden, D. J. *Practical Business Statistics.* Englewood Cliffs, N.J., Prentice-Hall, 1960.

Spurr, W. A. and Others. *Business and Economic Statistics.* 2d ed. Homewood, Ill., Irwin, 1960.

Use of Government Sources

Andriot, John L. *Guide to U.S. Government Statistics.* 3d ed. Arlington 10, Mass., Documents Index, 1961.

Hauser, Philip M. and Learned, William L., editors. *Government Statistics for Business Use.* 2d ed. New York, Wiley, 1956.

6

FINANCIAL INFORMATION

The operations involved in business financing fall into three major classifications: bank and installment credit, corporation finance, and investments. However, it is extremely difficult to make a distinction between general business, banking, and investments when the literature is discussed. Although bank and corporation investments are important, a very large proportion of the literature in this field is concerned with advising the individual on wise investment of his own funds.

All of these activities are so interrelated that any discussion of one must include references to the other two. This is particularly true of magazines which carry information on business forecasts and trends, security analyses, financial information, and security quotations.

There is no current bibliography comparable to Roy B. Westerfield, *Select Bibliography of Money, Credit, Banking and Business Finance,* Cambridge, Mass., Bankers Publishing Company, 1940, which has come to light. However, all of the general bibliographies described in Chapter 2 have sections dealing with finance and should be utilized. Of these, the *Business Methods Index* has a section on finance which covers books, pamphlets, and periodical articles. Two current publications, although primarily concerned with investment information, do cover areas of corporate finance. A third publication deals primarily with monetary policy.

Index of Corporations and Industries. Weekly with monthly cumulative indexes and irregular supplements. Detroit 26, 286 Penobscot Building, Funk & Scott.

This index is divided into two sections, an industry section and a corporation section. It indexes sixty-seven financial publications and services and those of one hundred and eighty investment houses. Coverage includes the leading financial publications in the United States, Canada, and abroad, plus investment services, speeches before societies of security analysts and brokerage firm reports. This service enables the reader to locate financial information in a large variety of publications. It is most useful as a source of locating information in periodicals when there is a large and current file of brokers memorandums available to the user.

U.S. Board of Governors of the Federal Reserve System Library. *Selected Bibliography on Monetary Policy and Management of the Public Debt 1947–1960.* Washington, D.C., Board of Governors of the Federal Reserve System Library, 1961. Mimeographed.

This bibliography is composed of titles drawn from government reports, hearings, symposia, books, and periodical articles. It is a handy selected *finding* list of current information on these topics.

Dougall, H. E. and Jordan, D. F. *Investments.* 7th ed. Englewood Cliffs, N.Y., Prentice-Hall, 1960.

One long chapter describes in detail and evaluates investment services and sources of investment information. A thorough and excellent treatment of the subject.

It is always helpful to have some work to turn to for definition of terms in their particular application to an activity. This information can be found in:

Clark, D. T. and Gottfried, B. A. *Dictionary of Business and Finance.* New York, Crowell, 1957.

The specialized meanings of terms used in business and finance. Both the broad meaning and its more restricted application are defined and explained. The many cross references lead the reader to varying or related usage of the term. An indispensable volume for the businessman's desk.

Three other works both define financial terms and supply information on methods and practices in the field of finance.

Garcia, F. L. and Munn, G. G. *Encyclopedia of Banking and Finance.* 6th ed. New York, The Bankers Publishing Company, 1962.

The author goes considerably beyond the bare definition of terms. He illustrates the definition with examples and discusses the use of the term in order to make the meaning clear. Reference to an encyclopedia of this kind makes for a more intelligent understanding of current events, particularly today when financial terms occur so frequently in the news. The bibliographies included in the longer articles are very helpful.

Bogen, J. I. et al. eds. *Financial Handbook*. 3d rev. ed. New York, Ronald, 1957.

This handy reference book defines and explains financial practices. It is most valuable to the businessman because it provides him with exact information on financial activities and the proper form or procedure necessary to solve a particular financial problem. The sections on corporate organization and procedures, financing, various phases of financial control, mergers and reorganizations, and banking practice bring together in one volume much valuable information. This handbook eliminates an immense amount of searching through many works and provides sufficient facts to make an intelligent decision relative to a financial problem.

Doris, L. ed. *Business Finance Handbook*. Englewood Cliffs, N.J., Prentice-Hall, 1953.

The presentation is a practical treatment of all phases of finance and financial management written by persons of wide experience. It contains explanations, suggestions and forms on control of budgets and inventories along with plans for handling financing and avoiding financial hazards. This book provides both useful information and suggestions as to how the businessman can avoid costly mistakes.

Of the many excellent books on the subject of banking and money a few are mentioned here as being among the best in the field. In addition there are publications, especially of the American Institute of Banking, such as its *Bank Administration,* New York, American Institute of Banking, 1938, and *Credit Administration,* New York, American Institute of Banking, 1940, which are largely involved in the mechanics of operation of a bank. The titles listed will give the businessman sufficient information to gain a general understanding of the subject.

American Bankers Association. *Present Day Banking*. New York, American Bankers Association, 1954–1958. 6 vols.

A very thorough presentation of banking and monetary theory, policies, and practices. It brings up to date previous studies of the Association.

American Bankers Association. Economic Policy Commission. *Monetary Studies,* Nos. 1–6. New York, American Bankers Association, 1954.

These studies are designed to bring banking executives up to date on factors affecting bank policies; they include material on the financial system as a whole, reserve bank operations, interest rates, effects of federal reserve and treasury operations, and basic issues of monetary policy.

American Institute of Banking. *Analyzing Financial Statements*. New York, American Institute of Banking, 1939.

Although published before World War II, this book, in an excellent and clear-cut presentation, points up sound principles of credit and statement analysis for the operation of credit departments.

Bradford, F. A. *Money and Banking.* 6th ed. New York, Longmans, 1949.

A practical discussion of monetary and banking operations. The condensed accounts of the historical development of these activities are useful to nonbankers who wish to gain the proper perspective.

As an outgrowth of the studies of the financial system undertaken by the Commission on Money and Credit, Prentice-Hall published in 1962 and 1963 eighteen volumes dealing with their investigations.

Prentice-Hall History of Money and Credit. Englewood Cliffs, N.J., Prentice-Hall, 1962–1963. 18 vols.

These volumes grew out of the research for the Commission on Money and Credit and formed the basis of its final report: *Money and Credit: Their Influence on Jobs, Prices and Growth.* This is the most exhaustive study that has been made of our monetary and credit system since the early 1920's. In the main, these volumes are the result of a team effort and from six to a dozen authors contributed, titles published in 1962 are: *The Commercial Banking Industry; The Consumer Finance Industry; Life Insurance Companies as Financial Institutions; Management Investment Companies; Mortgage Companies, Their Place in the Financial Structure; Mutual Savings Banks, Basic Characteristics and Role in the National Economy; Property and Casualty Insurance Companies; Their Role as Financial Intermediaries; The Savings and Loan Business; Its Purposes, Functions and Justification;* Fifty-nine essays by scholars and economists appeared in the nine volumes published in 1963. Titles of these are: *Impacts of Monetary Policy; Monetary Management; Fiscal and Debt Management Policies; Federal Credit Agencies; Federal Credit Programs; Prorate Capital Markets; Private Financial Institutions; Inflation Growth and Employment; The Federal Reserve and the Treasury;* and *Answers to the Questions from the Commission on Money and Credit.*

Fischer, G. C. *Bank Holding Companies.* New York, Columbia University Press, 1961.

The only up-to-date general study of bank holding companies. The first six chapters cover the history and development of bank holding companies. The competitive position, effect on the stockholders and community, and regulations enacted to control bank holding companies comprise the remainder of this book.

Hart, A. G. *Money, Debt and Economic Activity.* 2d ed. Englewood Cliffs, N.J., Prentice-Hall, 1953.

Much of the earlier material on money and banking has been retained, but more material has been added and greater emphasis is placed on current monetary policies and their effects on the banking and monetary systems.

Banking activities are closely regulated by state and federal laws, and a knowledge of these laws and regulations is vital to the successful operation of a banking business. Eight services provide basic and current information on this subject.

Commerce Clearing House Federal Banking Law Reports. Chicago, Commerce Clearing House, Inc., 4 vols. with weekly supplements.

The regulations of the federal banking system and the various loan laws under which the banking communities operate come within the scope of this reporter. The requirements of the National Bank Acts and the Federal Reserve System are clearly explained. The detailed subject arrangement of the contents makes for easy reference, and the thorough discussion of each requirement permits the application of these requirements to everyday bank operations.

Prentice-Hall Federal Bank Service. New York, Prentice-Hall, Inc. 2 vols. with biweekly supplements.

Anyone seeking information on the various federal laws that govern loans and other banking operations will find this service especially useful. The arrangement of the material and the concise explanations make it easy to see how the following laws, which are included in full, affect banks: National Banking Act, Federal Reserve Act, Federal Deposit Insurance Act, Bank Conservation Act, Home Owners Loan Act (Section V), Reconstruction Finance Act, Farm Loan Acts, Federal Gold and Silver Legislation, National Housing Act, Export-Import Bank Act, Bretton Woods Agreement Act, and Servicemen's Readjustment Act (Title III).

Small loans, a specialized field of lending, are regulated chiefly by the individual states.

Prentice-Hall Installment and Conditional Sales Service. New York, Prentice-Hall Inc. with biweekly supplements.

In clear, simple business English, the service describes the nature of installment sales, the procedure in financing them, the laws, regulations and rules that govern them in each of the states in the United States and Canada. All laws relating in any way to installment sales are given in full. Forms and charts highlight the steps that should be taken in making a safe and legal installment sale in any state. A complete index makes the answer to any question instantly available.

Commerce Clearing House Conditional Sale—Chattel Mortgage Reports. Chicago, Commerce Clearing House, Inc. 3 vols. with current supplements.

There is a wide variance in the provisions of state laws regulating installment sales contracts. All these state statutes are analyzed and interpreted. A helpful collection of forms adopted for use in various parts of the country, and the sales of different kinds of products, is a part of this service.

Prentice-Hall Wills, Trusts and Estates Service. New York, Prentice-Hall, Inc.

The very complete set of guides and forms for wills, estate planning, and trust agreements make this a most helpful service. All of this information is keyed into the pertinent federal and state statutes and court rulings which are fully annotated. The excellent locator index makes this service easy to use.

Commerce Clearing House Inheritance, Estate and Gift Tax Reports. Chicago, Commerce Clearing House, Inc. 7 vols. with current supplements.

All of the laws, regulations, and court decisions of the federal and state governments are brought together in this service. Their application to particular problems is clearly explained and the many cross references bring in additional relevant material.

Commerce Clearing House Trust and Estate Law Reports. Chicago, Commerce Clearing House, Inc. 3 vols. with frequent current supplements.

The statutes and rules of law are published in full for all states dealing with descent, wills, estates, distribution, and corporate fiduciaries. Many forms and examples provide practical information.

Commerce Clearing House Federal Banking Law Reports. Chicago, Commerce Clearing House, Inc. 4 vols. with weekly reports.

All federal statutes and regulations concerned with banking and loans by banks and other lending institutions are covered by this service. Texts of laws and regulations with interpretations and suggested applications are grouped under easy-to-locate topical headings.

Another widely quoted service is *Pick's World Currency Report.*

Pick's World Currency Report. Annually. New York 6, 75 West Street, Pick's Currency Report with Pick's Currency Yearbook.

This is the most widely used source for information on world currencies. It presents the history of seventy-four currencies, describes exchange controls of fifty-three countries and rules for transferability. Additional information is supplied on currency administration in these countries, statistics on circulation, official and black market exchange rates. The *Yearbook* contains a directory of banks which make foreign exchange markets and the names of leading foreign exchange traders in addition to a complete directory of all banks with foreign exchange departments. Trade and payment agreements are described and changing discount rates are listed.

Statistics on money and banking are found largely in the publications of the Federal Reserve Board and the various foreign central banks.

U.S. Board of Governors of the Federal Reserve System. *Banking and Monetary Statistics.* Washington, D.C., The Board, 1943.

A useful cumulation of statistics largely for the period 1914 to 1941 inclusive. Certain series deal with debits and deposit turnover, bank earnings, suspensions, branch, group and chain banking, money rates and security markets, and international statistics. The average monthly foreign exchange rates supply a handy cumulation of these figures over a period of years.

U.S. Board of Governors of the Federal Reserve System. *All Bank Statistics, 1896–1956.* Washington, D.C., U.S. Board of Governors of the Federal Reserve System, 1959.

Statistics of all banks in a state are followed by a breakdown by type of bank—national, state, savings, and unincorporated. All states are covered plus Puerto Rico, American Samoa, Canal Zone, and Virgin Islands. Figures are comparable, and there is a complete definition of balance sheet items.

Federal Reserve Bulletin. Monthly. Washington, D.C., U.S. Board of Governors of the Federal Reserve System.

This is the best single source of banking and monetary statistics. The large amount of data provided on all phases of business make this publication one of the first to turn to in searching for facts. *The Federal Reserve Bulletin* picks up information in *Banking and Monetary Statistics* from 1941. Many of these series also appear in the annual and monthly issues of the *Federal Reserve Chartbook on Financial and Business Statistics.*

Savings Banks Fact Book. Annually. New York, Savings Bank Trust Co.

Compilations of data on resources, loans and other operations of savings banks appear in this publication each year.

The following publications supply information on individual banks:

The Bankers' Almanac and Year Book. Annually. New York 6, 111 Broadway, Skinner & Co. Ltd.

Information includes names of officers and partners of banks, addresses, data as to capitalization, assets and liabilities of 34,000 banks throughout the world. The names and telegraphic addresses of 3,100 banks are in another section. Discount rates and banking statistics are also covered.

Polk's Bankers Encyclopedia. Semiannually. Detroit and New York, R. L. Polk & Co., 1896–.

All federal credit institutions and their officers are included. Bank statements for all banks in each locality, officers of the bank, and directories of attorneys and leading security dealers are also furnished. The present status of absorbed and closed bank (i.e., who is controlling or directing them) is indicated. This publication supplies no information as to earnings, dividends of banks, or the market for bank stock. It does supply a complete directory of all American banks.

Polk's Bankers Information Bulletin. Monthly. Detroit and New York, R. L. Polk & Co.

Monthly supplements of current information for *Polk's Bankers Encyclopedia.*

Polk's Bank Information Service. Daily. Detroit and New York, R. L. Polk & Co.

Supplement to the monthly *Bulletin.*

Rand McNally Bankers Directory. Semiannually. New York, Rand McNally Co., 1927–.

As its name implies, this is more a directory than a statistical source. Bank statements are included for all American and Canadian banks.

Moody's Investors Service. *Moody's Manual of Investments, American and Foreign Banks, Insurance Companies, Investment Trusts, Real Estate Finance and Credit Companies.* Annually. New York, Moody's Investors Service, 1928–.

Detailed information is supplied on only 2,000 of the banks in the United States and condensed balance sheets for 2,500 additional banks. The information on the 2,000 banks is more complete than in the sources mentioned above. Not only are balance sheets given but earning statements as well, along with dividends, description of securities, and market prices. The ten-year price range of individual stocks is useful. Similar information is included for foreign, central, and commercial banks.

Similar information on the larger American banks is contained in Standard and Poor's *Standard Corporation Record.* International banking statistics of a general nature are:

United Nations. *Statistical Yearbook.* Annually. New York, United Nations.

Statistics as to the currency situation, gold reserves assets of central banks, and balance of payments are of the most interest to the American businessman.

United Nations. *Monthly Bulletin of Statistics.* Monthly. New York, United Nations.

Supplements the above on a current basis.

Bank for International Settlements Annual Report. Basel, Bank for International Settlements. Published annually since 1920.

The world fiscal situation is analyzed, and statistics include data on the currency situation, prices, the condition of central banks, and statements of a selected group of commercial banks.

International Financial Statistics. Monthly with annual supplements. Washington, D.C., International Monetary Fund.

Data appear in this publication on the International Monetary Fund, International Bank for Reconstruction and Development, International Finance Corporation, European Fund and on interest rates, gold reserves, changes of cost of living and prices, trade, and freight rates in individual countries.

The publications of the various central banks are packed with statistics on currency, circulation, and the financial condition of the country. All the central banks of the larger European and South American countries issue bulletins on statistical studies. Bank statements of the larger commercial banks appear each year in a supplement to the *Statist.*

The International Banking Section of the Statist. Annually. London, Statist.

The information on banks within the British Commonwealth is more complete than for other areas. The brief historical sketches of each bank and tables of liabilities and assets of each for a five-to-ten-year period provide statistical information in a most convenient form.

Bank of Canada Statistical Summary. Monthly. Ottawa, Bank of Canada.

There are excellent tables and charts of all phases of Canadian governmental fiscal activities and, in addition, trends and activities in the private financial and commercial realm.

Bank of England Quarterly Bulletin. Quarterly. London, Bank of England.

Short articles commenting on the general economic and financial situation and other topics of current interest are followed by statistics on governmental financial operations and those of banks.

Many of the leading business magazines, especially those devoted to investments, carry articles on banking and finance. The *Wall Street Journal, Barrons',* and *Forbes* frequently have excellent articles on banking and monetary developments, even though they are predominately concerned with investment news. The following are the major banking periodicals:

American Banker. Daily. New York, American Banker, Inc.

The only daily publication in this field, it supplies news of new banking developments pending legislation and regulations affecting banks, news of individual banks, and short articles on individuals active in banking. Each issue carries a short list of bank stock quotations.

Bankers Monthly. Chicago, Rand McNally & Co.

Regular features are "Top of the Financial News," "Washington Report," "Operating News and Trends," "Bankers and Brokers," and "Calendar of Special Events." Special articles on topics of interest to bankers appear in each issue.

Banking Journal of the American Bankers Association. Monthly. New York, American Bankers Association.

This official publication of the American Bankers Association is a good source of information for banking trends, new and improved banking techniques, activities of bankers' associations, and notes on individual banks and bankers.

Banking Law Journal. Monthly. Cambridge, Mass., Bankers Publishing Co.

The first section is given over to general articles on banking; the bulk of the magazine (formerly *The Bankers Magazine*) is devoted to court decisions involving banks.

The Commercial and Financial Chronicle. Two issues weekly. New York, W. B. Dana Company.

The Thursday issue each week provides the broadest and most reasoned presentation of finance and business appearing in any business publication. All viewpoints are represented in articles written by leaders in their respective fields. This magazine is "must" reading, not only for bankers, but for every businessman who attempts to understand the current economic situation. The Monday issue is devoted to corporation statements, stock and bond quotations, and general investment news.

Credit and Financial Management. Monthly. 229 Fourth Avenue, New York, National Association of Credit Men.

Because this is the official publication of the National Association of Credit Management the activities of the Association are reported fully. Washington news, management and credit policies, and techniques primarily concerned with short-term financing are discussed in other sections.

Journal of Finance. Quarterly. Chicago, The American Finance Association.

The well-written articles on all aspects of finance are on a broad and sometimes theoretical basis. The book reviews are excellent.

Monetary Times. Monthly. Toronto, Monetary Times.

Information is provided on the financial situation in Canada along with bank clearings, price indexes for Canada and exchange quotations.

Savings Bank Journal. Monthly. New York, Natamsa Publishing Co.

Articles of general interest to officers of savings banks are the major feature.

Trust Companies Monthly. Monthly. New York, Trust Companies Publishing Association.

The authoritative publication on all phases of trust company operations.

Trust Bulletin. Monthly except for July and August. New York, American Bankers Association, Trust Division.

News of the Division and articles on topics of interest to trust officers are included.

Trusts and Estates. Monthly. New York, Fiduciary Publishers.

The most important feature for the businessman is the information on the performance of mutual and common stock funds. General business comments and suggestions as to the operation of trust funds are also a part of each monthly issue.

There are three publications which can be extremely helpful to corporate officers and these are:

Doris, L. *Corporate Treasurers' and Controllers' Encyclopedia.* Englewood Cliffs, N.J., Prentice-Hall, 1958. 4 vols.

Long articles replete with forms and suggestions as how to apply the information which comes to them are most helpful to both the controller and the treasurer. The suggestions and data enable these officers to improve the operations of their offices and broaden their horizons. All phases of their duties are covered.

Doris, L. *Corporate Treasurers' and Controllers' Handbook.* Englewood Cliffs, N.J., Prentice-Hall, 1950.

All of the activities of the treasurer and controller are described with many practical suggestions as to how to handle specific problems.

Doris, L., Friedman, E. J. and Spellman, H. H. *Corporate Secretary's Manual.* Rev. ed. Englewood Cliffs, N.J., Prentice-Hall, 1949.

A ready reference book for the corporate secretary, lawyers, and the average businessman. Much detailed information is supplied on the handling of corporate meetings and the keeping of corporate records, with many full references to legal and regulatory practices and citations of many legal decisions.

Corporation finance has an extensive literature, but the following are standard works that treat the subject broadly with a minimum of discussion of technicalities. They supply the information needed by the general reader.

Buchanan, Norman S. *The Economics of Corporate Enterprise.* New York, Holt, 1940.

The broad economic relationships of corporation finance are considered from the viewpoint of the law, and the economy as a whole. In addition, the problems and principles of corporate reorganizations are presented. The value of this book to the businessman lies in his ability to gain an over-all conception of the principles of corporate finance stated clearly and with a minimum of detail.

Dauten, C. A. *Business Finance.* 2d ed. Englewood Cliffs, N.J., Prentice-Hall, 1956.

A clearly written exposition of the various methods of financing a business which provides descriptions of various types of financing including leasing and sale and leasebacks. Credit policies and sources are also discussed, along with various types of financial organization and reorganization.

Gerstenberg, C. W. *Financial Organization and Management.* 4th rev. ed. Englewood Cliffs, N.J., Prentice-Hall, 1959.

The financial management of corporate finances rather than their forms is stressed. Advantages and disadvantages of different types of organization are clearly brought out, and the effects of various financial policies are emphasized. A valuable work for any businessman starting his own business or investing funds.

Dewing, A. S. *The Financial Policy of Corporations.* 5th ed. New York, Ronald, 1953.

Written from the business executives' viewpoint, this book gives the principles which form the basis of sound financial planning. The financial pitfalls which beset a corporation are vividly portrayed. The wealth of examples of corporate policies drawn from every type of business plus the analysis and comparisons of each with standards of efficient operation and social values enable the executive to plan his financial course intelligently. As one reads the book the history of American finance is unfolded. He learns what kinds of financial management will and will not work.

Guthmann, H. G. and Dougall, H. E. *Corporate Financial Policy.* 3d ed. Englewood Cliffs, N.J., Prentice-Hall, 1955.

    This work deals with all aspects of corporation finance. After all forms
of business organization are considered, the types of financing both through
issuance of securities and through other types of financing are described and
discussed along with the different types of enterprises for which they are
suitable. Distribution of securities, corporate mergers, and reorganizations are
treated in an excellent fashion. This book is notable for its splendid up-to-date
bibliography.

Husband, W. H. and Dockery, J. C. *Modern Corporation Finance.* 4th ed. Homewood, Ill., Irwin, 1957.

    The corporation is described historically as to its various forms. All kinds
of corporate financing are described followed by chapters on organization,
financing, management of corporations, sale and regulation of securities, income and working capital, expansion, failure and reorganization, and public
policy.

Johnson, R. W. *Financial Management.* Boston, Allyn and Bacon, 1959.

    Although written on a somewhat elementary level, this book differs from
the average one on finance in that it treats all phases from the viewpoint of
the financial manager.

Before the businessman utilizes the various investment advisory services and security analyses in the financial journals, he should learn the
basic principles of investments. By so doing he may avoid some of the
pitfalls that beset the way of even the shrewdest investor. The following
publications provide a sound groundwork for the planning of an individual investment program.

Jordan, D. F. and Willett, E. F. *Managing Personal Finances.* 3d ed. Englewood
Cliffs, N.J., Prentice-Hall, 1951.

    All forms of investment and personal financial operations from making
up a budget to starting a business are considered. The simple direct style and
illustrations drawn from everyday life enable the reader to grasp the fact that
there are many forms of investment other than stocks and bonds. The advantages and disadvantages of each type of investment are clearly brought
out. A most helpful work for the young man starting his business career and
for others who want to keep a proper perspective on investments.

Graham, B. *The Intelligent Investor.* 3d ed. New York, Harper, 1959.

    Written somewhat along the same lines as the previous citation, this
book gives straightforward and understandable advice as to how to invest one's
funds. It candidly emphasizes the uncertainties of investments and investing.

Cooper, R. U. *Investments for Professional People.* Rev. ed. New York, Macmillan,
1959.

Written by a layman in layman's language, this doctor points up the investment problems of a professional man and indicates avenues of investment. A helpful book to young doctors and other professional men starting their careers.

Dowrie, George W., Fuller, D. R. and Calkins, F. J. *Investments.* 3d ed. New York, Wiley, 1961.

These authors stress the fundamentals of investment in an unusually clear style. The mechanism, policy, and analysis of investments are discussed with emphasis on the underlying factors. After describing various investment media and the methods of marketing, the authors discuss investment policies to fit different needs. The illustrations, based on securities of well-known companies, drive home the principles under consideration and enable the reader to relate these principles to his own operations. Various methods and criteria of investment selection are analyzed. The breadth of view and clarity of presentation make this book an excellent starting point in a study of the field.

Graham, B., Dodd, D., Cottle, S. L. with the collaboration of C. Totham, *Security Analysis: Principles and Techniques.* 4th ed. New York, McGraw-Hill, 1962.

Completely brought up to date, this fourth edition continues the arrangement of the earlier editions. The first three sections resemble the earlier treatment in that broad principles of investment are laid down and various types of securities are described and analyzed along with the analysis of financial statements. The data and yardsticks have all been updated as have been the illustrations. The last three sections dealing with common stocks and market studies have been completely rewritten in the light of changed conditions and criteria. There are no chapter references, but the footnotes provide many useful current references.

Grodinsky, J. *Investments.* New York, Ronald, 1953.

This book contains an excellent discussion of investment principles plus data on the rise and decline of industries. The suitability of various types of investment for particular situations is thoroughly treated. There is a very good analysis of investment services.

Jordan, David F. and Dougall, H. C. *Investments.* 7th ed. Englewood Cliffs, N.J., Prentice-Hall, 1960.

The basic principles of investment are very clearly presented. This is followed by a detailed description of various types of securities with a discussion of their suitability for the investor. The chapters on security analysis are excellent. The chapter on investment services gives a very complete listing and analysis, and the bibliography is up-to-date and complete.

Plum, L. N. *Investing in American Industry.* New York, Harper, 1960.

The nonferrous metal, steel, business machine, chemical, paper, electric utilities, petroleum, aircraft and insurance industries are analyzed as to their investment qualities. These analyses are on a broad basis of the history and characteristics of the industry, its earnings, prospects, and peculiar hazards.

This gives the investor background information rather than the principles of investment. The "Sources of Further Information and Reading" section is useful.

The financial statement is the basic ingredient of all investment analysis. Businessmen, whether they invest or not, should obtain a working knowledge of all the elements that comprise a financial statement, and learn to evaluate their significance in the financial analysis of a firm. Two works are available on this subject which should prove helpful.

Foulke, R. A. *Practical Financial Statement Analysis.* 4th ed. New York, McGraw-Hill, 1957.

The technique used is to get behind the figures in financial statements, and the material is set forth in nontechnical language. The balance sheet, income statement, retained earnings, the source and application of funds are all analyzed as the basis for interpretating the financial conditions of a business. The earnings, inventory, and capital ratios are indicated for a large number of kinds of businesses.

Guthmann, H. G. *The Analysis of Financial Statements.* 4th ed. Englewood Cliffs, N.J., Prentice-Hall, 1953.

Each item of the balance sheet and earnings statement is carefully analyzed and its relationship to the current position of the firm is pointed out. The principles of analysis are set forth clearly and simply. The second section is the most helpful to the investors: it discusses the financial statements of various industries and provides yardsticks for analyzing the statements of companies within the group.

If the individual is doing any considerable amount of investing, he should know something about security market operations, and it follows that to understand the financial sections of newspapers and business magazines he must be familiar with the meaning of stock-market terms. This information is supplied in:

Dice, C. A. and Eiteman, W. J. *The Stock Market.* 3d ed. New York, McGraw-Hill, 1952.

Not only are the terms used in security transactions explained, but also the operating methods of exchanges and stock brokers. Various types of stock-market operations are also illustrated. Fortified by the knowledge gained from the general works on invesment and having in mind the general principles involved, any businessman will be in a better position to evaluate the tremendous amount of information available in this field.

Leffler, G. L. *The Stock Market.* 2d ed. New York, Ronald, 1957.

After a description of security markets and securities, the author goes into great detail about the operations of various components of security markets and their mechanics of operation. There are excellent chapters on over-the-counter markets, analysis of stock prices, investing, and trading.

Friend, I. and others. *The Over-the-Counter Securities Market.* New York, McGraw-Hill, 1958.

   An exhaustive treatment of all aspects of this market and its operation.

ADVISORY AND STATISTICAL PUBLICATIONS

Probably no business activity is as well supplied with advisory and statistical publications as the investment field. This information falls into several categories: (1) the state of the stock market and its probable trends, (2) the outlook for specific industries, (3) stock and bond quotations, and (4) the description and analysis of individual companies. All investment publications reinforce their recommendations with indexes and statistics, which make it difficult to separate the purely statistical from the more general publications.

   The best source catalog of investment services is Special Libraries Association, *Directory of Business and Financial Services,* New York, Special Libraries Association, 1963, mentioned in Chapter 5. The *Index of Corporations and Industries* described in the early part of this chapter indexes a very large amount of investment information and is a great help in locating information.

Special Libraries Association, *Directory of Business and Financial Services.* New York, Special Libraries Association, 1963.

   This expanded and current edition of two previous issues makes this publication useful again. This is a selective list of newsletters, bulletins, reports, and other published services covering business economics and finance. The names and addresses of five hundred publishers are supplied along with the title and content of the service, frequency of publication, and cost. There are 1,050 services listed.

A recent publication on investment services is:

Walter, H. C., ed. *Directory of Investment Advisory Services.* 1962 edition. Rochester, N.Y., 520 Granite Bldg., Fir Publishing Company, 1962.

   Over two hundred services are grouped under nine headings which enable the user to locate the service most useful to him. The information supplied is the address and cost of the service followed by a description of the kind of service supplied. The breakdown of services under type of information supplied is a very helpful feature of this service.

Each investment advisory service has its loyal clientele who believe that the suggestions offered are the best available market predictions. The user of any service should recognize, however, that none is infallible and that, if the system of investment were foolproof, it would be far more profitable to speculate in the market than to sell the service. The best procedure for the would-be investor is to read several services, learn as many facts as possible about the companies in which he intends to invest, become thoroughly familiar with the leading investment journals, make a careful analysis of annual reports, and then draw his own conclusions.

A service which analyzes and interprets the daily news is the *Daily News Service* of Phelan's Statistics, Ltd., 637 Craig Street West, Montreal 3, Canada. Important business, government, corporation news and developments, and investment news are analyzed and interpreted daily. Both Canadian and foreign news are covered.

The Index of Corporations and Industry cited at the beginning of this chapter also indexes sources of investment information.

A very complete service which locates investment information in a wide variety of media is:

The Financial Index. Weekly. New York 28, 1295 Madison Ave., Financial Index Company, Inc. (Absorbed by *Funk and Scott Index* in 1963.)

A weekly publication with quarterly cumulations, it indexes the following; thirty-five financial magazines, reports of 350 brokerage houses, sixty bank letters, ten financial newspapers, and books and pamphlets of over 500 publishers. Names and addresses and subscription rates of publications and services are given. Addresses of brokerage houses are also supplied. Coverage includes periodicals published in Canada, Great Britain and Japan as well as in the United States. Part I contains references to industry surveys, Part II to individual corporations. The kind of information in each article is indicated.

Another service which is helpful is:

Silverman, C., ed. *The Cumulative Financial Index.* Woodstock, Vermont, The Financial Index. Annually.

An index to financial publications which contain data on companies and industries.

The stock-market analyses provided by the leading investment services follow much the same pattern but do not always agree as to their conclusions. No attempt will be made here to include all investment advisory services but a few of the better-known and readily available ones are listed.

GENERAL MARKET FORECASTS

Babson's Reports, Wellesley Hills, Mass.

Investment and Barometer Letter. This confidential weekly letter is issued in connection with Babson's Personal Investment Service. It is largely concerned with investment advice but includes reports on commodity and labor markets and on general business conditions.

Arnold Bernard & Co. Inc., Value Line Survey Bldg., 5 E. 49th St., New York 17.

The Value Line Investment Survey appears in six parts:

Part 1. "Ratings and Reports" on 600 leading stocks, supplies rating, background, prospects, and analysis of developments.

Part 2. "Analyses of 55 Leading Industries."

Part 3. "Special Situation Reports" which discuss unusually favorable or unfavorable conditions of stocks and companies.

Part 4. "Supervised Account"—an example of the operation of a model account.

Part 5. "Weekly Supplement" which keeps the other four parts up to date.

Part 6. "Fortnightly Commentaries." Opinions on economic and political conditions which affect price trends.

Guenther Publishing Corporation, 17 Battery Place, New York.

Financial World Stock Factographs appear annually with brief data on companies whose stocks are listed on the New York and American Stock Exchanges which includes full name, address, number of stockholders, and capitalization, business and financial position, dividend record, outlook, brief comment, and earnings, dividends, and price range.

Magazine of Wall Street, 90 Broad Street, New York 4.

The Investment and Business Forecast of the Magazine of Wall Street. Each week, an analysis and forecast is made of the securities market. The Dow-Jones averages are charted for industrials, rails, and utilities; specific stocks are recommended for income and for capital appreciation, and there is a list of low price stocks. Features are: "Outlook for Business," "Washington Letter," and "Statistical Background with Charts and Comments."

Moody's Investors Service, 65 Broadway, New York 6.

Moody's Stock Survey. Weekly. Information includes trends of security markets, analysis of industries, and recommendations for sale, purchase, or exchange of stocks.

Moody's Bond Survey. A weekly service for bonds similar to the preceding item.

Standard and Poor's Corporation, 345 Hudson Street, New York 14.

Weekly Outlook for the Securities Market. A general market forecast.

Monthly Earnings and Ratings Stock Guide. The earnings, buy, qualified or switch ratings are given on approximately 5,000 common and preferred stocks. Data are arranged on one line to make analysis easy.

These two services are a part of the Standard and Poor's Trade and Securities Service.

Facts and Forecasts. This is a daily service published by Standard and Poor's Corporation every day the New York Stock Exchange is open. It supplies information as to the current market movements, analyzes conditions in the leading industries, and recommends the purchase and sale of stocks and bonds.

United Business Service, 210 Newberry Street, Boston, Mass. *Weekly Forecasts Based on the United Opinion of Recognized Business and Economic Authorities.*

This compilation of forecasts from nine different sources provides the businessman with a quick summary of opinion. It also contains brief surveys, commodity and stock market situations, and recommendations for purchase and sale of stocks.

American Institute for Economic Research, Great Barrington, Mass. *The Investment Bulletin Service.* Biweekly.

Provides investment planning for those dependent on income from investments and municipals; bank insurance, real estate, investment trusts; induscan afford greater risks.

SECURITY SERVICES

Since the Fitch Publishing Company was absorbed by Standard and Poor's Corporation in 1962, there are now only two leading security services—Moody's, and Standard and Poor's—which attempt to give as complete a picture on all phases of investment as possible. The heart of each service is the data assembled on individual companies. The information is also cumulated for industry statistics, business indexes, and forecasts as to trends of specific industries and concerns within these industries. These publications are kept current through loose-leaf services with periodic cumulations.

Moody's Investors Service, 65 Broadway, New York 6. *Moody's Manual of Investments, American and Foreign.*

These annual volumes are kept current by semiweekly bulletins. Governments and municipals; bank insurance, real estate, investment trusts; industrials; public utilities; and transportation, represent the subdivision of the security field. A brief history of each company and its operations, description of plants and products, names of officers, five-year comparison of income ac-

count, and balance sheet for larger companies and two-year comparisons for
smaller companies comprise the basic information. The detailed description of
each type of security includes a complete dividend record over the past fifteen
years in the industries and a ten-year quotation of individual security prices.
Moody's Dividend Record is a semiweekly, cumulative record of dividends
and dates of payments and corporate meetings.

Moody's Bond Record. Semimonthly quotations on 12,000 corporate, government, and municipal bonds are supplied by this booklet. Detailed statistical information as to earnings, markets, and amount outstanding is given for 4,000
bonds. The coverage is by far the largest of any of these all-in-one-line pocket
guides. Ratings are also given on municipal bonds.

The Moody's organization also supplies specialized services to large
investors and financial organizations.

Standard and Poor's Corporation, 345 Hudson Street, N.Y. 14.

Standard Corporation Records includes complete factual information on 6,000
major American and Canadian corporations and important developments affecting 5,000 smaller concerns. Six loose-leaf volumes, revised monthly, supply the
bulk of the data on balance sheets, earnings, and market prices. Each set of
figures is carried back for a longer period than for any other service. It makes
comparisons easier, particularly when figures go back through 1921, 1929, and
1932. These volumes are kept up to date by the "Daily News Section," which
highlights the day's important corporation news. And this information is
cumulated monthly into loose-leaf supplements. The "Dividend Section," daily
and weekly, completes the information necessary to keep this service up to date.

Standard and Poor's Trade And Securities.

The first two sections, *Weekly Outlook for Security Markets* and *Monthly
Earnings and Ratings Stock Guide* have already been discussed on page 28
under "General Market Forecast." The third, "Statistical Section," continues
indexes of employment, prices, business activity in various lines, stock price
indexes for all industries, and prices, production, and inventories of commodities. The figures are carried forward each month.

Standard and Poor's Bond Guide. Semimonthly.

The *Guide* supplies essential information of call price, interest dates, twelve-
year high and low rating, five-year earnings, and bid-and-asked price for a
large number of corporate, municipal, and real estate bonds and preferred
stocks. It is another pocket-size booklet with information all on one line.

Standard and Poor's Corporation publish nineteen other services
which are either designed for very specialized situations or reproduce in
part information supplied in the complete Standard Corporation Records.

A local service most helpful to Westerners is *Walker's Manual:*

Walker's Manual of Pacific Coast Securities. San Francisco, Calif., 363 Pine Street, Walker's Manual Inc.

This annual volume supplies very complete data on the companies in the area whose securities are in the hands of the public. It is particularly helpful for information on real estate and irrigation district securities.

Walker's Cumulative Summary of Pacific Coast Securities. A monthly supplement which keeps the *Manual* up to date.

The U. S. Securities and Exchange Commission publishes periodicals which provide statistics helpful to the businessman and investor. Three of these are purely factual whereas the fourth includes some comment and interpretation.

U.S. Securities and Exchange Commission.
Plant and Equipment Expenditures of United States Business. Quarterly. Washington, D.C., and Securities and Exchange Commission.
—— *Net Working Capital of United States Corporations.* Quarterly. Washington, D.C., U.S. Securities and Exchange Commission.
—— *Quarterly Financial Report of U.S. Manufacturing Corporations.* Quarterly. Washington, D.C., U.S. Securities and Exchange Commission.
—— *Statistical Bulletin.* Monthly. Washington, D.C., U.S. Securities and Exchange Commission.

The periodical carries financial series, information on new offerings and trading on the various exchanges, stock price indexes, special offerings, and further information.

Many valuable studies and analysis of industries as well as market studies have been made by the research departments of banks and investment houses. Among those widely used are:

Bankers Trust Company Economics Department.
The Investment Outlook. Annually. New York, Bankers Trust Company, 1948–.
This annual survey is primarily concerned with trends and sources of supply of funds for the investment market. The tables of sources of investment funds are complete, current, and give an eight-year comparison.
Bankers Trust Company. Investment Research Division.
Industry Study. Annually. New York, Bankers Trust Company.
Up-to-date brief analyses of the immediate prospects of twenty-seven industries. The situation of the leading companies in each industry is discussed. Financial and earnings data, are shown in charts and tables from 1946 to date.
Morgan Guaranty Trust Company.
The Morgan Guaranty Survey. Monthly. New York, Morgan Guaranty Trust Company.
Excellent, brief analyses of business and financial conditions, money and

credit are featured plus articles on special situations. An index of business activity and "Monetary Indicators" are also part of this publication. The *Monthly Statistical Supplement* adds statistical detail and indexes of business activity and wholesale price comparisons..

Notable among the studies published by investment houses are those of Merrill, Lynch, Pierce, Fenner and Smith.

For the chart-minded investor there are several visual analyses of the market and individual securities. One of the best known of these is Investograph Service.

Investographs. 31 Gibbs Street, Rochester, N.Y. Investograph Service.
This is a partially supervised weekly loose-leaf service. The complete service analyzes 250 stocks and 22 industries, whereas the junior service covers 110 stocks. Sections of this service are as follows:
"Investograph Comparative Market Charts," monthly, depicts relative market action, current earnings, and trends of 250 stocks.
"Corporate Investographs," weekly, provides current charts on the first item; trends are recorded from 1919 on.
"Industry Composites," quarterly, charts earning trends from 1919 on 22 industry groups and earning factors.
"General Business," is charted from 1919 and issued monthly.

The broadening of interest in foreign securities requires that some way be found to get data on them. The previously mentioned surveys treat some foreign securities. The following publications have more complete coverage:

Stock Exchange Official Year Book. Annually. New York, Skinner & Co., Ltd.
Information is supplied on 13,000 British, dominion, and foreign companies and their securities. This includes name and address of company, type of business, capital, earnings, dividends, transfers of funds, reserves and stock prices. A quarterly "Supplementary Index" provides current data.
Yamaichi's Manual of Japanese Corporations. Tokyo, Yamaichi Securities Company Ltd., 1960.
This is the first English edition of the leading Japanese publication in this field. This manual provides for 811 Japanese companies the name, address, names of two or three principal officers, capitalization, par value of shares, type of business, number of stockholders, balance sheet, production, earnings per share and price range of the stock. Additional features are digests of information on laws governing investment by foreigners, discussion of Japanese business practices, review of business conditions in Japan, taxes on securities and other data. The most complete information on Japanese companies available in English.

Services that specialize in certain investments often supply additional information not found in the more general coverage services.

INVESTMENT TRUSTS

American Institute for Economic Research, Great Barrington, Mass.
Investment Trust Stockholders Service.

A monthly business review with a quarterly analysis of results of fifty leading investment trusts; the performance records are compared.
Investment Trusts and Funds from the Buyers Point of View.

An annual summation of the results of leading investment trusts. The publication also describes activities of investment trusts, their place in an investment program and adds a recommended list of these securities.

Finance. Monthly. Chicago, Finance Publishing Company.

In addition to general news of banks, finance and insurance companies, mutual investment company news is covered.

Arthur Wiesenberger and Company, 61 Broadway, New York 6.
Investment Companies.

An annual publication that compares the performance of approximately 150 investment trust funds. The general comparisons are useful, but the individual analyses vary as to quality. Information includes simplified balance sheets, summary of capitalization, operating results as compared to the Dow-Jones averages and earnings, asset value per share of common stock and the market position. In many instances the year-end portfolio is included.

MINING SECURITIES

Robert D. Fisher Mining Manual. New York, Robert D. Fisher, 1940–.

An annual list of reports on 12,000 American, Canadian, and Alaskan mining Companies.

The Mining Yearbook. London, Walter E. Skinner, 1896–.

This annual British publication supplies brief financial information on mining companies. Past two-year earnings, selected items from the balance sheet, dividends, high and low prices for the past three years, are all tabulated. The greater number of the mines listed are located in the British Commonwealth.

MUNICIPAL AND GOVERNMENT BONDS

The Bond Buyer, 67 Pearl Street, New York 4.
Daily Bond Buyer.

Special news on federal, state, and municipal bonds is supplied for each business day. A monthly indexed cumulation is included with the service.

C. F. Childs & Co., Chicago.
Investment Bulletin.

A monthly rundown on the situation of bonds of political subdivisions.

C. J. Devine and Company, 148 Wall Street, New York 5.

United States Government Securities.

This annual survey of securities issued by the federal government gives complete descriptions of each security, market prices, receipts and expenditures of the government, and government corporations.

QUOTATIONS

Blue List Publishing Company, 55 Liberty Street, New York 5.

The Blue List of Current Municipal Offerings.

Here is daily compilation of offerings of 350 of the larger municipal bond houses.

William B. Dana Company, 25 Spruce Street, New York 7.

Commercial and Financial Chronicle.

Twice-weekly. The Monday issue carries quotations for the week on the New York Stock Exchanges and the week's high and low on eight leading American stock exchanges and Montreal and Toronto.

Bank and Quotation Record. Each month this publication cumulates the information on high, low and last prices for the year and month, and share turnover on the major American and Canadian exchanges. State and municipal bonds are also quoted as are inactive and defaulted bonds.

National Quotation Bureau, 46 Front Street, New York 4.

National Daily Quotation Service. Wire service quoting wants and offerings of 1,000 leading investment houses in the country, gives the bid and ask price with the date of bid for 5,000 invested stocks and 2,050 unlisted bonds.

Monthly Corporation Bond Summary. This cumulation, issued every six months, includes data on thousands of *unlisted* and *inactive* stocks. Otherwise it is similar to the *Bond Survey.*

Monthly Municipal Bond Summary. A similar six months cumulation on the market for municipals.

RAILROAD SECURITIES

James H. Oliphant Co., 61 Broadway, New York.

Oliphant's Earning Power of Railroads. An annual publication presents in tabular form the essential statistics, operating and financial, for analyzing the situation of the road.

Standard and Poor's Corporation, 345 Hudson Street, New York 14.

Standard and Poor's Railroad Securities consists of eleven sections (1) "Weekly Survey," (2) "Traffic Section," (3) "Earnings Section," (4) "Position of Securities," (5) "Revenues and Expenses," (6) "Railroad Earnings Forecasters," (7) "Rail Equipment Bulletin," (8) "Freight Commodity Statistics," (9) "Guaranteed Stock Bulletin," (10) "Railway Economic Review," (11) "Reorganization Plans."

Unlisted Securities

Over-The-Counter Securities Review, Box 12, Jenkintown, Pa.

Over-The-Counter Securities Review. A monthly publication provides a factual review of prices and earnings of securities dealt in the over-the-counter market without any recommendations or ratings.

Standard and Poor's Corporation, 345 Hudson Street, New York 14.

Unlisted Bond Reports. Five hundred companies whose securities are not listed on any stock exchange are analyzed. Information on each security includes quality and market ratings, opinion, earnings, forecast, fundamental position, earnings, and price record. Reports are continuously revised.

Unlisted Stock Reports. This service supplies the same type of information for 750 stocks that the *Unlisted Bond Survey* does for bonds. It is kept current through daily revisions.

The larger metropolitan daily newspapers, especially the *New York Times* and *New York Herald-Tribune,* carry a large amount of investment news and stock and bond quotations. Almost every business publication prints some investment news. The periodicals devoted almost exclusively to investments are mentioned below:

The Analysts' Journal. Five times a year. New York, Society of Security Analysts.

Various methods of security and stock market analyses are critically evaluated by working experts in the field of security analysis. Also publishes evaluations of individual companies and their current activities.

Barrons National Financial Weekly. New York, Barrons Publishing Company.

The analysis of the general investment situation is amplified by résumés of general business, commodity, political, and foreign conditions. Financial prospects of various companies and industries are discussed. The "Stock Market at a Glance" section is a most convenient tabulation of prices, earnings, and dividends. The treatment is general, with recommendations to buy or sell securities.

Commercial and Financial Chronicle. Twice weekly. New York, William B. Dana Company.

The Monday issue each week consists of brief notes on individual companies and quotations of securities listed on all the leading exchanges in the United States and Canada. Over-the-counter and municipal bond quotations are included. The Thursday release deals with fundamentals of finance and business. Recommendations for buying or selling are not included in either issue.

Financial Times. Daily except Saturday and Sunday. London, The Financial Times.

News of the London market is the principal information supplied by this publication. Much news of European and Commonwealth exchanges and

quotations of stocks listed on them are published in each issue. Commodity
prices are thoroughly covered. Longer articles treat financial and monetary
situations. An excellent source to be used for price quotations on foreign
securities and a fresh viewpoint on United States and world financial affairs.

Financial World. Weekly. New York, Guenther Publishing Corporation.

This publication reports on the investment scene with comments on the
economy, stock market, individual companies, and stocks, daily except Saturday
and Sunday.

Journal of Commerce. Daily. New York, B. J. Ridder Publisher.

Although focused on commodities, commerce and manufacturing news,
it contains much general business news and financial comment. It is an unusually good source for daily over-the-counter security quotations.

Magazine of Wall Street and Business Analyst. Biweekly. New York, Ticker Publishing Co.

General news on the state of business and the stock market is followed by
descriptions of individual company activities and their prospects with recommendations to buy or sell their securities.

Monetary Times. Monthly. Toronto, Monetary Times.

The financial situation in Canada, bank clearings, indexes for industrial
activities and prices in Canada and stock quotations appear in this publication.

Wall Street Journal. Daily every weekday. New York, Chicago, San Francisco, and
Los Angeles, Dow-Jones and Co., Inc.

The accounts of current business and political trends and developments
are unusually fine. The sketches of financial situations of various companies
are brief but good. The editorials and staff writers reflect the views of the
more thoughtful and reasonable businessmen. The various editions carry
special news of companies and activities in their localities. The "New York
Edition" is the one indexed.

LOOSE-LEAF SERVICES

Investment houses, banks, legal firms concerned with corporate business, and corporations issuing securities will find these three services
helpful.

Prentice-Hall Securities Regulation Service. New York, Prentice-Hall, Inc. 2 vols.
with current supplements.

Brokers, dealers, investment companies, corporations, and attorneys who
must know how the laws, regulations, rules, opinions, and court decisions
affect securities use this service to keep up to date on the requirements. Concise
editorial comments help clear the way to quick understanding.

Commerce Clearing House Federal Securities Law Reports. Chicago, Commerce
Clearing House Inc. 4 vols. with current supplements.

The statutes administered by the Security and Exchange Commission respecting the issuance of and trading in securities are very closely analyzed in this service.

Prentice-Hall Capital Adjustments Service. New York, Prentice-Hall, Inc. 2 vols. with current supplements.

Ready reference tables provide a record of changes in the capital investment of stocks and securities of individual companies. The treatment of reorganizations, exchanges, and distribution of stock dividends and rights for federal income tax purposes is also analyzed in detail.

Commerce Clearing House Blue Sky Law Reports. Chicago, Commerce Clearing House, Inc. 2 vols. with current supplements.

These reports show how to qualify securities under state blue sky laws. All state statutes are reproduced in full with their pertinent regulations and other applicable data.

SUMMARY

Persons interested in securing practical information on banking should thoughtfully read a general text such as F. A. Bradford's *Money and Banking,* 3d ed., New York, Longmans, 1949. This should be supplemented by reference to Glenn G. Munn's *Encyclopedia of Banking and Finance,* 6th ed., New York Bankers Publishing Company, 1962. *The Federal Reserve Bulletin, Commercial and Financial Chronicle, Polk's Bankers Encyclopedia, Barron's, American Banker,* and the *Banking Journal* supply current information.

For an understanding of corporation finance, the information contained in the following will be useful: Jules I. Bogen *et al.,* eds. *Financial Handbook,* 3d rev. ed., Englewood Cliffs, N.J., Prentice-Hall, 1957; Charles W. Gerstenberg, *Financial Organization and Management,* 4th rev. ed., Englewood Cliffs, N.J., Prentice-Hall, 1959; Arthur S. Dewing, *The Financial Policy of Corporations,* 5th ed., New York, Ronald, 1953; and Roy A. Foulke, *Practical Financial Statement Analysis,* 4th ed., New York, McGraw-Hill, 1957.

Books that will provide information on the background and principles of investment activities include the following titles: G. W. Dowrie, D. R. Fuller and F. J. Calkins, *Investments,* 3d ed., New York, Wiley, 1961; D. H. Jordan and H. E. Dougall, *Investments,* 7th ed., Englewood Cliffs, N.J., Prentice-Hall, 1960; J. Grodinsky, *Investments,* New York, Wiley, 1953; and H. G. Guthmann, *The Analysis of Financial Statements,* 4th ed., Englewood Cliffs, N.J., 1953.

For general news on the stock and bond market the larger metropolitan newspapers and the *Commercial and Financial Chronicle, Barron's,* and the *Wall Street Journal* should prove adequate. Forecasts and analyses of the market and individual stocks are covered by *Moody's Investors Service, Poor's Trade and Securities,* and the *United Business Service.* In making a study of individual companies, *Moody's Manual of Investments* and *Standard and Poor's Corporation Records* are essential. Recommendation for purchase and sale of securities should be checked in the *United Business Service, Moody's Stock Survey, Moody's Bond Survey,* Poor's Corporation *Monthly Earnings and Ratings Stock Guide,* and the *Magazine of Wall Street.* Quotations can be found in the *Commercial and Financial Chronicle, Bank and Quotation Record, National Daily Quotation Service* and its *Monthly Corporation Bond Summary, Monthly Stock Summary,* and *Monthly Municipal Bond Summary.*

CHECKLIST OF FINANCIAL BOND SUMMARY

BIBLIOGRAPHIES AND INDEXES

The Financial Index. Weekly. New York, Financial Index Company, Inc. (Absorbed by *Funk and Scott Index,* 1963.)

Index of Corporations and Industries. Weekly with monthly cumulations. Detroit, Funk & Scott.

Silverman, C., ed. *The Cumulative Financial Index.* Woodstock, Vt. Financial Index Company, annually.

Special Libraries Association. *Directory of Investment Advisory Services, 1962.* New York, Special Libraries Association, 1963.

U.S. Federal Reserve System Library. *Selected Bibliography on Monetary Policy and Management.* Washington, D.C., Board of Governors of the Federal Reserve System, 1961. Mimeographed.

Walter, H. C. ed. *Directory of Investment Advisory Services,* ed. Rochester, N.Y., Fir Publishing, 1962.

Westerfield, R. B. *Selected Bibliography of Money, Credit, Banking and Business Finance.* Boston, Bankers Publishing Company, 1940.

CORPORATION FINANCE—BOOKS

Buchanan, Norman S. *The Economics of Corporate Enterprise.* New York, Holt, 1940.

Dauten, C. A. *Business Finance.* 2d ed. Englewood Cliffs, N.J., Prentice-Hall, 1956.

Dewing, A. S. *The Financial Policies of Corporations.* 5th ed. New York, Ronald, 1953.

Gerstenberg, C. W. *Financial Organization and Management.* 4th ed. Englewood Cliffs, N.J., Prentice-Hall, 1959.

Guthmann, H. G. and Dougall, H. E. *Corporate Financial Policy*. 3d ed. Englewood Cliffs, N.J., Prentice-Hall, 1955.

Husband, W. H. and Dockery, J. C. *Modern Corporation Finance*. 4th ed. Homewood, Ill., Irwin, 1957.

Johnson, R. W. *Financial Management*. Boston, Allyn and Bacon, 1959.

HANDBOOKS AND ENCYCLOPEDIAS

Bogen, J. I. and others, eds. *Financial Handbook*. 3d ed. New York, Ronald, 1957.

Clark, D. T. and Gottfried, D. A. *Dictionary of Business and Finance*. N.Y., Cromwell, 1957.

Doris, L., ed. *Business Finance Handbook*. Englewood Cliffs, N.J., Prentice-Hall, 1953.

———, Friedman, E. J. and Spellman, H. H. *Corporate Secretary's Manual*. Rev. ed. Englewood Cliffs, N.J., Prentice-Hall, 1949.

———. *Corporate Treasurer's and Controller's Encyclopedia*. Englewood Cliffs, N.J., Prentice-Hall, 1958. 4 vols.

———. *Corporate Treasurer's and Controller's Handbook*. Englewood Cliffs, N.J., Prentice-Hall, 1950.

Garcia, F. L. and Munn, G. G. *Encyclopedia of Banking and Finance*. 6th ed. New York, The Bankers Publishing Company, 1962.

INVESTMENTS—BOOKS

Cooper, R. V. *Investments for Professional People*. Rev. ed. New York, Macmillan, 1959.

Dice, C. A. *The Stock Market*. 3d ed. New York, McGraw-Hill, 1952.

Dowrie, G. W., Fuller, D. R. and Calkins, F. J. *Investments*. 3d ed. New York, Wiley, 1961.

Foulke, R. A. *Practical Financial Statement Analysis*. 4th ed. New York, McGraw-Hill, 1957.

Friend, I. and others. *The Over-the-Counter Securities Market*. New York, McGraw-Hill, 1958.

Graham, B., Dodd, D., Cottle, S. L. with the collaboration of C. Tatham. *Security Analysis Principles and Techniques*. 4th ed. New York, McGraw-Hill, 1962.

Graham, B. *The Intelligent Investor*. 3d ed. New York, Harper, 1959.

Guthmann, H. G. *The Analysis of Financial Statements*. 4th ed. Englewood Cliffs, N.J., Prentice-Hall, 1953.

Grodinsky, J. *Investments*. New York, Ronald, 1953.

Jordan, D. F. and Dougall, H. E. *Investments*. 7th ed. Englewood Cliffs, N.J., Prentice-Hall, 1960.

——— and Willetts, E. F. *Managing Personal Finances*. 3d ed. Englewood Cliffs, N.J., Prentice-Hall, 1951.

Leffler, G. L. *The Stock Market*. 2d ed. New York, Ronald, 1957.

Plum, L. V. *Investing in American Industry*. New York, Harper, 1960.

INVESTMENTS—PERIODICALS

The Analysts' Journal. Five times a year. New York, Society of Security Analysts.
Barron's National Financial Weekly. Weekly. New York, Barron's Publishing
Company.
Commercial and Financial Chronicle. Twice weekly. New York, William B. Dana
Company.
Financial Times. Daily except Saturday and Sunday. London, The Financial Times.
Financial World. Weekly. New York, Guenther Publishing Corporation.
Journal of Commerce. Daily except Saturday and Sunday. New York, B. J. Ridder
Publisher.
Magazine of Wall Street and Business Analyst. Biweekly. New York, Ticker
Publishing Co.
Monetary Times. Monthly. Toronto, Monetary Times.
Wall Street Journal. Daily every weekday. New York, Chicago, San Francisco and
Los Angeles, Dow-Jones and Co. Inc.

INVESTMENTS—STATISTICS

U.S. Securities and Exchange Commission. *Net Working Capital of United States
Corporations.* Quarterly. Washington, D.C., U.S. Securities and Exchange
Commission.
———. *Plant and Equipment Expenditures of United States Business.* Quarterly.
Washington, D.C., U.S. Securities and Exchange Commission.
———. *Quarterly Financial Report of U.S. Manufacturing Corporations.* Quarterly.
Washington, D.C., U.S. Securities and Exchange Commission.
———. *Statistical Bulletin.* Monthly. Washington, D.C., U.S. Securities and Ex-
change Commission.

MONEY AND BANKING—BOOKS

American Bankers Association. *Present Day Banking.* New York, American Bank-
ers Association, 1954–1958. 6 vols.
———. Economic Policy Commission. *Monetary Studies,* Nos. 1–6. New York,
American Bankers Association, 1954.
American Institute of Banking. *Analyzing Financial Statements.* New York, Amer-
ican Institute of Banking, 1939.
Bradford, F. A. *Money and Banking.* 6th ed. New York, Longmans, 1949.
Fischer, G. E. *Bank Holding Companies.* New York, Columbia University Press,
1961.
Hart, A. G. *Money, Debt and Economic Activity.* Englewood Cliffs, N.J., Prentice-
Hall, 1953.
Prentice-Hall Library of Money and Credit. Englewood Cliffs, N.J., Prentice-Hall,
1962–1963.

Money and Banking—Periodicals

American Banker. Daily. New York, American Banker, Inc.

Bankers Monthly. Monthly. Chicago, Rand McNally & Co.

Banking Journal of the American Bankers Association. Monthly. New York, American Bankers Association.

Banking Law Journal. Monthly. Cambridge, Mass., Bankers Publishing Company.

The Commercial and Financial Chronicle. Two issues a week. New York, Wm. B. Dana Company.

Credit and Financial Management. Monthly. New York, National Association of Credit Men.

Journal of Finance. Quarterly. Chicago, American Finance Association.

Monetary Times. Monthly. Toronto, Monetary Times.

Savings Bank Journal. Monthly. New York, Natamsa Publishing Company.

Trust Bulletin. Monthly except for July and August. New York, American Bankers Association.

Trusts and Estates. Monthly. New York, Fiduciary Publishers.

Trust Companies Monthly. Monthly. New York, Trust Companies Publishing Company.

Money and Banking—Statistics

Bank for International Settlements Annual Report. Basle, Bank for International Settlements.

Bank of Canada Statistical Summary. Monthly. Ottawa, Bank of Canada.

Bank of England Quarterly Bulletin. Quarterly. London, Bank of England.

Bankers Almanac and Year Book. Annually. New York, Skinner & Co., Ltd.

Federal Reserve Bulletin. Monthly. Washington, D.C., U.S. Board of Governors of the Federal Reserve System.

The International Banking Section of the Statist. Annually. London, The Statist.

International Financial Statistics. Monthly with an annual supplement. Washington, D.C., International Monetary Fund.

Moody's Investors Service. *Moody's Manual of Investments, American and Foreign Banks and Insurance Companies, Investment Trusts, Real Estate Finance and Credit Companies.* New York, Moody's Investors Service, 1928–.

Polk's Bank Information Service. Daily. Detroit and New York, R. L. Polk and Co.

Polk's Bankers Encyclopedia. Semiannual. Detroit and New York, R. L. Polk and Co., 1896–.

Polk's Bankers Information Bulletin. Monthly. Detroit and New York, R. L. Polk and Co.

Rand McNally Bankers Directory. Semiannual. New York, Rand McNally and Company, 1927–.

Savings Banks Fact Book. Annually. New York, Savings Bank Trust Co.

United Nations. *Monthly Bulletin of Statistics.* Monthly. New York, United Nations.

United Nations. *Statistical Yearbook*. Annually. New York, United Nations.

U.S. Board of Governors of the Federal Reserve System. *All Bank Statistics, 1896–1956*. Washington, D.C., U.S. Board of Governors of the Federal Reserve System, 1959.

U.S. Board of Governors of the Federal Reserve System. *Banking and Monetary Statistics*. Washington, D.C., U.S. Board of Governors of the Federal Reserve System, 1943.

U.S. Board of Governors of the Federal Reserve System. *Federal Reserve Bulletin*. Monthly. Washington, D.C., U.S. Board of Governors of the Federal Reserve System.

7

REAL ESTATE
AND INSURANCE

Real estate is the oldest and most widely held form of investment. Furthermore, dealings in it are still characterized by direct bargaining between the buyer and the seller rather than the more impersonal operation of organized exchanges. Because most real estate sales and purchases are on an individual basis, it is quite desirable that the seller, and practically imperative that the buyer, have as many of the facts in hand as possible before entering into the transaction.

The buyer should have certain basic principles firmly in mind before purchasing or building. Real estate values fluctuate in cycles of from fourteen to twenty years and would-be purchasers should consider the period of the cycle before buying or building. Other factors which affect real estate costs and prices are building codes, trends in community developments, zoning laws, improvements, and union labor agreements. In many instances, land has been purchased without a complete investigation of the foregoing, and the new owner has found that the building code requires a much more expensive type of construction than he had anticipated. In other cases he has discovered that zoning laws prohibit the type of building he had planned to construct. The purchase of real estate in advance of a street or utility improvement program may saddle the new owner with a heavy outlay in assessments which will reduce the earning power of his property and seriously lower his cash position. Property bought in a new subdivision or sparsely settled area is hazardous, because it may develop in a fashion that will depreciate property values. Some unwary buyers have found that they cannot get a clear title without buying off other owners or that heavy unpaid tax liens have accumulated.

Books, statistical surveys, magazines, and the local newspapers can all aid the real estate investor in acquiring information that will enable him to evaluate the real estate situation. However, several facts must be gained through personal inquiry and observation. The city building inspector can supply information as to the requirements of the building codes, zoning restrictions can be obtained from the planning commission, and the assessor or tax collector can furnish information as to the tax rate. Classified ads and other items in local newspapers usually reflect activity in the local real estate market and give some indication of prices. After acquiring this information, an individual is ready to do business with either a broker or the owner of the property. In selecting a broker it is always advisable to deal with one who has become well established over a considerable period of time and who enjoys a reputation for efficient service and fair dealing. Local banks are usually willing to advise persons on brokers in their area.

Anyone concerned with real estate must know what is happening in the building industry. Because this subject is discussed fully on pages 243–248, the statistical and other references are not included here. The following four books stress the basic principles of land economics and land use, thus giving the real estate buyer an over-all picture of the factors that affect real estate.

Ely, R. T. and Wehrwein, G. S. *Land Economics.* New York, Macmillan, 1940.
   Although published in 1940, the book still has the sound basic principles of land use. Every type of land use is discussed by these authors. The effects of various kinds of utilization on the land, the individual, and the nation are clearly expressed. This book enables the individual to see what is happening to the nation's inheritance in land.

Hoagland, H. E. *Real Estate Principles.* 3d ed. New York, McGraw-Hill, 1955.
   A descriptive history of real estate activities and organizations is combined with a general statement of real estate principles. This work gives the reader a general background and the facts are presented clearly in nontechnical language.

North, N. L. and Ring, A. A. *Real Estate Principles and Practices.* 5th ed. Englewood Cliffs, N.J., Prentice-Hall, 1960.

> Although the authors had the realtor rather than the investor in mind
> when they wrote this book, the chapters on contracts, taxation, deeds, leases,
> and solutions provide much helpful information for would-be purchasers.

Husband, W. H. and Anderson, F. R. *Real Estate.* 3d ed. Homewood, Ill., Irwin,
1960.

> After discussing titles and property interests, the authors treat the financing
> of real estate, the real estate market and appraisals, land values, land develop-
> ment and subdivisions, real estate management, investment in real estate
> securities, and regulation of real estate by zoning. The references bring together
> the latest information on real estate practices.

All aspects of real estate activities are dealt with in the following
handbook.

Holmes, L. G. and Jones, C. M., eds. *The Real Estate Handbook.* 2d ed. New York,
Prentice-Hall, 1948.

> The information contained in this volume is supplied by experts in every
> phase of real estate activity. It is designed as a reference book for real estate
> men, lawyers, bankers, and real estate operators. The chapter bibliographies
> and multitude of forms and illustrations make it a most practical work for
> any person dealing in real estate.

The correct valuation of the property is perhaps the most important
step in any real estate transaction. Since there is no regularly published
set of quotations, as there is for securities, it is up to the investor to acquire the rudiments of the appraisal technique. The following books
explain the elements affecting the value of real estate.

Bonbright, J. C. *The Valuation of Property.* New York, McGraw-Hill, 1937. 2 vols.

> This treatise goes far beyond the valuation of the land and buildings. The
> technicalities in capitalization of value, values for appraising earning power,
> for rate-making, for taxation, and in reorganization are treated exhaustively.
> Because of the approach used, this work is probably more useful to the corpo-
> ration lawyer and the accountant than to the individual realty purchaser.

McMichael, S. L. *McMichael's Appraising Manual.* 4th ed. Englewood Cliffs, N.J.,
Prentice-Hall, 1951.

> The elements affecting the appraisal of every type of property are out-
> lined clearly. Methods of appraisal are described in detail with numerous
> illustrations. Farm, residential, and business properties are included. The
> evaluation of odd-shaped bits of property, special conditions affecting values,
> and unusual rental and investment conditions make this manual more useful
> to the real estate investor than most books on real estate. Numerous useful

tables add to the value of this work, making it indispensable for any large real estate operator.

May, A. A. *The Valuation of Residential Real Estate*. 2d ed. Englewood Cliffs, N.J., Prentice-Hall, 1953.

> By confining himself to the residential market, the author has presented a very thorough examination of valuation in this particular phase of real estate activity. The "Data Program" in a single table brings together factors affecting residential real estate valuation and much sound advice for home owners is offered in the chapters analyzing city neigborhoods and property values. The addition of case studies in valuation enhances the usefulness of the book.

If a transaction involves a considerable investment one is wise to enlist the services of a professional appraiser or of an appraising firm. The American Appraisal Company, 525 E. Michigan Street, Milwaukee 2, Wisconsin, will provide reports on costs and values of industrial and residential properties and analyze depreciation and other charges for accounting, tax, insurance purposes and for purchase, sale, and condemnation. *The Appraisal Journal,* Chicago, American Institute of Appraisers of the National Association of Real Estate Boards, each quarter provides up-to-date information on appraising and factors which affect appraisals. This keeps the appraiser abreast of trends and developments in the field.

The complete source book on appraising is:

Friedman, E. J. *Encyclopedia of Real Estate Appraising*. Englewood Cliffs, N.J., Prentice-Hall, 1959.

> The discussion of all the factors which go into or affect the appraisal is thorough and very readable. Examples of special problems of appraisal are helpful.

The mass of legal rights and restrictions which have grown up in connection with real property require some general information on the law, legal terms, and forms of various contracts. However, the individual should not rely on books alone, and any important or complicated contract should be drawn up by a competent lawyer.

Kratovil, R. *Real Estate Law*. 3d ed. Englewood Cliffs, N.J., Prentice-Hall, 1958.

> In simple, nontechnical language, the author has defined and illustrated the law and legal terms pertaining to real property. The clarity of the definitions and the ease in which topics can be located should appeal to the nonlegal user.

Grange, W. J. *Real Estate—A Practical Guide to Ownership, Transfer, Mortgaging, and Leasing of Real Property*. New York, Ronald, 1940.

The legal aspects of all kinds of real estate transactions are discussed at length in nontechnical language. Not as many topics covered as in Kratovil, but those which are included are more fully discussed.

Friedman, E. J. *Handbook of Real Estate Forms*. Englewood Cliffs, N.J., Prentice-Hall, 1957.

Examples of every type of contract, lease, conveyance form, and agreements are illustrated. The forms should be used for guidance largely, as individual contracts should be drawn up with competent legal advice and in compliance with local laws and regulations.

In large real estate transactions involving factories, shopping centers, and large retail establishments, location is very important. The literature on this subject is brought together in two recent bibliographies.

University of California, Los Angeles. Real Estate Research Program, Graduate School of Business Administration. *Industrial Location Bibliography*. Los Angeles, Graduate School of Business Administration, 1959.

References are to postwar publications on location theory, site selection, development of individual industries, and to assist firms in the location of plants. Helpful to those who are engaged in area planning and zoning. Detailed subject classification makes for easy location of topics.

U.S. Department of Commerce. *Data Sources for Plant Location*. Washington, D.C., U.S. Department of Commerce, 1959.

Primarily a directory of agencies which can assist in locating a plant, these agencies include state planning boards, chambers of commerce, banks, railroads, and public utilities.

Two books "treat" the subject of plant location.

Losch, A. *The Economics of Plant Location*. 2d ed. New Haven, Yale University Press, 1954.

This is a brilliant discussion and analysis of the theory of the location of industry and regional development. Agricultural regions as well as industrial are included. There is much data on transportation costs as they affect mobility of products and people as well as the location of industry.

Bogue, D. J. and Beale, C. L. *Economic Areas of the United States*. Glencoe, Ill., Free Press, 1961.

This is a study in depth of geographical regions which are more or less economic units. Much descriptive, economic, and statistical information is supplied on each region. This book is an excellent starting point for gathering data on planning the relocation of a plant or industry.

When it comes to the actual selection of a plant location, the following service can save much time and money.

Fantus Factory Locating Service, 139 North Clark Street, Chicago, and Empire
State Building, New York.
    Specialists will make surveys as to the feasibility of present and new
locations of plants as to production costs, costs of raw materials, transportation,
labor, and markets. This information can be supplied on every community over
2,500 population. Active files are maintained on available industrial properties.

After settling the location, appraisal and legal aspects, the next step
is the financing.

McMichael, S. L. and O'Keefe, P. T. *How to Finance Real Estate.* Englewood Cliffs,
N.J., Prentice-Hall, 1953.
    Advantages and disadvantages of all types of financing are emphasized
in this work, plus the financial aspects of various types of real estate investments.

American Savings and Loan Institute. *Savings and Loan Principles.* 2d ed. Chicago,
American Savings and Loan Institute Press, 1960.
    Although primarily concerned with savings and loan management, the
chapters on mortgage loan services, lending policies, and the business and real
estate cycles are helpful to any person interested in real estate.

American Institute of Banking. *Home Mortgage Lending.* New York, American Institute of Banking, 1953.
    This book reflects the modern approach of banks to home mortgage lend-
ing. Information includes principles of real estate credit, legal aspects, mortgage
contract, and principles of servicing real estate loans.

A book written primarily for the real estate broker contains suggestions helpful to property owners and real estate investors.

McMichael, S. L. *Selling Real Estate.* 3d ed. Englewood Cliffs, N.J., Prentice-Hall,
1950.
    This narrative account of real estate selling contains useful suggestions
on sales organization and methods.

Current information on real estate is provided in the following periodicals. Other periodicals concerned more directly with building construction will be found on pages 246–248.

American Builder. Monthly. New York, Simmons, Boardman Publishing Company.
    Building developments, opportunities for purchase of property, descriptions
of new building materials and techniques are published in a New York, Mid-
west, and West Coast edition. Each edition carries an expanded section on
news and statistics of the area.

The Appraisal Journal. Quarterly. Chicago, 36 So. Wabash Avenue, American
Institute of Appraisers of the National Association of Real Estate Boards.

Up-to-date information is published on methods of appraising and factors which affect appraisals, which keeps the appraiser abreast of trends and developments in the field.

Building Reporter and Realty News. Monthly. New York, 285 Madison Avenue, Building Reporter & Realty News Inc.

The national magazine for owners of income-producing properties. Covers all aspects of real estate and building industry.

Buildings. Monthly. Cedar Rapids, Iowa, 427 Sixth Avenue. S.E., Stamats Publishing Co.

This publication has combined with the *National Real Estate and Building Journal.*

Engineering News-Record. Weekly. New York, 330 W. 42d Street, McGraw-Hill.

This magazine supplies information on building costs, trends, and construction awards. The February issue is the "Annual Report and Forecast." The June issue cumulates statistics and other data.

Journal of Property Management. Quarterly. Chicago, Institute of Real Estate Management, National Association of Real Estate Boards.

Construction, factors affecting real estate values, maintenance, and management problems are the principal topics discussed. The semiannual survey of the real estate market is an aid to real estate owners and brokers.

Land Economics. Quarterly. Madison, Wis., University of Wisconsin.

Long articles on the more theoretical aspects of land use, plus those on utility valuations, operations, and land reform are discussed.

Mortgage Banker. Monthly. Chicago, Mortgage Bankers Association of America.

Underlying factors affecting the bank's mortgage operations and news of people and events make up the content of this publication.

National Real Estate and Building Journal. Monthly. Cedar Rapids, Iowa, 427 Sixth Ave., S.E., Stamats Publishing Co.

Over-all trends in real estate, news of real estate activities, and personalities in the real estate field are discussed in this magazine. Items on management of commercial properties are helpful to those who construct, equip, maintain, and manage these properties.

Realty, Brokerage, Building, Investments, Management, Modernization. Biweekly. New York, 251 W. 40th Street, Bensenson Publications, Inc.

As the title implies, this periodical attempts to supply information on all aspects of real estate activities. The frequency of publication makes the news very current.

Residential Appraiser. Monthly. Chicago, 7 So. Dearborn Street. Society of Residential Appraisers.

The appraiser is kept informed of the trends in valuations and appraising methods in this magazine.

Savings and Loan Factbook. Annually. Rockford, Ill., United States Savings and Loan League.

This publication brings together much information on mortgages and amount of mortgage credit outstanding, in addition to statistics on the savings and loan industry.

Savings and Loan News. Monthly. Rockford, Ill., United States Savings and Loan League.

Although this publication is designed primarily for savings and loan executives, it contains many good articles on long-term realty trends and realty financing. It also carries indexes of building activities and trends.

Construction Review. Monthly. Washington, D.C., U.S. Business and Defense Services Administration.

All current government statistics on building are brought together in this publication. Topics include "Construction at a Glance," "The Economy at a Glance," and "Construction Comments," a feature article and statistics on total construction, housing, building permits, contract awards, costs, prices, cost of construction materials, and construction employment. The data is on a monthly basis for the past year, with a five year annual average for earlier periods, and much is on a state or area basis.

Housing Statistics. Monthly. Washington, D.C., U.S. Housing and Home Finance Agency.

Most of the data on housing published by the government and private agencies are brought together in this publication. There is a considerable amount of statistical material, particularly on financing of real estate.

For more specific information needed by real estate operators the following services are useful.

Prentice-Hall Real Estate Service. New York, Prentice-Hall. 1 vol. with monthly supplements.

This service brings together in one work all the information on real estate activities and general business which affects real estate. The monthly *Report* presents, in concise form, charts of business activities, building indexes, tables of building costs and mortgage recordings and any news that has a bearing on the building business. The supplementary material is carefully cross-indexed to relate it to the basic information in the volume. The main sections cover: selling, advertising, management, financing, federal regulation, federal taxation, federal aids to financing, rent control, state laws, appraising, and new ideas in relation to real estate. This service contains many practical suggestions and illustrations as to how the reader can apply this information to his own problems.

Roy Wenzlick & Co., 706 Walnut St., St. Louis 1, Mo.

This company publishes a number of studies on all aspects of the real estate situation and these include:

Real Estate Analyst. Monthly. Statistics and tables which support analyses of factors influencing real estate and construction activities on a national and city-by-city basis.

As I See It Bulletin. Monthly. Current real estate problems are discussed.
Appraisal Bulletin. Monthly. Consists of appraisal techniques and problems.
Agricultural Bulletin. Irregular. Prices and trends of farm property.
Construction Bulletin. Monthly. Construction in 168 metropolitan areas.
Mortgage Bulletin. Irregular. Developments in and state of mortgage market.
Real Estate Tax Bulletin. Irregular.

The securities of publicly held real estate companies are described in:

Moody's Manual of Investments, American and Foreign Banks, Insurance Companies, Investment Trusts, Real Estate Finance and Credit Companies and *Standard and Poor's Corporation Records.*

No book or magazine, of course, is a substitute for personal knowledge of the local real estate situation and the profits relating to a particular piece of property. But the reader can gain an idea of the principles involved and apply the acquired knowledge to the local situation.

INSURANCE

Since the bulk of property insurance is closely tied in with real property and real estate sales and leasing, the topic deserves discussion here.

The businessman's knowledge of insurance is apt to be sketchy, and he is prone to regard his insurance premiums as an expense to be kept at the lowest possible figure. This may be the most expensive form of protection, particularly if a loss occurs during a period of rising realty and building values.

Each unit of insurable property has its own peculiarities to be considered in drawing up the contract. The wide variety of risks and policy provisions make it advisable to employ the services of a well-trained broker. The latter will endeavor to get the best coverage at the lowest cost; furthermore, he will analyze the situation for any unusual hazards or unprotected risks and draw up a policy that assures ample protection. Many a business has been protected against fire and flood damage only to lose heavily from overhead costs that went on during the rebuilding after the loss. Use and occupancy insurance can substantially reduce this loss by paying overhead costs during the shutdown period.

Insurance policies are filled with many technical terms which can be confusing to the layman. The following books provide definitions of words and phrases peculiar to insurance:

Gallagher, V. L. and Heath, J. R. *Insurance Words and Their Meanings.* 5th ed. Indianapolis, Rough Notes, 1961.

> Brief and simple definitions of words commonly used in a technical sense in all forms of insurance except life.

Crobaugh, C. J. *Handbook of Insurance.* 2d ed. Englewood Cliffs, N.J., Prentice-Hall, 1949.

> Terms found in all types of insurance are defined and illustrated. This book, compiled by one of the leading authorities on insurance, is unusually helpful in explaining the various policy options and provisions in simple, easily understood language.

There are two publications of the Special Libraries Association which are helpful in locating and evaluating books on insurance.

Special Libraries Association Insurance Group. *Creation and Development of an Insurance Library.* New York, Special Libraries Association, 1949.

> Very practical suggestions are given as to how to organize and build up an insurance library. A comprehensive bibliography of books and periodicals in all fields of insurance are included.

Special Libraries Association Insurance Group. *Insurance Book Reviews.* Ten times a year. Newark, N.J., Mutual Benefit Life Insurance Co.

> Books and periodicals in all fields of insurance are reviewed. The annotations are brief and to the point.

There are a number of organizations which publish statistics on insurance. A forthcoming publication of Special Libraries Association, Insurance Division, *Sources of Insurance Statistics* will prove helpful in locating statistical data.

Of the various annual statistical publications in the field of insurance those published by the Alfred M. Best Company, The Spectator Company, and the Underwriter Printing and Publishing Company are the most complete and have been issued for the longest period of time.

The Insurance Almanac; Who, What and Where in Insurance. New York, The Underwriter Printing and Publishing Company, 1912-.

> This annual compilation contains a larger amount of information than any other single volume in the insurance field. The two "Who's Who" sections—the first for insurance company officials, the second for agents and brokers—are both directories with brief biographical accounts of the part these persons play in the insurance world. The head office address, officers and directors, types of insurance written, branches and territory covered, are given for all kinds of insurance companies. Capital, total assets, reserves for reinsurance, net surplus, net premiums written, and net losses paid are given for many

companies for a nine-year period. Fraternal, mutual, and reciprocal organizations are included. Lists of companies which have been merged or absorbed during the year, insurance associations, and insurance periodicals are other features. A handy section is the listing by type of insurance, of all companies that write a given type of policy.

Insurance news of general interest is published in the "Insurance Section" of the *Journal of Commerce* and in the *Wall Street Journal.* The annual insurance supplement of the *Journal of Commerce* summarizes all types of insurance activities for the year. The *Weekly Underwriter* carries information on all types of insurance and statistics of the industry. The *Underwriters' Report,* a weekly, covers insurance activities and personalities on the Pacific Coast. The *Insurance Post,* published monthly to inform buyers of large lines of property insurance, supplies up-to-date information from the viewpoint of the buyer.

FIRE AND MARINE INSURANCE

Bests Insurance Reports (Fire and Marine edition). New York, Alfred M. Best Co., 1899–.
    The instructions for analyzing the statement of an insurance company enable the layman to interpret intelligently the information set forth in this volume. A greater amount of information is given on history and management than in the Insurance Almanac. Useful data for the current year are supplied in the balance sheet, income statement, and on underwriting results. Stock, mutual, and reciprocal companies are included, and each is rated. The list of insurance companies that have retired during the past ten years makes this publication the first place to look when searching for a defunct company.
The Spectator Insurance Yearbook—Fire and Marine volume. Philadelphia, Pa., The Spectator, 1873–.
    In contrast to the Best publications, this work makes no attempt to rate individual concerns. The factual information is more complete as to balance sheet and profit-and-loss statements. All types of underwriters are included. A unique feature is the classification of net premiums and losses paid by each company during the year and the table of each company's premium writings in each state. A complete list of fire insurance companies that have failed, retired, or merged appears in each issue.

Pocket-sized digests of the financial information in the *Spectator Insurance Yearbook—Fire and Marine* volume are published as *The Spectator Financial and Underwriting Analysis* of *Fire and Marine*

Insurance Companies. The Argus Fire Chart: Financial Statements, Operating Reports and Underwriting Results is a similar publication issued by the National Underwriter Company. The annual digests each contain similar data: tables of premiums, losses, underwriting expenses, and loss and expense rates indicate the standing of each company.

Many books on insurance are so concerned with an analysis of the insurance contract that they are not only very dull reading but they lack explanations of the principles involved. The books cited below are the least subject to criticism. The five best books on property insurance for the general reader are the following:

Riegel, R. and Miller, J. S. *Insurance Principles and Practices.* 4th ed. Englewood
     Cliffs, N.J., Prentice-Hall, 1959.
          This comprehensive basic text deals with all the important branches of
     the insurance business. Each chapter is closed with a brief summary outline
     of the principles and practices discussed, a list of readings, and problems.
Magee, J. H. *Property Insurance.* 3d ed. Homewood, Ill., Irwin, 1955.
          This is probably the best, most helpful, general textbook available on the
     subject. The author's treatment of all types of property insurance is crystal
     clear, his style is most readable, and his points are well illustrated by examples.
     The risks and policy provisions are analyzed in detail in the early chapters
     which are followed by chapters on the development of insurance, types of
     carriers, insurance practices, and financing of insurance. The selected references
     at the end of each chapter are unusually well-chosen and are up to date.
Huebner, S. S. and Black, K. *Property Insurance.* 4th ed. New York, Appleton-
     Century-Crofts, 1957.
          This book brings up-to-date information on all forms of property insurance
     and discusses insurable risks, forms of contract, types of protection for fire,
     marine, automobile, surety bonding, burglary and theft, and title insurance.
     The discussion of the insurance contract and the author's more technical
     approach results in a book that still appeals more to the insurance fraternity
     than the general public. However, it does contain a mine of information on
     insurance practice and theory.
Schultz, R. E. and Backwell, E. C. *Property Insurance.* New York, Rinehart & Co.,
     1959.
          Fire, inland marine, casualty, property and multi-peril coverages are treated
     along with policy provisions, risks, and coverages. Business interruption in-
     surance is fully dealt with in two chapters.
Myers, L. S. *The Manufacturer and His Insurance.* Rev. ed. Cincinnati, The Na-
     tional Underwriter, 1948.
          One of the most valuable features of this book are the pointers given by
     the author on various hazards ordinarily not apparent to the average insurance

buyer. He indicates what risks are not covered by standard policy forms and suggests combination of policies to give the best protection at the lowest costs. In nontechnical language, Mr. Myers describes the operation of various clauses of insurance policies in event of loss. All kinds except life insurance policies are discussed.

Current activities in the field of property insurance are recorded in the *National Underwriter, Fire and Casualty Issue,* which appears every Thursday. The two leading property insurance monthly publications are *The Spectator Property* and *Best's Insurance News—Fire and Casualty Edition.* Both periodicals publish very complete statistics on losses, underwriting results, as well as profits of the entire industry and individual companies. They also print copies of new insurance contracts.

MARINE INSURANCE

The oldest form of property insurance is marine insurance, and it is one which requires more skill and experience on the part of the underwriter than any other type of insurance. The British have been leaders in this field and the best works on marine insurance are by British authors.

Lloyd's Register of Shipping is a "must" book for the marine insurance office and the large ship-owner. It lists all vessels by name, and gives information on the owner, date of building or launching, name of builder, and home port. A comprehensive set of symbols describes the vessel and its equipment. The following books state the basic principles of marine insurance and interpret the policy:

Dover, B. *Elements and Practice of Marine Insurance.* Rev. ed. London, H. F. & J. Witherby, 1957.
    A current description of the operation of marine insurance and the principles governing it. The approach is from British experience and practice.
Winter, W. D. *Marine Insurance, Its Principles and Practices.* 3d ed. New York, McGraw-Hill, 1952.
    In a readable and current presentation with a minimum of technical detail, the author provides the general reader with information on marine insurance. American practice is brought out as against the British.

Current information on activities in the field of marine insurance is carried in the *Journal of Commerce, Weekly Underwriter* and the monthly *Spectator Property Insurance Review.*

INLAND MARINE INSURANCE

Inland marine insurance, an outgrowth of marine insurance, has developed to a substantial business. This type of coverage protects goods in warehouses and in transit on inland carriers. The "floater" policies are a form of inland marine insurance which is becoming increasingly popular. Inland marine insurance is discussed in: Magee's *Property Insurance,* Huebner and Black, *Property Insurance,* and Schultz and Backwell, *Property Insurance.* An up-to-date treatment of this subject is:

Rhodda, W. H. *Inland Marine and Transportation Insurance.* 2d ed. Englewood Cliffs, N.J., Prentice-Hall, 1958.
    The author describes the different types of coverage and policies available.

The *Journal of Commerce* and other general magazines dealing with property insurance are sources of current information on inland marine insurance.

CASUALTY INSURANCE

As business became increasingly complex, there arose the need for protection against various hazards which do not fall within the categories of property, life, or marine insurance. Such risks evolved from the possibilities that a businessman could become liable to others for damages due to his own actions or those of his employees. Businessmen and firms had to protect themselves against losses arising from a contractor's inability to fulfill contracts and from dishonesty of employees.

Because this type of risk was totally different from that handled by fire, marine, and life companies, these companies did not branch out into the casualty and surety field. Instead new companies were formed, which in recent years have developed close affiliations with fire insurance companies. The automobile liability, other liability, fidelity, burglary, property damage, surety and performance bonds, accident, and health protection are today some of the largest lines in the casualty insurance field. Statistical data compiled by companies writing casualty insurance will be found in the publications mentioned below:

The Spectator Insurance Yearbook—Casualty and Surety volume. Philadelphia,
The Spectator, 1872–.

The information in this volume has the same arrangement as that of the
Spectator fire and marine volume. History of the company, analyses of investment portfolios, balance sheets, income statements, and underwriting results
for the preceding year supply the most essential information on each company.

*The Spectator Financial and Underwriting Analysis of Casualty Insurance Com-
panies.* Philadelphia, Pa., The Spectator, 1872–.

Published annually as Section II of *The Spectator Insurance Yearbook—
Casualty and Surety* volume, this pamphlet supplies financial and underwriting
information in handy tabular form.

Bests Insurance Reports (Casualty and Surety). New York, Alfred M. Best Company, 1899–.

An annual publication which supplies information similar to the *Spectator*
volume plus ratings on each company.

Argus Casualty and Surety Chart with Special Accident and Health Section.
Cincinnati, Ohio, The National Underwriter, 1899–.

This annual publication presents a handy compilation of financial and
underwriting records. An excellent general work on casualty insurance is:

Kulp, C. A. *Casualty Insurance, An Analysis of Hazards, Policies, Companies and
Rates.* 3d ed. New York, Ronald, 1956.

The author discusses the principles of casualty insurance. Under each risk
he explains the policy provisions and the proper type of coverage, and in a
chapter on casualty companies he weighs the merits of the different types of
casualty insurance carriers. This is a surprisingly readable book in spite of the
somewhat dry topics considered.

Automobile liability insurance is probably the largest single kind of
coverage handled by casualty companies. E. W. Sawyer's book remains
one of the few works which deal with this subject exclusively.

Sawyer, E. W. *Automobile Liability Insurance, An Analysis of the National
Standard Policy Provisions.* New York, McGraw-Hill, 1936.

The value of this book is in its very excellent explanations of the rights
and the responsibilities of both the insured and the company under the terms
of the policy.

Although accident and health insurance is now being written by life
insurance companies, it was originally developed by casualty underwriters
or concerns especially organized for this purpose. A good survey of all
kinds of accident and health insurance can be found in McCahan's
Accident and Health Insurance.

McCahan, D. *Accident and Health Insurance.* Philadelphia, University of Pennsylvania Press, 1954.

   The historical development of health and accident insurance is described. The various types of coverage are then taken up and the need for such protection is pointed out, thus making this book useful both to the insurance specialist and the layman. The insurance buyer is able to gain some idea of the available types of coverage from this book.

Surety underwriters maintain that their business does not properly come under the casualty heading. However, it is partially an outgrowth of certain phases of the casualty business and, therefore, will be included with it in this book. This form of protection is of great importance to the businessman because it indemnifies him for many losses that commonly occur in the ordinary course of his business, or it enables him to meet certain conditions required by law.

   Although it is thirty years old, Lunt's book still has value.

Lunt, E. C. *Surety Bonds, Nature, Functions, Underwriting Requirements.* Rev. ed. New York, Ronald, 1930.

   The author offers reasons for the purchase of surety protection, describes the kinds of risks—indicates how they affect a person's business—and outlines the terms of the contract. The effective use of illustrations and a slightly humorous approach drive home the writer's points.

Current news of the casualty and surety business can be found in the *Journal of Commerce, The National Underwriter, Spectator Property Insurance Review, Best's Insurance News—Fire and Casualty Edition, Accident and Health Review* and the *Casualty Insurer.*

CHECKLIST OF PROPERTY INSURANCE

BACKGROUND AND PRINCIPLES

Riegel, R. and Miller, R. S. *Insurance Principles and Practices.* 4th ed. Englewood Cliffs, N.J., Prentice-Hall, 1959.

BIBLIOGRAPHY

Special Libraries Association. Insurance Group. *Creation and Development of an Insurance Library.* New York, Special Libraries Association, 1949.
Special Libraries Association. Insurance Division. *Insurance Book Reviews.* Ten times a year. Newark, N.J., Mutual Benefit Life Insurance Co.

Special Libraries Association. Insurance Division. *Sources of Insurance Statistics.*
New York, Special Libraries Association, in process.

Definition of Terms

Crobaugh, C. J. *Handbook of Insurance.* 2d. ed. Englewood Cliffs, N.J., Prentice-
Hall, 1949.
Gallagher, B. L. and Heath, G. R. *Insurance Words and Their Meaning.* 5th ed.
Indianapolis, Rough Notes, 1961.

Financial and Underwriting Information

Best's Insurance Reports (Fire and Marine) and (Casualty and Surety). New York,
Alfred M. Best Co., 1899–.
*Moody's Manual of Investments, American and Foreign, Banks, Insurance Com-
panies, Investment Trusts, Real Estate. Finance and Credit Companies.* New
York, Moody's. Investor Service, 1928–.
Spectator Insurance Yearbooks, Fire and Marine Volume. Philadelphia, The Spec-
tator, 1892–.

General Information and Statistics

The Insurance Almanac. New York, The Underwriter Printing and Publishing
Company, 1912–.

Types of Insurance

ACCIDENT AND HEALTH

McCahan, D. *Accident and Health Insurance.* Philadelphia, University of Pennsylvania Press, 1954.

AUTOMOBILE

Sawyer, E. W. *Automobile Liability Insurance, An Analysis of the National
Standard Policy Provisions.* New York, McGraw-Hill, 1936.

CASUALTY

Argus Casualty and Surety Chart with Special Accident and Health Section.
Cincinnati, Ohio, The National Underwriter, 1899–.
Best's Insurance Reports (Casualty and Surety). New York, Alfred M. Best Co.,
1899.
Kulp, C. A. *Casualty Insurance Principles, An Analysis of Hazards, Policies, Com-
panies and Rates.* 3d ed. New York, Ronald, 1956.
The Spectator Insurance Yearbook—Casualty and Surety volume. Philadelphia,
Pa., The Spectator, 1872–.

The Spectator Financial and Underwriting Analysis of Casualty Insurance Companies. Philadelphia, The Spectator, 1872–.

FIRE

Argus Fire Chart: Financial Statements, Operating Reports, Underwriting Results. Cincinnati, Ohio, National Underwriter, 1899–.

Best's Insurance Reports (Fire and Marine Edition). New York, Alfred M. Best Co., 1899–.

Spectator Financial and Underwriting Analysis of Fire and Marine Insurance Companies. Philadelphia, The Spectator, 1872–.

Spectator, Insurance Yearbook—Fire and Marine volume. Philadelphia, The Spectator, 1872–.

HANDBOOKS

Crobaugh, C. J. *Handbook of Insurance.* 2d ed. Englewood Cliffs, N.J., Prentice-Hall, 1949.

INLAND MARINE

Rhodda, W. H. *Inland Marine and Transportation Insurance.* 2d ed. Englewood Cliffs, N.J., Prentice-Hall, 1958.

MARINE

Dover, V. *Elements and Practice of Marine Insurance.* Rev. ed. London, H. F. and J. Witherby, 1957.

Lloyd's Register of Shipping. Annually. London, Lloyd's Register of Shipping.

Winter, W. D. *Marine Insurance, Its Principles and Practices.* 3d ed. New York, McGraw-Hill, 1952.

PERIODICALS

Best's Insurance News—Fire and Casualty Edition. Monthly. New York, Alfred M. Best Co.

Journal of Commerce. Daily. New York, B. J. Ridder Publisher.

National Underwriter. Fire and Casualty Issue. Weekly. Cincinnati, National Underwriter.

The Spectator. Monthly. Philadelphia, Chilton Co., Inc.

PROPERTY INSURANCE—GENERAL

Huebner, S. S. and Black, K. *Property Insurance.* 4th ed. New York, Appleton-Century-Crofts, 1957.

Magee, J. H. *Property Insurance.* 3d ed. Homewood, Ill., Irwin, 1955.

Myers, L. S. *The Manufacturer and His Insurance.* Rev. ed. Cincinnati, The National Underwriter Company, 1948.

Schultz, R. E. and Backwell, E. C. *Property Insurance*. New York, Rinehart & Co., 1959.

SURETY

Lunt, E. C. *Surety Bonds, Nature Functions, Underwriting Requirements*. Rev. ed. New York, Ronald, 1930.

YEARBOOKS

The Insurance Almanac. New York, Underwriters Printing and Publishing Company 1912–.

Associations

CASUALTY

Association of Casualty and Surety Companies, 60 John Street, New York, N.Y.
Health Insurance Association of America, 1701 K. Street, N.W., Washington, D.C.
International Association of Accident and Health Underwriters, 330 South Wells Street, Chicago, Ill.
National Bureau of Casualty and Surety Underwriters, 60 John Street, New York, N.Y.

FIRE AND MARINE

Association of Marine Underwriters, 99 John Street, New York, N.Y.
Board of Fire Underwriters of the Pacific, 215 Battery Street, San Francisco, Calif.
Fire Underwriters Association of the Northwest, 310 So. Michigan Avenue, Chicago, Ill.
Inland Marine Underwriters Association, 161 William Street, New York, N.Y.
Insurance Institute of America, 3924 Walnut Street, Philadelphia, Pa.
National Automobile Underwriters Association, 125 Maiden Lane, New York, N.Y.
National Board of Fire Underwriters, 85 John Street, New York, N.Y.
Stock Company Association, 1422 K. Street, N.W., Washington, D.C.

CHECKLIST OF REAL ESTATE SOURCES

Background and Principles

Ely, R. T. and Wehrwein, G. S. *Land Economics*. New York, Macmillan, 1940.
Hoagland, H. E. *Real Estate Principles*. 3d ed. New York, McGraw-Hill, 1955.
Holmes, L. G. and Jones, E. M. eds. *The Real Estate Handbook*. Englewood Cliffs, N.J., Prentice-Hall, 1948.

Husband, W. H. and Anderson, F. R. *Real Estate*. 3d ed. Homewood, Ill., Irwin, 1960.

North, N. L. and Ring, A. A. *Real Estate Principles and Practices*. 5th ed. Englewood Cliffs, N.J., Prentice-Hall, 1960.

FINANCING

American Institute of Banking. *Home Mortgage Lending*. New York, American Institute of Banking, 1953.

American Savings and Loan League. *Savings and Loan Principles*. 2d ed. Chicago, American Savings and Loan Press, 1960.

McMichael, S. L. and O'Keefe, P. T. *How to Finance Real Estate*. Englewood Cliffs, N.J., Prentice-Hall, 1953.

LEGAL

Friedman, E. J. *Handbook of Real Estate Forms*. Englewood Cliffs, N.J., Prentice-Hall, 1957.

Grange, W. J. *Transfer, Mortgaging and Leasing of Real Property*. N.Y., Ronald, 1940.

Kratovil, R. *Real Estate Law*. 3d ed. Englewood Cliffs, N.J., Prentice-Hall, 1957.

LOCATION OF PLANTS

Bogue, D. J. and Beale, C. L. *Economic Areas of the United States*. Glencoe, Ill., Free Press, 1961.

Losch, A. *The Economics of Plan Location*. 2d ed. New Haven, Conn., Yale University Press, 1954.

U.S. Department of Commerce. *Data Sources for Plant Location*. Washington, D.C., U.S. Department of Commerce, 1959.

University of California, Los Angeles Real Estate Research Program. Graduate School of Business Administration. *Industrial Location Bibliography*. Los Angeles, Graduate School of Business Administration, 1959.

PERIODICALS

American Builder. Monthly. New York, Boardman Publishing Company.

The Appraisal Journal. Quarterly. Chicago, 36 Wabash Avenue, American Institute of Appraisers of the National Association of Real Estate Boards.

Building Reporter and Realty News. Monthly. New York, 285 Madison Avenue, Building Reporter & Realty News Inc.

Engineering News-Record. Weekly. New York, 330 West 42nd Street, McGraw-Hill Publishing Company.

Journal of Property Management. Quarterly. Chicago, 36 South Wabash Avenue, Institute of Real Estate Management, National Association of Real Estate Boards.

Land Economics. Quarterly. Madison, Wis., University of Wisconsin.

Mortgage Banker. Monthly. Chicago, Mortgage Bankers Association of America.

National Real Estate and Building Journal. Monthly. Cedar Rapids, Iowa, 427 Sixth Ave., S.E., Stamats Publishing Co.

Realty: *Brokerage, Building, Investments, Management, Modernization.* Biweekly. N.Y., 251 W. 40th Street, Bensenson Publications, Inc.

Residential Appraiser. Monthly. Chicago, 7 South Dearborn Street, Society of Residential Appraisers.

Savings and Loan Fact Book. Annually. Rockford, Ill., United States Savings and Loan League.

Savings and Loan News. Monthly. Rockford, Ill., United States Savings and Loan League.

Securities of Real Estate Concerns

Moody's Manual of Investments. American and Foreign Banks, Insurance Companies, Investment Trusts, Real Estate Finance and Credit Companies. N.Y., Moody's Investors Service.

Standard and Poor's Corporation Records. New York, Standard and Poor's Corporation.

Selling and Management

McMichael, S. L. *Selling Real Estate.* 3d ed. Englewood Cliffs, N.J., Prentice-Hall, 1950.

Services

Dodge Statistical Research Service. F. W. Dodge Corporation, 113 West 40th Street, New York 18, N.Y.

Fantus Factory Locating Service, 139 North Clark Street, Chicago, Ill., and Empire State Building, New York.

Prentice-Hall Real Estate Service. Prentice-Hall, Inc., 70 Fifth Ave., New York 11, N.Y.

Roy Wenzlick & Co., 706 Walnut Street, St. Louis 1, Mo. publishes the following:
Agricultural Bulletin
Appraisal Bulletin
As I See It Bulletin
Construction Bulletin
Mortgage Bulletin
Real Estate Tax Bulletin

Real Estate Research Corporation, First National Bank Building, Chicago, Ill., publishes the *National Market Letter.*

Statistics

Construction Review. Monthly. Washington, D.C., U.S. Business and Defense Services Administration.

Dodge Statistical Research Service. Bimonthly. New York, 119 West 40th Street, New York 18. F. W. Dodge Corporation.

Engineering News-Record. Weekly. New York, 330 West 42d Street, McGraw-Hill Publishing Company.

Federal Home Loan Bank Review. Monthly. Washington, D.C., Federal Home Loan Bank Board.

Housing Statistics. Monthly. Washington, D.C., U.S. Housing and Home Finance Agency.

Monthly Labor Review. Monthly. Washington, D.C., U.S. Department of Labor.

Survey of Current Business. Monthly. Washington, D.C., U.S. Office of Economics.

VALUATION

Bonbright, J. C. *The Valuation of Property*. New York, McGraw-Hill, 1937. 2 vols.

Friedman, E. J. *The Encyclopedia of Real Estate Appraising*. Englewood Cliffs, N.J., Prentice-Hall, 1959.

McMichael, S. L. *McMichael's Appraising Manual*. 4th ed. Englewood Cliffs, N.J., Prentice-Hall, 1951.

May, A. A. *The Valuation of Residential Real Estate*. 2d ed. Englewood Cliffs, N.J., Prentice-Hall, 1953.

ASSOCIATIONS

American Institute of Real Estate Appraisers, 36 South Wabash Avenue, Chicago, Ill.

National Association of Real Estate Boards, 36 South Wabash Avenue, Chicago, Ill.

Property Owners Association of America, Rialto Building, Kansas City, Missouri.

Society of Residential Appraisers, 7 South Dearborn Street, Chicago, Illinois.

8

THE LITERATURE
OF ACCOUNTING

Probably no field of business has such a prolific literature nor as long a history as does accounting. As soon as man's economic activity developed beyond the simple barter stage, it became necessary for him to keep some record and recapitulation of his transactions in order to know the condition of his business. As business grew in complexity, he realized the desirability of more closely controlled operations, so he expanded and refined his accounting system in order to reflect his costs more accurately. The expansion of a credit economy also stimulated the businessman to utilize more uniform accounting methods.

Present-day accounting has progressed far beyond those rudiments of double entry bookkeeping that were devised by Genoese merchants. Not only has the technique of accounting and auditing been developed to a high level, but better methods of cost control and many specialized accounting systems have been evolved to meet the needs of particular kinds of business.

The accountant is fortunate in that the published materials in his field are very completely recorded in excellent, up-to-date bibliographies and indexes. The best of these are published by the American Institute of Certified Public Accountants and the National Association of Accountants. The first organization publishes a bibliography on all phases of accounting;

the second is limited to indexes of articles on cost accounting published in the bulletins of the Association.

American Institute of Certified Public Accountants. *Accountant's Index.* New York, American Institute Publishing Company, 1921–.

The first volume covers books in English which were in print in 1912 and all material published from that date to 1920. This volume is kept up to date by the issuance of periodic supplementary volumes. All accounting literature (books, pamphlets, periodical articles) published in English is indexed. The material is classified under an unusually well-conceived list of subjects. A most useful feature is the reference to portions of books dealing with specific subjects. A large number of references to accounting articles which have appeared in publications not strictly in the accounting field are included. The lists of uniform systems of accounts are an aid to the small businessman who wishes to establish a system adapted to his needs.

Coe, C. E. *Bibliography of Accounting and Tax Articles.* Inglewood, Calif., Cecil E. Coe, 1953–. Loose-leaf.

This service represents an attempt to supply a current service to periodical articles in the fields of taxation and accounting. The monthly issues are cumulated and supplements are issued periodically.

Institute of Internal Auditors. *Bibliography of Internal Auditing to December 31, 1955.* New York, Institute of Internal Auditors, 1956.

An annotated list of articles in books and periodicals on internal auditing arranged by subject which includes title of industry served. References are complete through December 31, 1955.

National Association of Accountants. *Complete Topical Index.* 1920–1942. New York, National Association of Accountants, 1943.

This index, kept up to date by leaflets issued quarterly, is the key to the very valuable articles published in the Bulletin of the National Association of Accountants. The latter is the most important in its field. Articles appear in it at an earlier date than they do in other accounting journals. The very detailed subject classification adds greatly to the value of the index.

The businessman seeking information on accepted practices in accounting and to knowledge of forms and procedures will find that the handbooks provide the maximum of facts with the minimum of effort. Furthermore, references to all phases of accounting are presented briefly within the covers of one book.

Barker, M. ed. *Handbook of Modern Accounting Theory.* Englewood Cliffs, N.J., Prentice-Hall, 1955.

The editor has brought together twenty-one chapters written by experienced accountants in which they endeavor to depict the relationship of the accountant to both the organization and outside agencies. The broad treatment deals with the origin and development of basic concepts.

Dukey, R. L. ed. *Accountants Cost Handbook*. 2d ed. New York, Ronald, 1960.

   Since this handbook deals primarily with cost accounting in manufacturing industries, the data are of direct value to the businessman. The operations of the various components of a cost accounting system are explained and illustrated along with brief descriptions of the duties of the employee concerned. This book is a handy reference for the definition of terms and procedures.

Fiske, W. P. and Beckett, J. A. *Industrial Accountants' Handbook*. Englewood Cliffs, N.J., Prentice-Hall, 1954.

   The increasing specialization of business functions has created a need for publications in various areas of business. This handbook meets the need for concise and authoritative information on accounting for industry. After the initial chapters on concepts, definitions, and organization of industrial accounting, there are helpful sections on controlling overhead costs, standard costs, inventory and material control, and the keeping of plant records.

Kane, R. L. Jr. ed. *CPA Handbook*. New York, American Institute Publishing Company, 1952. 2 vols. loose-leaf

   A practical reference work for the accountant in which the everyday aspects of his work is related to theory

Lasser, E. K. *Handbook of Accounting Methods*. 2d ed. New York, Van Nostrand, 1954.

   The accounting systems for eighty-four types of businesses have been brought up to date in line with improved practices and recent regulatory legislation.

Wixon, R. ed. *The Accountants' Handbook*. 4th ed. New York, Ronald, 1956.

   This is the latest edition of this work formerly edited by Paton. It is the authoritative work of its kind because the contributing and consulting editors include the majority of the outstanding accountants of the country. It provides information on principles, rules, methods, and procedures for the solution of problems in the broad field of accounting. Excellent examples illustrate the body of the text. This handbook is most useful to the accountant; the businessman and the engineer will also turn to it for aid.

For a definition of accounting terms the following is helpful:

Kohler, E. L. *Dictionary for Accountants*. 3d ed. Englewood Cliffs, N.J., Prentice-Hall, 1963.

   A current list of accounting terms and phrases which are defined in nontechnical language. The explanations range from one sentence to several pages with forms and charts.

Another work of a more extensive nature is:

Encyclopedia of Accounting. Edited by R. I. Williams and L. Doris. Englewood Cliffs, N.J., Prentice-Hall, 1956. 5 vols.

This work is designed to help the accountant set up an accounting system for a particular type of business. Systems of accounts for sixty-seven businesses and professions are described in great detail. The peculiarities of each business are brought out, and the system best suited for each business is explained and illustrated by forms and charts.

Two books have appeared to assist managers in understanding and utilizing accounting information without taking accounting courses. R. N. Anthony in his *Management Accounting,* Homewood, Ill., Irwin, 1956 has designed a book to provide managers with the ability to draw information from accounting statements and enable them to interpret the information supplied by the accounting department. H. S. Wittner, *Executives' Guide to Accounting,* Englewood Cliffs, N.J., Prentice-Hall, 1958 performs a similar function for the executive without an accounting background.

The increasing complexity of business, the demands of government agencies for accurate business facts and the necessity for the businessman constantly to know the condition of his business, all require at best a basic knowledge of accounting. For those who wish to gain an understanding of the general principles of accounting, the following books should prove adequate:

Noble, H. S. and Niswonger, R. *Accounting Principles.* 7th ed. Cincinnati, O. South-Western Publishing Co., 1957.

> This standard text is brought up to date. It is designed to give businessmen and economists a better understanding of accounting as a business tool and to enable professional men to measure their financial progress; it also presents the fundamentals of accounting from the layman's viewpoint. The illustrations are drawn from actual business situations, and the principles of accounting are presented with a minimum of theory. The function of accounting as a service to management is emphasized.

Paton, W. A. and Dixon, R. L. *Essentials of Accounting.* New York, Macmillan, 1958.

> This is an elementary text of unusual clarity and penetration. Basic principles and pertinent accounting theory are presented in a clear logical manner, enabling even the individual with a minimum of experience in accounting procedures to grasp the fundamentals. The illustrations and approach are for the practical accountant and the businessman.

Other good elementary accounting texts are: H. A. Finney and H. E. Miller, *Principles of Accounting—Introductory,* 5th ed., Englewood Cliffs,

N.J., Prentice-Hall, 1957; A. W. Holmes and others, *Elementary Accounting,* rev. ed., Homewood, Ill., Irwin, 1956; and G. A. MacFarland and B. S. Ayars, *Accounting Fundamentals,* 3d ed., New York, McGraw-Hill, 1957.

For works on more advanced accounting operations and more technical in character, Finney's *Principles of Accounting* and Noble's *Advanced Accounting* are standards.

Finney, H. A. and Miller, H. E. *Principles of Accounting Intermediate.* 5th ed. Englewood Cliffs, N.J., Prentice-Hall, 1958; *Principles of Accounting—Advanced,* 5th ed. Englewood Cliffs, N.J., Prentice-Hall, 1960.

In their manner of presentation the authors assume that the reader has a knowledge of the fundamentals of corporate accounting. In the "intermediate" volume, the accounting for stock issues and dividends is treated thoroughly as is accounting for inventories, installment sales, fixed assets, investments and reserves. Five chapters have been added to the fifth edition, namely; "Statements from Incomplete Records," "Cash-Flow Statement," "Quasi-Reorganizations," "Business Combinations," "Income Tax Allocation," and "Price-level Impact on Financial Statements." The "advanced" book is concerned with accounting techniques involved in the formation and dissolution of partnerships, and special kinds of accounts such as insurance, foreign exchange, and liquidation. The earlier material on parent company and subsidiary accounting has been expanded to ten chapters to give a very thorough coverage.

Noble, H. S. and others. *Advanced Accounting.* 2d ed. Cincinnati, O., South-Western Publishing Co., 1955.

The treatment is much the same as that of the preceding title reference with reference to the formation of a business, its dissolution, or consolidation.

Bierman, H. *Managerial Accounting.* New York, Macmillan, 1959.

This work is designed to assist the manager to set up accounting controls and deals with financial accounts, cost, and inventory control and depreciation.

For general current reading on accounting the following magazines are especially recommended:

The Journal of Accountancy. Monthly. New York, American Institute Publishing Co.

This magazine, the official publication of the American Institute of Certified Public Accountants, is concerned with practical accounting problems from the viewpoint of the CPA and company accountant. It has recently become a slick paper journal with more general news, more emphasis on the managerial side of accounting, and an expanded book and periodical review section. Its factual content still recommends it to the business reader.

The Accounting Review. Quarterly. Columbus, Ohio, American Accounting Association, c/o R. C. Cox, College of Commerce, Ohio State University.

> Designed more for teachers and students of accounting rather than for
> the practicing accountant. Each issue, however, usually carries one or two
> articles of interest to businessmen and accountants. The authors' approach is
> inclined to be more theoretical than practical.

The Accountants' Digest. Quarterly. Burlington, Vt., 13 Bay View Street, L. L.
Briggs.

> The brief digests of significant articles published in English keep the
> reader abreast of accounting developments here and abroad. A particularly
> useful feature of this publication is its index to periodical accounting literature
> grouped under broad subjects.

Accounting Research Bulletins. Irregularly. New York, Committee on Accounting
Procedure, American Institute of Certified Public Accountants.

> These bulletins contain statements by representative accountants on ac-
> counting methods and procedures for handling current problems. The objective
> is to encourage clarity and uniform treatment of balance sheets and earning
> statements. Accountants and others are shown how to handle controversial
> problems in accounting.

The small businessman can receive definite assistance with his particular accounting problems if he contacts his own trade association. Many
trade associations have financed studies that have developed uniform
systems embodying accepted accounting practice but modified to meet
the peculiarities of the particular business concerned. The systems evolved
by the United Typothetae of America for printers and the National Paper
Box Manufacturers Association are samples.

He can also turn to the U.S. Small Business Administration, Washington, 25, D.C. for help.

The accounting department is usually the first of the office departments to use extensively automated equipment. The subject of automation will be discussed in Chapter 9. The following named work will be
mentioned here as directly pertaining to the accounting side of a business.

Johnson, E. A. *Accounting Systems in Modern Business.* New York, McGraw-Hill,
1959.

> This is an excellent discussion of mechanical devices used in accounting
> and includes programmed computers. The author presumes that the reader
> has some knowledge of computers and binary arithmetic.

The budget is an essential feature of any accounting system. Although
budgeting will not solve all the troubles of the businessman, it will, when

properly used with a sound system of accounts, assist him in planning intelligently.

Bartizal, J. R. *Budget Principles and Procedure.* New York, Prentice-Hall, 1940.
    By following through the various steps required in building up the budget for a small manufacturing concern, the author simply and clearly illustrates the principles of budgeting. This book is excellent for the individual who has a general knowledge of accounting and desires an understanding of the fundamentals of budgeting.

Dean, Joel. *Capital Budgeting: Top-management Policy on Plant, Equipment and Product Development.* New York, Columbia University Press, 1951.
    The author takes a broad view of a system of capital budgeting based on economic analysis. This procedure requires a knowledge of the internal demand for capital investment, the supply of funds, the allocation of funds, and the timing of capital investment. The emphasis is placed on the different factors in various industries which affect capital budgeting.

Welsh, J. A. *Budgeting, Profit-Planning and Control.* Englewood Cliffs, N.J., Prentice-Hall, 1957.
    A reference work for businessmen and accountants.

A natural outgrowth of general accounting and budgeting has been the development of cost accounting. This refining of accounting procedures has enabled the businessman to watch his costs more closely and in general to have up-to-the-minute knowledge of his business: current position, trend, and so on. The books whose descriptions follow will furnish the reader with the essential principles of cost accounting.

Blocker, J. G. *Essentials of Cost Accounting.* New York, McGraw-Hill, 1942.
    This book, a simplification of an earlier work by the same author, presents the basic essentials of cost accounting. It is useful to the individual who desires a general knowledge of cost accounting but has neither the background nor the time for studying more technical works.

Gillespie, C. M. *Cost Accounting and Control.* Englewood Cliffs, N.J., Prentice-Hall, 1957.
    The author is concerned with cost accounting, cost control, and the use of costs in business planning. Approximately half of the book deals with uses and classifications of cost, job order costing, joint-product and by-product costing. The remainder of the volume is given over to cost control. An annotated bibliography on cost accounting is included.

Neuner, J. J. W. *Cost Accounting Principles and Practice.* 5th ed. Homewood, Ill., Irwin, 1957.
    Brought up to date by the inclusion of the latest practices developed by the National Association of Accountants, this book has also been expanded

to include material on managerial control and new material on accelerated depreciation and automation as they affect cost accounting.

A number of specialized works have been published on accounting systems and cost accounting for particular industries. Accounting practices and tax laws have changed in the years since World War II and many of the works mentioned in the previous edition of this book have become outdated. This gap in the field of specialized accounting has been largely filled by J. K. Lasser, *Handbook of Accounting Methods,* New York, Van Nostrand, 1954, and the *Encyclopedia of Accounting,* Englewood Cliffs, N.J., Prentice-Hall, 1956. One work that is of value to firms selling securities to the public is:

Rappaport, L. H. *S.E.C. Accounting.* New York, Ronald, 1956.
> This work develops in detail all the accounting practices required by the S.E.C. for the registration of securities. It also includes the regulations under the 1933 and 1934 Acts.

A general discussion of the principles basic to setting up accounting systems for a business appears in:

Heckert, J. B. and Kerrigan, H. D. *Accounting Systemss Design and Installation.* 2d. ed. New York, Ronald, 1953.
> Methods and procedures in setting up cost accounting systems are discussed by the authors. Up-to-date new developments are brought out.

Auditing represents the final step in the utilization of accounting by business. The audit is not only a periodic summing up of the operations of a business, but it also provides a check on the efficiency of the accounting system and an opportunity to correct practices which lead to loss or invite dishonesty on the part of employees. Auditing is usually done by individuals outside the concern, thereby rendering the audit a more objective process than if it were a part of the regular business routine. Although the author is deceased, Montgomery's work on auditing continues to be the standard work on this subject.

Lenhart, N. J. and Defliese, P. L. *Montgomery's Auditing.* 8th ed. New York, Ronald, 1957.
> Initial chapters describe the objectives, methods, and procedures of auditing and the auditor. Each item in the audit is carefully analyzed and sound auditing principles indicated. This edition includes current material on the impact of rising price levels, legislation, taxes, rulings of government agencies and accounting societies. The questionnaire on internal checks and controls

and the detailed discussion of the requirements for reports to be filed with the S.E.C. should be especially useful to businessmen.

Another book which has received favorable acceptance is E. L. Kohler, *Auditing*. 2d ed., Englewood Cliffs, N.J., Prentice-Hall, 1954. J. K. Lasser *Handbook of Auditing Methods,* New York, Van Nostrand, 1953, is also useful.

The tremendous increase in size of American corporations and the great increase in their overseas operations have brought to the fore the need for adequate internal audits. Two excellent books on internal auditing are:

Brink, V. Z. *Internal Auditing.* 2d. rev. ed. New York, Ronald, 1958.
    The principles and practices of internal auditing are presented in an organized fashion for the benefit of those working in this field. In addition, internal auditing is emphasized as a management tool for more effective control of operations.
Institute of Internal Auditing. *Internal Auditing in Industry.* New York, The Institute, 1950.
    The reasons for internal audits and the uses to which they can be put are presented in this book. The organization of an internal auditing department is described. The usefulness of the internal audit as a management tool is emphasized.

In recapitulation the best books for one who desires a simple introduction to the subject of accounting and related fields are:

Bartizal, J. R. *Budget Principles and Procedure.* New York, Prentice-Hall, 1940.
Blocker, J. G. *Essentials of Cost Accounting.* New York, McGraw-Hill, 1942.
Paton, W. A. and Dixon, R. L. *Essentials of Accounting.* New York, Macmillan, 1958.

TAX SERVICES

In recent years federal and state tax regulations have increased tremendously in scope and complexity. Many of these levies are collected by the businessman for the taxing agencies. The accounting methods and system are directly affected and regulated by the tax laws. In order to minimize their own taxes and to comply with the law, it is most necessary that businessmen and accountants have access to the latest texts of laws, regulations, and rulings pertaining to tax matters. The most current and best sources of this information are the tax services.

The services described in the following list which are shown to have periodical supplements are loose-leaf publications. See pages 23–29 for a complete description of this type of publication. Other sources that may be useful to the accountant are listed on pages 192–194.

Prentice-Hall Accountants Weekly News Letter. New York, Prentice-Hall, Inc.
      This news letter enables accountants to grasp readily the current happenings in taxation. New laws, regulations, and decisions affecting taxation are explained and analyzed.

Prentice-Hall Federal Tax Course. New York, Prentice-Hall, Inc. 1 vol. Annually.
      This course enables beginners and others to learn the federal income tax principles either by self-study or in one of the universities or colleges that use the course as a text. It also serves as a handy portable reference book for tax men and business executives. Simple examples make each of the explanations easy to understand. Each of the thirty chapters has its own set of problems and solutions. Explanations of the federal estate tax, gift tax, and Social Security laws are also included.

Commerce Clearing House Tax Course. Chicago, Commerce Clearing House, Inc. 1 vol. Annually.
      Self-training in federal tax principles is made possible by this publication which explains how the federal tax system developed and what it is today. This unit is also used in universities and colleges for the teaching of federal taxation. Citation of authorities and a supplementary full text of the Internal Revenue Code make it easy to get down to the basis of the federal tax system. Problems and solutions of actual tax questions are provided to test the user's knowledge.

Prentice-Hall Federal Tax Guide. New York, Prentice-Hall, Inc. 1- and 2-vol. editions with weekly supplements.
      In the one-volume edition, the publishers have simplified the federal income tax for businessmen, accountants, lawyers and anyone who needs tax information. The plainly written explanations guide the user in reporting the common minimum tax due. Completed specimen returns make it easy to see how returns are made out.
      The two-volume edition includes the same type of explanations for the following federal taxes: estate, gift, excise, admissions and dues, windfall, and stamp taxes. The publishers also issue a complete Federal Tax Service in five volumes, with weekly supplements.

Commerce Clearing House Federal Tax Guide Reports. Chicago, Commerce Clearing House, Inc. 2 vols. with weekly supplements.
      Week by week the *Federal Tax Guide Reports* keep subscribers in touch with new developments in federal taxation which may affect their business and personal activities. The service is designed for all persons who must know taxes in order to handle their business affairs properly. It contains nothing

technical or verbose—just the practical, easily understood information that is
needed in keeping taxes down and making out correct tax returns. (The
publishers also issue a complete Standard Federal Tax Reports for subscribers
with all-embracing tax interests.)

Prentice-Hall Payroll Service. New York, Prentice-Hall, Inc. 1 vol. with frequent
supplements.

In this single volume anyone handling payrolls will find all the information needed to comply with all the tax laws and the wage-hour laws affecting
payrolls. Withholding taxes under federal, state and local laws, and deductions
for old-age benefits and unemployment insurance are explained concisely. The
rules on wage-hour limitations are described and analyzed. Numerous payroll
systems and ideas to help save time and money are given.

Commerce Clearing House Payroll Tax Guide. Chicago, Commerce Clearing
House, Inc. 1 vol. with frequent supplements.

This operating manual is widely used by payroll departments because of
its prompt, factual coverage of federal and state laws affecting deductions and
special pay computations. All kinds of tax withholding systems under state,
federal, and local laws are included. The various payroll taxes for Social
Security, together with the records to be kept and forms to be filed, and the
wage-and-hour laws so important in figuring overtime and other wage computations are also covered.

Prentice-Hall Social Security Tax Service. New York, Prentice-Hall, Inc. Available
for any or all states. For all states—6 vols., for one state—2 vols., with weekly
supplements.

The federal government and each state have laws that impose payroll
taxes for Social Security purposes. In this service the federal and state laws,
with the rulings, regulations, and court decisions pertaining to them, are
compiled and explained. A thorough analysis of the statutes takes employers'
problems and experiences into account and stresses the practical application of
each provision of the various laws. Useful charts and tables clarify this mass
of important information.

Commerce Clearing House Unemployment Insurance Reports. Chicago, Commerce
Clearing House, Inc. 7 vols. with weekly supplements.

Payroll taxes imposed on employers and employees under the Federal
Social Security program have given rise to a complex regulatory system. Here
all the federal developments and the laws of all the states affecting unemployment insurance and old-age benefits are arranged for quick reference by
employers and other interested persons. The information provided assists the
subscriber in computing taxes and in managing payrolls for tax minimization.

Prentice-Hall State and Local Tax Service. New York, Prentice-Hall, Inc. Available
for any of all states and the District of Columbia. 22 vols. cover all the states,
with weekly supplements.

In this service tax regulations imposed by state and by local governmental units are assembled and simplified by rearrangement, ingenious indexing, and clear explanations. Regulations, rulings, opinions, and court decisions are reported, new opportunities are pointed out, and pitfalls to avoid are indicated. Charts, forms, tables, calendars, and other handy guides for quick reference save the reader hours of laborious searching. Under the uniform scheme of explanations, each topic has an identical number in each state section, making it simple to compare requirements in several states.

Commerce Clearing House State Tax Guide. Chicago, Commerce Clearing House, Inc. 1 vol. with supplements when needed.

This state taxation service shows at a glance what taxes are imposed in each of the states. Coverage is "by states" to show the panorama of tax types, and focused treatment "by taxes" analyzes the main feature of each kind of tax. Everything is arranged by subjects for easy reference.

Commerce Clearing House All State Tax Reports. Chicago, Commerce Clearing House, Inc. Individual loose-leaf units with separate current supplements when needed.

Each of the states and the District of Columbia is distinguished by its own taxing system, which may include property, income, sales, franchise, etc., taxes. How these taxes affect business and other interests, as well as individual tax-payers, is made plain in the separate units of the *All State Tax Reports.* Each reporting system is complete, but designed for use with the units of the other states by reason of uniform arrangements. Supplement issues insure the immediate receipt of all new developments in the state, while the State Tax Review provides the all-important bird's-eye view of new tax law developments in all states.

Prentice-Hall Sales Tax Service. New York, Prentice-Hall, Inc. 2 vols. with weekly supplements.

This service, compiled especially to serve businesses shipping goods in interstate commerce, gives complete information (laws, regulations, court decisions, special rulings, forms and editorial explanation) for all state-imposed sales and use taxes.

Commerce Clearing House & Interstate Sales Tax Reports. Chicago, Commerce Clearing House, Inc. 1 vol. with current supplements.

When business travels across state lines, it may become liable for sale and use taxes—artificial barriers to the free flow of trade. How the sales and use taxes affect interstate business is the subject matter of this service which is designed for business and its interests.

Commerce Clearing House Accountancy Law Reports. Chicago, Commerce Clearing House, Inc. 1 vol. with current supplements.

Laws of all states regulate the practice of accountancy. This service, which is published in coöperation with the American Institute of Accountants, shows the qualifications for registration and practice in the various states, together with the various regulations of state accountancy commissions.

CHECKLIST OF ACCOUNTING SOURCES

BIBLIOGRAPHY

American Institute of Certified Public Accountants. *Accountants' Index*. New York, American Institute Publishing Co., 1921–.
Coe, C. E. *Bibliography of Accounting and Tax Articles*. Inglewood, Calif., Cecil E. Coe, 1953–.
Institute of Internal Auditors. *Bibliography of Internal Auditing to December 31, 1955*. New York, Institute of Internal Auditors, 1956.
National Association of Accountants. *Complete Topical Index, 1920–1942*. New York, National Association of Accountants, 1943. Brought up-to-date by quarterly supplements.

AUDITING

Kohler, E. L. *Auditing*. 2d ed. Englewood Cliffs, N.J., Prentice-Hall, 1954.
Lasser, J. K. ed. *Handbook of Auditing Methods*. New York, Van Nostrand, 1953.
Lenhart, N. J. and Defliese, P. L. *Montgomery's Auditing* 8th ed. New York, Ronald, 1957.

BUDGETING

Bartizal, J. R. *Budgeting Principles and Procedure*. New York, Prentice-Hall, 1940.
Dean, Joel. *Capital Budgeting. Top Management Policy on Plant, Equipment and Product Development*. New York, Columbia University Press, 1951.
Welsh, G. A. *Budgeting, Profit-Planning and Control*. Englewood Cliffs, N.J., Prentice-Hall, 1957.

COST ACCOUNTING

Blocker, J. G. *Essentials of Cost Accounting*. New York, McGraw-Hill, 1942.
Gillespie, C. M. *Cost Accounting and Control*. Englewood Cliffs, N.J., Prentice-Hall, 1957.
Neuner, J. J. W. *Cost Accounting Principles and Practice*. 5th ed. Homewood, Ill., 1957.

DICTIONARIES

Kohler, E. L. *Dictionary of Accounting Encyclopedia*. 3d ed. Englewood Cliffs, N.J., Prentice-Hall, 1963.
Encyclopedia of Accounting. Edited by R. I. Williams and L. Doris. Englewood Cliffs, N.J., Prentice-Hall, 1956. 5 vols.

GENERAL WORKS

Anthony, R. N. *Management Accounting*. Homewood, Ill., Irwin, 1956.

Bierman, H. *Managerial Accounting*. New York, Macmillan, 1959.

Finney, H. A. and Miller, H. E. *Principles of Accounting*. 5th ed. Vol. I, *Intro-ductory*. Vol. II, *Intermediate*. Vol. III, *Advanced*. Englewood Cliffs, N.J., Prentice-Hall, 1957–1960.

Holmes, A. W. and others. *Elementary Accounting*. Rev. ed. Homewood, Ill., Irwin, 1956.

———. *Intermediate Accounting*. Rev. ed. Homewood, Ill. Irwin, 1954.

MacFarland, G. A. and Ayars, B. S. *Accounting Fundamentals*. 3d ed. New York, McGraw-Hill, 1957.

Noble, H. S. and Niswonger, R. *Accounting Principles*. 7th ed. Cincinnati, O., South-Western Publishing Co., 1957.

Noble, H. S. and others. *Advanced Accounting*. 2d ed. Cincinnati, O., South-Western Publishing Co., 1955.

Paton, W. A. *Essentials of Accounting*. New York, Macmillan, 1958.

Wittner, H. S. *Executive's Guide to Accounting*. Englewood Cliffs, N.J., Prentice-Hall, 1958.

HANDBOOKS

Barker, M. ed. *Handbook of Modern Accounting Theory*. Englewood Cliffs, N.J., Prentice-Hall, 1955.

Dickey, R. L. ed. *Accountants' Cost Handbook*. 2d ed. New York, Ronald, 1960.

Fiske, W. P. and Beckett, J. A. *Industrial Accountants' Handbook*. Englewood Cliffs, N.J., Prentice-Hall, 1954.

Kane, R. L. Jr. ed. *CPA Handbook*. New York, American Institute Publishing Company, 1952. 2 vols. loose-leaf.

Lasser, J. K. *Handbook of Accounting Methods*. 2d ed. New York, Van Nostrand, 1954.

Wixon, R. ed. *The Accountants' Handbook*. 4th ed. New York, Ronald, 1956.

SPECIALIZED ACCOUNTING

Although many of these books are becoming quite old, very often they are the only detailed treatment of the accounting requirements of individual industries. In many instances changes in methods and later developments can be picked up in Lasser's *Handbook of Accounting Methods* or Williams and Doris, *Encyclopedia of Accounting System*.

BANKING

Langston, Lloyd H. *Bank Accounting Practice*. New York, Ronald, 1937.

Potts, James E. *Bank Accounting and Audit Control*. Boston, Bankers Publishing Company, 1938.

BROKERAGE

Langer, Charles H. *Stock Brokerage Accounting.* Chicago, Walton, 1940.
Pace, Homer St. C. *Brokerage Accounting.* New York, Business Text-Book Publishers, 1938.
Rappaport, L. H. *S.E.C. Accounting.* New York, Ronald, 1956.
Todman, Frederick S. *Wall Street Accounting.* New York, Ronald, 1921.

CHEMICAL INDUSTRIES

Prochazka, George A., Jr. *Accounting and Cost Finding for the Chemical Industries.* New York, McGraw-Hill, 1928.

CEMETERIES

Mucklow, Walter, *Cemetery Accounts.* New York, American Institute Publishing Co., 1935.

DRUGSTORES

Heckert, J. Brooks and Dickerson, William A. *Drug Store Accounting.* New York, McGraw-Hill, 1943.

ESTATES

Dodge, Chester J. and Sullivan, John F. *Estate Administration and Accounting.* New York, Clark Boardman Co. 1940.

FARM

Mitchell, Donald R. *Farm Accounting.* New York, McGraw-Hill, 1941.

FOREIGN EXCHANGE

Djorup, Christian. *Foreign Exchange Accounting.* New York, Prentice-Hall, 1926.

HOTEL

Horwath, Ernest B., and Toth, Louis. *Hotel Accounting Including Departmental Control, Food Costing, and Auditing.* New York, Ronald, 1928.

LUMBER

Eckardt, Hugo W. *Accounting in the Lumber Industry.* New York, Harper, 1929.
Mucklow, Walter. *Lumber Accounts.* New York, American Institute Publishing Co., 1936.

PATENTS

Klooster, Bert L. *Patent Accounting, A Phase of Cost Accounting.* New York, Prentice-Hall, 1930.

PETROLEUM

Humphreys, H. G. *The Accounts of an Oil Company.* New York, American Institute Publishing Co., 1934.

McKee, Raymond W. *Handbook of Petroleum Accounting.* New York, Harper, 1938.

Pitcher, Robert M. *Practical Accounting for Oil Producers.* Tulsa, Okla., Mid-West Printing Co., 1938.

REAL ESTATE

Mucklow, Walter. *Land Accounts.* New York, American Institute Publishing Co., 1935.

SECRETARIAL ACCOUNTING

Sherwood, John F., and Boling, Clem. *Secretarial Accounting.* Cincinnati, O., South-West Publishing Co., 1939.

TEXTILES

Lockwood, Jeremiah, and Maxwell, Arthur D. *Textile Costing.* Washington, D.C. The Textile Foundation, 1938.

Miller, Franklin, Bassett and Company. *Cost Control For Knit Underwear Factories.* New York, Ronald, 1924.

Szepesi, Eugene. *Cost Control and Accounting for Textile Mills.* New York, Brogdon, Lord and Nagle Co., 1922.

UNIVERSITY

Morey, Lloyd. *University and College Accounting.* New York, Wiley, 1930.

WATER WORKS

Municipal Finance Officers Association. *Manual of Water Works Accounting.* Chicago, The Association, 1938.

WINERIES

Maxwell, George A. *Winery Accounting and Cost Control.* New York, Prentice-Hall, 1946.

WHOLESALE TRADE

Heckert, J. Brooks, and Stone, Irving J. *Wholesale Accounting and Control.* New York, McGraw-Hill, 1935.

INTERNAL AUDITING

Brink, W. Z. *Internal Auditing.* 2d rev. ed. New York, Ronald, 1958.

Institute of Internal Auditors. *Internal Auditing in Industry.* New York, The Institute, 1950.

Walker, W. A. and Davies, W. R. *Industrial Internal Auditing.* New York, McGraw-Hill, 1951.

PERIODICALS

The Accountants' Digest. Quarterly. Burlington, Vt., 13 Bay View Street, L. L. Briggs.

Accounting Research Bulletin. Irregularly. New York, N.Y., Committee on Accounting Procedure, American Institute of Certified Public Accountants.

The Accounting Review. Quarterly. Columbus, Ohio, American Accounting Association, College of Commerce, Ohio State University.

Internal Auditor. Quarterly. New York, N.Y., Institute of Internal Auditors, Inc.

The Journal of Accountancy. Monthly. New York, N.Y., American Institute Publishing Company.

N.A.A. Bulletin. Semimonthly. New York, N.Y., National Association of Accountants.

Yearbook of the National Association of Accountants. New York, N.Y., National Association of Accountants.

SERVICES

Commerce Clearing House Accountancy Law Reports. Chicago, Commerce Clearing House, Inc. 1 vol. currently supplemented.

Commerce Clearing House All State Tax Reports. Chicago, Commerce Clearing House, Inc. Individual loose-leaf units with separate current supplements.

Commerce Clearing House Federal Tax Guide Reports. Chicago, Commerce Clearing House, Inc. 2 vols. with weekly supplements.

Commerce Clearing House Interstate Sales Tax Reports. Chicago, Commerce Clearing House, Inc. 1 vol. with current supplements.

Commerce Clearing House Payroll Tax Guide. Chicago, Commerce Clearing House, Inc. 1 vol. with frequent supplements.

Commerce Clearing House State Tax Guide. Chicago, Commerce Clearing House, Inc. 1 vol. with current issues.

Commerce Clearing House Tax Course. Chicago, Commerce Clearing House, Inc. 1 vol. up to date of publication.

Commerce Clearing House Unemployment Insurance Report. Chicago, Commerce Clearing House, Inc. 7 vols. with weekly supplements.

Prentice-Hall Accountant's Weekly Report. New York, Prentice-Hall, Inc.

Prentice-Hall Federal Tax Course. New York, Prentice-Hall, Inc. 1 vol. up to date of publication.

Prentice-Hall Federal Tax Guide. New York, Prentice-Hall, Inc. 1 and 2 vol. editions with weekly supplements.

Prentice-Hall Payroll Service. New York, Prentice-Hall, Inc. 1 vol. with frequent supplements.

Prentice-Hall Sales Tax Service. New York, Prentice-Hall, Inc. 2 vols. with weekly supplements.

Prentice-Hall Social Security Tax Service. New York, Prentice-Hall, Inc. Available for any or all states. For all states—6 vols., for one state—2 vols; with weekly supplements.

Prentice-Hall State and Local Tax Service. New York, Prentice-Hall, Inc. Available for any or all states and the District of Columbia. 22 vols. with weekly supplements cover all states.

ASSOCIATIONS

American Accounting Association, 1775 South College Road, Columbus, Ohio.

American Institute of Accountants (absorbed by American Institute of Certified Public Accountants).

American Institute of Certified Public Accountants, 270 Madison Avenue, New York, N.Y.

Institute of Internal Auditors, 20 Wall Street, New York, N.Y.

National Association of Accountants, 505 Park Avenue, New York 22.

National Association of Cost Accountants (has become National Association of Accountants).

National Society of Public Accountants, 919 Eighteenth Street, N.W., Washington 6, D.C.

9

AUTOMATION

The combination of the necessity of keeping track of the operations of billion dollar corporations spread around the world, a mass of reports required by law, and the increasing cost of overhead, has forced business to modernize clerical operations. Rising labor costs have made it necessary to make machines handle increased output on new products.

The new types of controls and computers have made it possible for businessmen to maintain quality of product and to obtain more accurate information more quickly on inventories, sales and profits. Many of the developments of World War II and the space age such as transistors, diodides, and printed circuits have been adapted to civilian use for speeding up production.

The emphasis in this chapter will be on the use of automation as a tool of management. The adaptation to manufacturing is even more technical and is in the realm of the engineer rather than that of the businessman. Even in the field of the office and managerial control the discussions are highly technical and not too easily followed by the average layman.

As yet there have been no very extensive bibliographies prepared on automation. Two rather inadequate ones are:

Lybrand, Ross Bros. & Montgomery, Management Services. *Electronic Data Processing Subject Bibliography of Periodical Literature, 1959.* N.Y., Lybrand, Ross Bros. & Montgomery, Management Services, 1960.

This useful subject arrangement is based on a survey of seventy-five periodicals for the year 1959. It is hoped that this will be continued.

Laurie, E. J. and Heald, R. W. *Data Processing Bibliography—Periodicals*. San Jose, Calif. Dept. of Business Management, San Jose State College, 1957.

An alphabetical listing, by author, of 1,348 periodical articles. This checklist would be more useful if it included a subject breakdown.

Two books treat the subject of automation broadly with some discussion of the effects on society. The first of these warns of the changes taking place in society because of new scientific developments.

Brady, R. A. *Organization, Automation, and Society. The Scientific Revolution in Industry*. Berkeley, Calif., University of California Press, 1961.

The author selects three kinds of activities which are revolutionizing industry. The chemical revolution is altering the fundamental materials of industry, changing standards and specifications and diversifying the means of selecting the best methods, processes, and products. Automation is changing processing methods, and the atomic revolution is altering systems of energy. All of these are creating basic changes in our society.

Jones, G. M. *Electronics in Business*. East Lansing, Mich., Michigan State University Press, 1960.

This is a nontechnical explanation and discussion of the potentialities of electronic data processing for the average businessman.

Another book which should be read by any businessman who is planning to automate is:

Bright, J. R. *Automation and Management*. Boston, Division of Research, Graduate School of Business Administration, Harvard University, 1958.

In this book management is informed that automation is a gradual process and has very definite drawbacks, particularly during the early stages of installation. Points to be considered before automating are: lack of flexibility, consequences of shut-downs, rearrangement of machinery, and the raw material requirements of automated machinery. Costs of developing automated machinery are considerable, and many problems must be solved before it is operating properly. Data on costs and problems are drawn from existing installations.

Perhaps the best introduction to data processing is:

Conning, R. G. *Electronic Data Processing for Business and Industry*. New York, Wiley, 1956.

Electronic data processing is defined, what it can do for a company is explained, and methods of investigating data processes are discussed. Clerical and other business operations are described in relation to kinds of equipment required. Any firm considering going into electronic data processing should make this book required reading for its executives.

The businessman as he digs deeper into automation literature immediately enters the space age and needs an engineering background to fully understand the operation of these mechanisms. The following works have been written with the businessman in mind.

McCracken, D. B., Weiss, H., and Lee, T. H. *Programming Business Computers.* New York, Wiley, 1959.

> In a sense this book is a primer for the person applying computers to business problems and those persons either to be involved in data processing or whose work is closely related to computer operations. It makes intelligible the application of electronic computers to business data processing. Background information is supplied on the nature of data processing, coding, and programming. There are details on advanced methods and a summary of the steps necessary to get a computor application going. This book has an up-to-date bibliography.

Gille Associates Inc. *Data Processing Handbook.* Detroit, Gille Associates, 1960. 13 vols.

> The first seven volumes deal with the utilization of data processing for various phases of a business. Topics covered are: accounts receivable, accounts payable, billing, inventory control, order processing, and tips on wiring and its techniques. The remaining six volumes are concerned with data processing in education, government, insurance, manufacturing, transportation, and utilities. Flow charts and diagrams indicate how to set up systems. Industry applications show what phases of operations can be automated and how.

Grabbe, E. M. and others, eds. *Handbook of Automation, Computation and Control.* New York, Wiley, 1958–1960. 3 vols.

> This is a somewhat more technical treatment of automation than the first work cited. It is a reference source book and manual for those involved in operating and servicing automatic equipment. It deals principally with computers, feedback control, and data processing.

Gille Associates Inc. *Data Processing Equipment Encyclopedia. Electro-Mechanical Systems, Punched Card, Punched Tape, Related Systems.* Detroit, Gille Associates, Inc., 1961. 2 vols.

> Primarily a description of "hardware," the first volume illustrates and describes the component parts of electro-mechanical systems. Specifications as to weight and size are included. Volume II is concerned with the different kinds of systems and components of each one.

Truxal, J. G. ed. *Control Engineer's Handbook.* New York, McGraw-Hill, 1958.

> As the title indicates, this book is largely for the engineer. It treats of servomechanisms, feedback controls, and regulators. The components of control systems are covered.

Another handbook which is less technical and has more information of immediate interest to the businessman is:

Lazzaro, V. ed. *Systems and Procedures. A Handbook for Business and Industry.* Englewood Cliffs, N.J., Prentice-Hall, 1959.

> A discussion of the principles involved in systems and their procedures is followed by descriptions of methods, forms, and equipment. This handbook does provide criteria for evaluating different systems and equipment.

The automation of a product line or even an entire factory is the responsibility of the engineer insofar as the mechanics are concerned. He in turn must explain the advantages and possibilities of automation to the general management. The office is one area where management is readily aware of increasing costs. Two books by R. Hunt Brown deal with office automation:

Brown, R. H. *Office Automation: Integrated and Electronic Data Processing.* New York, Automation Consultants, Inc., 1955 plus extra sheets to up-date.

> Discusses applications to particular operations, new hardware, and forms. The current and potential uses of equipment are brought out along with the sociological effects.

Brown, R. H. *Office Automation Applications.* New York, Automation Consultants, Inc., 1959. 2 vols.

> After a general discussion of automated systems, the author describes the application of automation to various industries and industrial processes. There is a good section on how to prepare for automation and the steps to be taken as one changes into an automated operation.

Johnson, E. A. *Accounting Systems in Modern Business.* New York, McGraw-Hill, 1959.

> Previously listed in Chapter 8, this book is mentioned again because it includes material on computers as used in accounting.

The computer industry is developing so rapidly and there are so many applications that books do not adequately keep up with the "state of the art." Furthermore, each installation must be custom made to fit the user's particular needs. Therefore, the businessman needs expert help in planning an installation. The companies' manufacturing computers have large staffs of highly trained people to assist in planning installations. In addition, they operate schools to train the people who will operate these machines.

International Business Machines has the most extensive training courses. Other firms which offer aid in planning and setting up installations are Burroughs and General Electric. They also have training programs. All these companies publish much material on systems and methods which is often the latest available.

It is in the periodicals that the new developments first appear and these are particularly helpful in this field.

American Documentation. Quarterly. Washington, D.C. American Documentation Institute.

Applications of data processing to various aspects of information retrieval are written up. Results of experiment and the type information which lends itself to data processing are reported.

Association for Computing Machinery Journal. Bimonthly. New York, 14 East 69th Street, Association for Computing Machinery.

This publication is concerned with the technical phases of computer operations. These include solutions of problems, information retrieval, etc.

Automation: The Magazine of Automatic Operations. Monthly. Cleveland, O., Penton Publishing Co.

The application of automation to specific manufacturing problems is described each month. There is also a section on the maintenance of automated systems.

Datamation. Monthly. Los Angeles, 10373 W. Pico Boulevard, Datamation.

Information on computer systems, equipment, problems, new research, and developments is supplied to manufacturers and users of automatic information handling equipment.

Data Processing. Monthly. Detroit, Mich., Gille Associates.

In addition to describing the uses of data processing in business and the utilization of forms and equipment, this publication deals with such things as employee attitudes toward automation and labor displacement. It contains a short book review section.

Data Processing and Microfilming Systems. Quarterly. New York, 10 East 40th Street, Data Processing Publishing Corp.

Aimed at those engaged in collecting, recording, and retrieving information, this publication presents case histories of how organizations handle their information management problems. Each issue lists free literature available on systems and equipment.

Data Processing Digest. Monthly. Los Angeles, 1140 South Robertson Boulevard, Canning, Sisson and Associates.

Books, periodical articles, and pamphlets on data processing are digested. Meetings of groups interested in data processing are listed, as are the names and addresses of the publishers of the material digested.

Electronics. Weekly. New York, McGraw-Hill.

News is provided on new developments (both technical and industrywise), new products and methods in the electronics industry.

Electronic Industry. Monthly. Philadelphia, Pa., Chilton Publications.

    General features include a news roundup, statistics on exports, Washington news and government contract awards. These topics are followed by numerous articles on the technical aspects of electronics. The June issue cumulates information on the electronics industry for the year and also includes a directory by product and the name of the manufacturer.

IBM Journal of Research and Development. Quarterly. New York, International Business Machines Corporation.

    This publication is primarily given over to the publication of technical papers on research done at I.B.M.

Journal of Machine Accounting. Monthly. Mount Prospect, Ill., Journal of Machine Accounting, Inc.

    Articles are on the utilization and operation of machines in accounting and, among other topics, the relationships, hook-up and operation of these machines is discussed. Data processing is included in the discussion.

Systems Management. Quarterly. New York, Data Processing Corporation.

    An attempt to keep abreast of new developments is the objective of this periodical. Industry uses of data processing equipment, new equipment, adaptation of equipment to special uses and microfilm and minor equipment items make up the bulk of the articles.

This fast growing field has a large periodical literature but by the very nature of its rapid development, there are not many books. Periodical literature is the best source for current information.

CHECKLIST OF AUTOMATION SOURCES

BIBLIOGRAPHY

Laurie, E. J. and Heald, R. W. *Data Processing Bibliography—Periodicals*. San Jose, Calif., Dept. of Business Management, San Jose State College, 1957.

Lybrand, Ross Bros. & Montgomery, Management Services. *Electronic Data Processing: Subject Bibliography of Periodical Literature, 1959*. New York, Lybrand, Ross Bros. & Montgomery, Management Services, 1960.

ENCYCLOPEDIA

Gille Associates, Inc. *Data Processing Equipment Encyclopedia Electro-mechanical Systems: Punched Card, Punched Tape, Related Systems*. Detroit, Gille Associates, Inc., 1961. 2 vols.

GENERAL WORKS

Brady, R. A. *Organization, Automation and Society. The Scientific Revolution in Industry*. Berkeley, Calif., University of California Press, 1961.

Bright, J. R. *Automation and Management.* Boston, Division of Research, Graduate School of Business Administration, Harvard University, 1958.

Canning, R. G. *Electronic Data Processing for Business and Industry.* N.Y., Wiley, 1956.

Jones, Z. M. *Electronics in Business.* East Lansing, Mich., Michigan State University, 1960.

McCracken, D. B., Weiss, H., and Lee, T. H. *Programming Business Computers.* New York, Wiley, 1959.

HANDBOOKS

Gille Associates, Inc., *Data Processing Handbook.* Detroit, Gille Associates, Inc., 1960. 13 vols.

Grabbe, E. M. and Others, eds. *Handbook of Automation, Computation and Control.* New York, Wiley, 1958–1960. 3 vols.

Lazzaro, V. ed. *Systems and Procedures. A Handbook for Business and Industry.* Englewood Cliffs, N.J., Prentice-Hall, 1959.

Truxel, J. G. ed. *Control Engineer's Handbook.* New York, McGraw-Hill, 1958.

OFFICE AUTOMATION

Brown, R. H. *Office Automation: Applications.* New York, Automation Consultants, Inc. 1959. 2 vols.

Brown, R. H. *Office Automation: Integrated and Electronic Data Processing.* New York Automation Consultants, Inc., 1955 plus extra sheets to update.

Johnson, E. A. *Accounting Systems in Modern Business.* New York, McGraw-Hill, 1959.

PERIODICALS

American Documentation. Quarterly. Washington, D.C., 2000 P Street, N.W., American Documentation Institute.

Association for Computing Machinery Journal. Quarterly. New York, 14 East 69th Street, Association for Computing Machinery.

Automation. The Magazine of Automatic Operations. Monthly. Cleveland, O., Penton Publishing Company.

Datamation. Monthly. Los Angeles, 10373 Pico Boulevard, Datamation.

Data Processing. Monthly. New York, 10 East 40th Street, Data Processing Publishing Company.

Data Processing Digest. Monthly. Los Angeles, 1140 South Robertson Boulevard, Cannon, Sisson and Associates.

Electronics. Weekly. New York, McGraw-Hill.

Electronics Industry. Monthly. Philadelphia, Chilton Publications.

IBM Journal of Research and Development. Quarterly. New York, International Business Machines Corporation.

Journal of Machine Accounting. Monthly. Mount Prospect, Ill., Journal of Machine
   Accounting, Inc.
SABE Data Processor. Quarterly. San Diego, Calif., San Diego State College.
Systems Management. Quarterly. New York, Data Processing Corporation.

ASSOCIATIONS

American Automation Control Council, c/o Control Engineering, 330 West 42d
   Street, New York 36, N.Y.
American Documentation Institute, 2000 P Street, N.W., Washington, D.C.
Association for Computing Machinery, 14 East 69th St., New York, N.Y.
Society for Automation in Business Education, San Diego State College, San Diego
   15, Calif.

10

MANAGEMENT

The increasing size, complexity, and world-wide operations of business firms have put increasing demands on management. In fact, the rapid development of technology, which brings forth a constant flow of both new products and new manufacturing methods, puts a premium on management excellence. The quality of management often spells the difference between the success or failure of a business.

The literature on business management has expanded greatly in recent years and there have been published some bibliographies and very useful guides to this material.

The best of these is:

Wasserman, Paul. *Information for Administrators. A Guide to Publications and Services for Management in Business and Government.* Ithaca, N.Y., Cornell University Press, 1956.

An unusually well-selected and annotated list of references basic to private and public management. The text both evaluates these sources and indicates how they can contribute to management. The six appendices list U.S. government depository libraries, U.S. Department of Commerce field offices, bureaus of business and governmental research in American universities, American Chambers of Commerce abroad, and bank publications on economic conditions in foreign countries. This is a most valuable source.

A second work by the same author which covers a narrower field is:

Wasserman, Paul. *Measurement Evaluation of Organizational Performance*. Ithaca, N.Y. Graduate School of Business and Public Administration, Cornell University, 1959.

> This highly selected list of books, periodical articles, and reports includes material published between 1945 and 1958. The excellent descriptive annotations make this book a splendid source for the location of data on organizational performance.

Another bibliography by this industrious compiler of bibliographies is:

Wasserman, P. and Silander, F. *Decision Making: An Annotated Bibliography*. Ithaca, N.Y., Graduate School of Business and Public Administration, Cornell University, 1958.

> A well-selected list of material which has a bearing on this major aspect of the duties of the executive.

Another bibliography on the same general topic is:

Georgi, C. et al. *The Literature of Executive Management*. New York, Special Libraries Association, 1963.

> A highly selected list of the best books in this field. The annotations are excellent and the information supplied on foreign management periodicals and publishers is especially useful.

The Baker Library of the Harvard Graduate School of Business Administration *Reference Lists* contain many references to management literature, among these are *Business Literature, Executive Development,* and *Executive Effectiveness.*

Three current bibliographies are:

American Management Association. *The Management Index 1932–1945, 1945–1955.* New York, American Management Association, 1955. 2 vols.

> All the publications of the American Management Association are covered in these volumes which provide a subject index to these books and pamphlets. The short, timely articles written by businessmen for businessmen represent the accumulated experience and judgment of managers in thousands of firms in all types of industry.

American Management Association. *AMA Management Bookshelf*. New York, American Management Association, annually.

> This publication is a current catalog of American Management Association publications and brings the preceding bibliography up to date.

American Management Association, *AMA Seminar Bibliographies*. New York, American Management Association, irregular.

These bibliographies supply the references to the various seminars held on topics of current interest to management.

Four current bibliographies cover the management field partially but are not as inclusive as the works by Wasserman. These are:

Controllership Foundation, Inc. *Management Planning and Control: An Annotated Bibliography* (Series II, Business Planning and Control, Report No. 4) New York, Controllership Foundation, Inc., 1955: Supplement No. 1, 1956.

An effort has been made to cover material on management planning and control published in Australia, Canada, France, Great Britain, New Zealand, and the United States. Citations are to books, periodical articles, and pamphlets. An alphabetical list of publications and publishers is appended to the main bibliography.

United States Government Advertiser, Inc., *Management Guide.* Monthly. Washington, D.C., 511 Eleventh Street, N.W., United States Government Advertisers, Inc.

This service digests current management articles from seventy-five important management journals. The fields covered are administrative management, building management, production and factory management, office and personnel management, purchasing and warehousing, and sales management. A subject index with frequent revisions is provided.

National Office Management Association. *NOMA Bibliography for Office Management.* Willow Grove, Pa., National Office Management Association, February, 1953, with annual supplements.

The first publication covers the period from 1949 to 1952. This is a classified list arranged under thirty-six headings of references to books, pamphlets, and reports.

Lewis, H. T., comp. *Where to Find It! Bibliography of Industrial Purchasing.* Rev. ed. New York, National Association of Purchasing Agents, 1955.

This is a listing of data for locating and evaluating industrial materials.

Many of the important pioneer works on management have gone out of print. Three recent books which provide an introduction to the classics of management and the contributors are:

Urwick, L. ed. *The Golden Book of Management. A Historical Record of the Life and Work of Seventy Pioneers.* London, Newman Neame, Ltd., 1956.

The International Committee of Scientific Management selected the men and women who made significant contributions to the science of management. The arrangement is chronological from James Watt, Jr., to Henry Pasdemodjian and is world-wide. Brief articles describe the work, life and personal characteristics of the individual and his most important publications. There are also lists of key books in management arranged chronologically and books dealing with the history of management.

Merrill, H. F. *Classics in Management.* New York, American Management Association, 1960.

This book recaptures the writings on management salient by the great names in the field. Many of their works have become unavailable. Although it covers fewer individuals than does Urwick, they are treated at greater length. The development of scientific management is traced in chronological order and the material is taken from the proceedings of technical societies, books, and congressional hearings and testimony. This account covers the writings of Robert Owen, Charles Babbage, Capt. Henry Metcalf, Henry Robinson Towne, Taylor, Gantt, Hamilton Church, Harrington Emerson, Leon Pratt Alford, Henri Fayol, Frank Gilbreth, Oliver Sheldon, Mary Parker Follett, Henry Arthur Hopf, and Elton Mayo. A bibliography of the important writings of these people is included.

Filipetti, A. *Industrial Management in Transition.* Rev. ed. Homewood, Ill., Irwin, 1953.

The kernel of the contributions of the leaders in the development of scientific management is presented along with comments as to the importance and effects of their work and thinking. Material is drawn from books and periodicals from the beginnings of scientific management to the date of publication. An excellent résumé of the development of scientific management.

Another work which makes available the publications of one of the important contributors to scientific management is:

Rathe, A. W. ed. *Gantt on Management: Guidelines for Today's Executives.* New York, American Management Association, 1961.

Selections are made from the most significant of Henry L. Gantt's writings in the field of management. They bring out his concern for the human element in productivity.

This book is organized into four parts. Scientific Approach in Management, Human Effort, Operating Effectively, and, Management and Society.

The books mentioned immediately above stress the principles and development of scientific management. The following publications describe how these principles can be applied and brings them up to date.

In recent years the number of excellent handbooks in all phases of business have increased greatly and management has its quota.

Lasser, J. K. ed. *Business Management Handbook.* 2d ed. New York, McGraw-Hill, 1960.

All aspects of organizing and operating a business are described in a "how to do it" manner. Each section has a checklist of salient points which are to be used to measure the success of business activities and to avoid difficulties.

Maynard, H. B. ed. *Top Management Handbook*. New York, McGraw-Hill, 1960.

This book contains a large body of material useful to the upper echelons of management. The chapters are drawn from the experience of successful managers and they are both a source of information and an inspiration to people faced with management decisions and problems. This can also be a source for those interested in giving some insight into the present-day activities of a manager.

Carson, G. B. ed. *Production Handbook*. 2d ed. New York, Ronald, 1958.

This thorough revision of Alford's "Production Handbook" represents the inclusion of a large amount of new material and an updating of the original sections. It represents the distillation of thousands of articles and studies. All phases of production from "Charting and Graphic Methods" to "Work Simplification" are treated in twenty-five sections. There is a section which provides sound information on electronic computers and suggestions as to their use.

Ireson, W. G. and Grant, E. L. *Handbook of Industrial Engineering and Management*. Englewood Cliffs, N.J., Prentice-Hall, 1955.

This handbook provides information for all those persons serving in management positions. The treatment is general with emphasis on the best practices in each subject area. Chapters not found in the average handbook of this type are on managerial economics and engineering economy, climate as it affects plant location and industrial activity, and, job evaluation and industrial engineering and the trade unions.

Dartnell Corporation. *Dartnell Office Manager's Handbook*. Chicago, Dartnell Corporation, 1958.

The first chapters point up the general principles of human relations. These are followed by a discussion of policies and the specific aspects of office relations. There are many outlines of forms and methods for improving the operations of the office as well as for solving particular problems. Many examples drawn from industry and large organizations illustrate the material effectively. This is an excellent reference book.

Aljian, G. W. ed. *Purchasing Handbook*. New York, McGraw-Hill, 1958.

As stated on the title page, this volume is the "Standard reference book on purchasing policies, practices, procedures, controls and forms." It takes its place with the other indispensable handbooks which provide quick answers to immediate problems.

AMA Encyclopedia of Supervisory Training. New York, American Management Association, 1961.

The text is intensely practical since it is based on successful training programs of leading firms. Exhibits and actual programs provide useful and helpful examples. The basic psychological factors involved in training programs are emphasized.

Other useful handbooks for particular phases of business are listed below:

Aspley, J. C. ed. *Handbook of Employer Relations*. Chicago, Dartnell Corporation, 1957.

Bogen, J. I. ed. *Financial Handbook*. 3d rev. ed. New York, Ronald, 1957.

Wixon, R. ed. *Accountant's Handbook*. 4th ed. New York, Ronald, 1956.

Yoder, J. and others. *Handbook of Personnel and Labor Relations*. New York, McGraw-Hill, 1958.

The literature of management has vastly increased in recent years because of the realization of its importance to the business enterprise, the training of a professional managerial class in schools of business, and the research which has been concerned with management principles and techniques. The number of good books which have been published in this field make selection difficult and the works discussed herein are in representative list rather than an exhaustive one.

Four books add background to the discussion of management principles.

Follett, M. P. *Dynamic Administration. The Collected Papers of Mary Parker Follett*. Edited by Henry C. Metcalf and L. Urwick. New York, Harper, 1941.

Mary Parker Follett's interest and research ranged over broad political, social, and industrial problems with special emphasis on organization and administration. Her basic tenet was that any enduring society must be grounded upon a recognition of the motivating desires of the individual and the group.

Harbison, F. H. and Myers, C. A. *Management in the Industrial World*. New York, McGraw-Hill, 1959.

Management is analyzed as an economic resource, a class, and a system of authority. This broad treatment is followed by surveys of management practices in eleven countries and the United States. This excellent book brings out the social and historical aspects of management.

Niles, M. C. H. *Essence of Management*. New York, Harper, 1958.

This book brings together the development and history of management. It represents a distillation of management practice and experience and brings out the human and social factors. It has an unusually good bibliography.

Tead, Ordway. *Administration: Its Purpose and Performance*. New York, Harper, 1959.

One of the leaders in the field of management gives the essence of his conception of dynamic but democratic administration.

The following books provide sources of information on organization and management in all their ramifications.

Peterson, E. and Plowman, E. G. *Business Organization and Management*. 4th ed. Homewood, Ill., Irwin, 1958.

In a definitive treatment of the principles of business organization, this work presents the elements of organization and management. These chapters are followed by discussions of the levels of management, the management organization, policy making, communication and control, and incentives. Two chapters on the management of association and government proprietary enterprises break new ground. Efficiency and automation as they are affected and promoted by the executive is another chapter brought up to date. The selected chapter references are up to date and basic.

Spriegel, W. R. and Davies, E. C. *Principles of Business Organization and Operation.* Englewood Cliffs, N.J., Prentice-Hall, 1960.

This standard text on the subject emphasizes the scientific approach to management. Principles and practices are presented on the basis of their successful application. A useful bibliography is included.

Davis, R. C. *Industrial Organization and Management.* 3d ed. New York, Harper, 1957.

This book is an excellent statement of the theory and practice of management. The material is clearly presented in logical sequence. This book has become a standard text on the subject of management.

Other good books on the general management field are R. N. Owens, *Management of Industrial Enterprises,* 3d ed., Homewood, Ill., Irwin, 1957; W. B. Cornell, *Organization and Management in Industry and Business,* 4th ed., New York, Ronald, 1958, and, R. L. Bethel and others, *Essentials of Industrial Management.* 2d ed., New York, McGraw-Hill, 1959.

One of the bases of scientific management is time and motion study and the following book has current information on the subject.

Barnes, R. N. *Time and Motion Study.* 4th ed. New York, Wiley, 1958.

Further research by the author in this field is embodied in this book. Consideration is given to the addition of indirect labor to the calculations and to the evaluation and control of machines and processes. All known systems of motion-time data are presented in outline and this work is replete with illustrations of methods.

Much study and research as to both the functions of the manager and improvement of management techniques has been undertaken by schools of business and the American Management Association. Two pioneer works which broke the ground for these studies are:

Barnard, C. I. *Functions of the Executive.* Cambridge, Mass., Harvard University Press, 1938.

This work broke new ground in the concept of the executive. The first half is concerned with the theory of coöperative action, and the latter part deals with factors affecting executive functions.

Holden, P. E., Fish, L. S., and Smith, H. L. *Top-Management Organization and Control*. Enlarged ed. Stanford, Calif., Stanford University Press, 1948.
    This research study of the policies and practices of thirty-one leading American industrial concerns brings together much factual data on important and complex management problems of large industrial organizations. The enlarged edition includes the data sheet used.

The functions of the manager and policies and practices governing his activities are described and evaluated in the books listed as follows:

McFarland, D. E. *Management Principles and Practices*. New York, Macmillan, 1958.
    The philosophy and activities of management are set forth in this book on the fundamentals of management. The treatment is purposely broad to encourage thinking on the part of the reader and not to obscure the principles of management by too many details.
Drucker, P. F. *Practice of Management*. New York, Harper, 1954.
    Thought-provoking chapters on concepts, actions, and the philosophy of management should put this book on the required reading list of any person in an administrative position. It contains a selected bibliography.
Brown, W. *Exploration in Management*. London, Heineman, 1960.
    Basic principles of management as related to the author's own company are discussed. Management organization and relationships, communication, policies, and inadequacies are treated thoughtfully and with clarity.

The selection and training of executives has become perhaps the most important function of top management. Many a business has failed because of either lack of effective management or no organized plan to development management succession. The following books provide suggestions as to how managers can be selected and developed.

Dooher, M. J. ed. *Selection of Management Personnel*. New York, American Management Association, 1957. 2 vols.
    Broad policies, specific objectives, methods of locating and evaluating executives, and the training of executives and supervisors are treated by forty-four individuals of wide experience.
Argyris, C. *Executive Leadership*. New York, Harper, 1953.
    This is a study in work and personal relationships between various levels of management. It describes the actions and reaction of an executive in terms of his effect on the organization. This book contains good suggestions on personal relationships in the plant.
Bursk, E. C. *Management Team*. Cambridge, Mass., Harvard University Press, 1955.
    Based on the Proceedings of the Twenty-fourth National Business Conferences sponsored by the Harvard Business School Association, this book is concerned with improving management. In the main, the author is concerned

with the maintenance of lines of communication and the effective delegation of authority.

Jones, M. H. *Executive Decision Making.* Rev. ed. Homewood, Ill., Irwin, 1962.

An excellent account of the factors that go into the making of decisions and the evaluation of executives. This book makes it possible for the executive to gain insight into the process of decision making, thereby enabling him to be a better executive. The author has drawn on the fields of psychology, philosophy, history, sociology, cultural anthropology, and others in developing a practical approach to his subject.

Christensen, C. R. *Management Succession in Small and Growing Enterprises.* Boston, Division of Research, Graduate School of Business Administration, Harvard University, 1953.

Perhaps the most important element in the survival of a small company, the development of competent management, is treated fully in this book. The development of policy, the training of younger executives, use of advisory sources outside the business, and, the willingness of the head to retire at the proper time are some of the topics discussed. A wealth of illustrations, drawn from the experiences of many small companies, make for interest. Every small businessman can profit from reading this book.

Smith, G. A. *Managing Geographically Decentralized Companies.* Boston, Harvard Graduate School of Business Administration, 1958.

The advantages and disadvantages of geographical decentralization are brought out along with effective management techniques.

Other aspects of management are management of the office and purchasing. In addition to *Dartnell's Office Manager's Handbook,* the office manager will find *The Office Supervisor* by H. E. Niles and others helpful.

Niles, H. E. et al. *The Office Supervisor.* 3d ed. New York, Wiley, 1959.

This book supplies much good information on the organization and administration of the office. Promotion and personnel policies are included as are suggestions as to improving efficiency and the introduction of automation.

The purchasing area of management is treated by the following publications:

Heinritz, S. F. *Purchasing Principles and Practices.* 3d ed. Englewood Cliffs, N.J., Prentice-Hall, 1959.

The earlier edition is brought up to date, and more illustrative cases have been added. There is greater emphasis on the managerial aspects of purchasing. The author takes note of the effects of inflation and changing trends in the buying habits of consumers.

National Association of Purchasing Agents, Bulletin. Weekly September to June, semi-monthly July and August. New York, National Association of Purchasing Agents.

Up-to-date data is supplied on changes in new orders, production, inventories, and prices which appear in a weekly commodity and price review.

Purchasing. Biweekly. New York, Conover-Mast Publications.

News of new products, articles on price trends, and activities of purchasing agents appear in this periodical. Methods and materials are described.

Purchasing Week. Weekly. N.Y., Purchasing Week.

Suggestions for better purchasing methods, prices of commodities, and accounts of activities of purchasing organizations and individuals comprise the bulk of the articles in this periodical.

As a business grows and diversifies it becomes necessary to enlarge the existing plant or establish branches nearer markets or sources of raw materials. The many factors which affect the location of a plant and data helpful in deciding where to locate can be found in Chapter 7, Real Estate and Insurance, page 115. Two additional publications which are useful are:

Yaseen, L. C. *Plant Location.* Rev ed. New York, American Research Council, 1960.

The author brings out clearly the basis principles of plant location. After considering the factors which determine plant location, such as transportation facilities, labor availability, costs and stability, power, fuel and water, taxes and labor laws, climate, and community analyzing, he discusses aids in getting data which include state development associations and special inducements. There are data also on locating in Puerto Rico and abroad. This book contains much useful factual information.

Plant Location. Annually. New York, Simmons Boardman.

Each year this publication updates information on industrial areas of the United States. The data supplied are on labor conditions including work force, hours, and wage rates. In addition, transportation, power and fuel supplies, availability of raw materials, industrial development organizations and climate are described.

Time and money can be saved by drawing on the wide experience and detailed information on cities and towns of the Fantus Factory Locating Service, 139 Clark Street, Chicago and Empire State Building, New York.

Articles on management—an integral part of all industry—appear in a great variety of business publications. Even magazines which discuss business in general terms such as *Business Week, Nation's Business,* and *Fortune,* frequently run articles on the subject or touch on it in articles dealing with other topics. Trade periodicals which are confined to a particular trade or industry carry these articles also. The following periodicals deal directly with management subjects:

Administrative Science Quarterly. Quarterly. Ithaca, N.Y., Cornell University, Graduate School of Business and Public Administration.

> The science of management is treated in depth and fundamental principles are discussed by the contributors to this publication.

Advanced Management. Monthly. New York, The Society for the Advancement of Management.

> A judicious blend of theory and practice in the articles published make this journal representative of the latest thinking in the field. Organization, personnel administration, cost control, and applications of sicentific management are the major subjects dealt with in each issue. Most of the authors are individuals with extensive practical management experience. A few penetrating reviews of new management literature comprise the final section. The change from quarterly to monthly publication makes more articles available and more quickly.

Business Journal for Management. Monthly. London, British Publications Ltd.

> A British periodical which treats business policies and problems at the management level.

CMR—California Management Review. Quarterly. Berkeley, Graduate Schools of Business Administration, University of California.

> The objectives of this periodical are: to publish the results of research in areas of knowledge which have significance for management of both public and private enterprises; to analyze economic, political, and social issues and trends which are important to management; to describe and evaluate new techniques of management; to discuss the theory, principles, and philosophy underlying business policies and operations. Reports of work in the other social sciences, humanities, and physical sciences having implications for management are included. This publication is designed to be of interest to active managers, scholars, teachers, and others concerned with management.

Factory. Monthly. New York, McGraw-Hill Publishing Company.

> Labor management and personnel administration bulk large in the management section. Each issue usually carries articles on costs, quality control, and production organization.

Industrial Management Review. Semiannually. Cambridge, Mass., Industrial Management Review Association, Massachusetts Institute of Technology.

> Long and scholarly articles are published on the theory and problems of management.

Journal of the Academy of Management. Quarterly. East Lansing, Mich., Michigan State University.

> This journal was founded to foster the philosophy of management, greater

understanding among executives of the application of the scientific method to the solution of managerial problems, and coöperation among those persons interested in the philosophy and science of management. Each issue usually contains one long article and four or five shorter ones.

Management Methods. Monthly. Greenwich, Conn., Management Publishing Group.

Suggestions to and for management and new methods and products are presented in a readable manner.

Management News. Monthly. New York, American Management Association.

Short, newsy articles on what is going on in management circles.

Management Personnel. Quarterly. Ann Arbor, Mich., University of Michigan.

The contributors to the first issue were prominent business leaders and members of the University of Michigan faculty. Articles were on the meaning of leadership, discipline, and arbitration. There is a good book review section.

Management Review. Monthly. New York, American Management Association.

In addition to special feature articles on management, this periodical includes digests of articles in other journals under the headings of "General Management," "Office Management," "Personnel," "Production Management," "Marketing Management," "Financial Management," and "Insurance." The "Month's Best Reading" plus the "Survey of Books for Executives" make this publication an excellent source for current literature.

Management Science: Journal of the Institute of Management Science. Quarterly. Baltimore 2, Md., Institute of Management Science, Mount Royal and Guilford Avenues.

A highly theoretical publication which is largely concerned with the application of mathematical formulae to management practices.

Mill & Factory. Monthly. New York, Conover-Mast Publications.

Designed for the factory manager, this periodical has material on methods, machinery, and equipment plus a "Report to Industry" and information on new products and new publications.

National Industrial Conference Board Management Record. Monthly. New York, National Industrial Conference Board.

Regular features are: "Briefs on Personnel Practices," "Labor Press Highlights," "Significant Labor Statistics," "Significant Pay Settlements," and "Management Bookshelf." Longer articles appear on subjects of general or immediate interest to management.

The Office Executive. Monthly. Willow Grove, Pa. National Office Management Association.

Articles on organization of the office, office layouts, personnel policies, records management, and news of new equipment and personnel comprise the content of this publication.

Supervisory Management. Monthly. New York, American Management Association.

This publication has excellent articles on the role of the supervisor including suggestions as to policies and costs and trouble-saving procedures.

The publications in the management field have become so numerous and are of such high quality that it is most difficult to make a selected listing. The books listed below will prove a basic collection.

J. B. Carson, ed. *Production Handbook*, 2d ed., New York, Ronald, 1958, and *Top Management Handbook*, New York, McGraw-Hill, 1960, edited by H. B. Maynard, are useful for quick reference.

The general principles of business management and industrial organization are presented in *Business Organization and Management*, 4th ed., by C. Peterson and E. G. Plowman, Homewood, Ill., Irwin, 1958; *Industrial Organization and Management*, 3d ed., by R. C. Davis, New York, Harper, 1957; *Top-Management Organization and Control*, enlarged ed., Stanford, Calif., Stanford University Press, 1948, by P. E. Holden, L. S. Fish, and H. L. Smith; and *Principles of Business Organization and Operation*, 3d ed., Englewood Cliffs, N.J., Prentice-Hall, 1960, by W. R. Spriegel and E. C. Davies.

Various elements of management are dealt with in the following books: R. M. Barnes' *Time and Motion Study*, 4th ed., New York, Wiley, 1958; H. E. Niles et al., *The Office Supervisor*, 3d ed., New York, Wiley, 1959; and E. F. Heinritz, *Purchasing Principles and Practices*, 3d ed., Englewood Cliffs, N.J., Prentice-Hall, 1959.

CHECKLIST OF MANAGEMENT SOURCES

ADMINISTRATION

Follett, M. P. *Dynamic Administration. The Collected Papers of Mary Parker Follett.* Edited by Henry C. Metcalf and L. Urwick. New York, Harper, 1941.
Harbison, F. H. and Myers, C. A. *Management in the Industrial World.* New York, McGraw-Hill, 1959.
Niles, M. C. H. *Essence of Management.* New York, Harper, 1958.
Tead, O. *Administration: Its Purpose and Performance.* New York, Harper, 1959.

BIBLIOGRAPHIES

American Management Association. *AMA Management Bookshelf.* New York, American Management Association. Annually.
—— *AMA Seminar Bibliographies.* New York, American Management Association. Irregular.
—— The Management Index, 1932–1945, 1945–1955. New York, N.Y., American Management Association, 1955. 2 vols.

Baker Library. Graduate School of Business Administration, Harvard University. *Reference Lists*. Boston, Mass., Baker Library. Irregularly.

Controllership Foundation, Inc. *Management Planning and Control: An Annotated Bibliography*. (Series II, Business Planning and Control, Report No. 4.) New York, Controllership Foundation, Inc., 1955. Supplement 1956.

Hopf, Harry Arthur. *Soundings in the Literature of Management, Fifty Books the Educated Practitioner Should Know*. (Hopf Institute of Management, Publication, No. 6.) Ossining, N.Y., Hopf Institute of Management, 1945.

Lewis, H. T. Comp. *Where to Find It! Bibliography of Industrial Purchasing*. Rev. ed. New York, National Association of Purchasing Agents, 1955.

National Office Management Association. *NOMA Bibliography for Office Management*. Willow Grove, Pa., February, 1953, with annual supplements.

United States Government Advertiser. *Management Guide*. Washington, D.C., United States Government Advertiser. Monthly.

Wasserman, Paul. *Information for Administrators. A Guide to Publications and Services for Management in Business and Government*. Ithaca, N.Y., Cornell University Press, 1956.

────── *Measurement Evaluation of Organizational Performance*. Ithaca, N.Y., Graduate School of Business and Public Administration, Cornell University, 1959.

────── and Silander, F. *Decision Making: An Annotated Bibliography*. Ithaca, N.Y., Graduate School of Business and Public Administration, Cornell University, 1958.

BUSINESS ORGANIZATION

Bethel, L. L. and Others. *Essentials of Industrial Management*. 2d ed., New York, McGraw-Hill, 1959.

Cornell, W. B. *Organization and Management in Industry and Business*. 4th ed. New York, Ronald, 1958.

Davis, R. C. *Industrial Organization and Management*. New York, Harper, 1957.

Owens, R. N. *Management of Industrial Enterprises*. 3d ed., Homewood, Ill., Irwin, 1957.

Peterson, E. and Plowman, E. G. *Business Organization and Management*. 4th ed. Homewood, Ill., Irwin, 1958.

Spriegal, W. R. and Davies, E. C. *Principles of Business Organization and Operation*. 3d ed. Englewood Cliffs, N.J., Prentice-Hall, 1960.

EXECUTIVE FUNCTIONS AND SELECTION

Argyris, C. *Executive Leadership*. New York, Harper, 1953.

Barnard, C. I. *Functions of the Executive*. Cambridge, Mass., Harvard University Press, 1938.

Bennett, W. E. *Manager Selection, Education and Training*. New York, McGraw-Hill, 1959.

Brown, W. *Explorations in Management:* London, Heineman, 1960.

Bursk, E. C. *Management Team.* Cambridge, Mass., Harvard University Press, 1955.

Christensen, C. R. *Management Succession in Small and Growing Enterprises.* Boston, Division of Research, Graduate School of Business Administration, Harvard University, 1953.

Dooher, M. J. and Marquis, V. *Development of Executive Talent: A Handbook of Development Techniques and Case Studies.* New York, American Management Association, 1952.

Dooher, M. J. ed. *Selection of Management Personnel.* New York, American Management Association, 1957. 2 vols.

Drucker, P. F. *Practice of Management.* New York, Harper, 1954.

Holden, P. E., Fish, L. S. and Smith, H. L. *Top-Management Organization and Control.* Enlarged ed. Stanford, Calif., Stanford University Press, 1948.

Jones, M. H. *Executive Decision Making.* Rev. ed. Homewood, Ill., Irwin, 1962.

McFarland, D. E. *Management Principles and Practices.* New York, Macmillan, 1958.

Smith, G. A. *Managing Geographically Decentralized Companies.* Boston, Harvard Graduate School of Business Administration, 1958.

HANDBOOKS

Aljian, G. W. ed. *Purchasing Handbook.* New York, McGraw-Hill, 1958.

AMA Encyclopedia of Supervisory Management. New York, American Management Association, 1961.

Aspley, J. C. ed. *Handbook of Employee Relations.* Chicago, Dartnell Corporation, 1957.

Bogen, J. I. ed. *Financial Handbook.* 3d rev. ed. New York, Ronald, 1957.

Carson, G. B. ed. *Production Handbook.* 2d ed. New York, Ronald, 1958.

Dartnell Corporation. *Dartnell Office Manager's Handbook.* Chicago, Dartnell Corporation, 1958.

Ireson, W. G. and Grant, E. L. *Handbook of Industrial Engineering and Management.* Englewood Cliffs, N.J., Prentice-Hall, 1955.

Lasser, J. K. ed. *Business Management Handbook.* 2d ed. New York, McGraw-Hill, 1960.

Maynard, H. B. ed. *Top Management Handbook.* New York, McGraw-Hill, 1960.

Wixon, R. ed. *Accountant's Handbook.* 4th ed. New York, Ronald, 1956.

Yoder, D. and others. *Handbook of Personnel and Labor Relations.* New York, McGraw-Hill, 1958.

OFFICE MANAGEMENT

Dartnell Office Manager's Handbook. Chicago, Dartnell Corporation, 1958.

Niles, H. C. and others. *The Office Supervisor.* 3d ed. New York, Wiley, 1959.

PLANT LOCATION

Plant Location. New York. Simmons Boardman. Annually.

Yaseen, L. C. *Plant Location.* Rev. ed. New York, American Research Council, 1960.

PLANT LOCATION SERVICE

Fantus Factory Locating Service, 139 North Clark Street, Chicago, Ill. and Empire State Building, New York, N.Y.

PURCHASING

Aljian, G. W. ed. *Purchasing Handbook.* New York, McGraw-Hill, 1958.

Heinritz, S. F. *Purchasing Principles and Practices.* 3d ed. Englewood Cliffs, N.J., Prentice-Hall, 1959.

PERIODICALS

Administrative Science Quarterly. Quarterly. Ithaca, N.Y., Cornell University, Graduate School of Business and Public Administration.

Advanced Management. Monthly. New York, Society for the Advancement of Management.

Business Journal for Management. Monthly. London, British Publications, Ltd.

CMR—California Management Review. Quarterly. Berkeley and Los Angeles, Graduate Schools of Business Administration.

Factory. Monthly. New York, McGraw-Hill Publishing Company.

Industrial Management Review. Semiannually. Cambridge, Mass., Massachusetts Institute of Technology.

Journal of the Academy of Management. Quarterly. East Lansing, Mich., Michigan State University.

Management Methods. Monthly. Greenwich, Conn., Management Publishing Group.

Management News. Monthly. New York, American Management Association.

Management Personnel. Quarterly. Ann Arbor, Mich., University of Michigan.

Management Review. Monthly. New York, American Management Association.

Management Science: Journal of the Institute of Management Science. Quarterly. Baltimore, Md., Mount Royal and Guilford Avenue, Institute of Management Science.

Mill & Factory. Monthly. New York, Conover-Mast Publications.

National Association of Purchasing Agents Bulletin. Weekly September to June, semimonthly July and August. New York, National Association of Purchasing Agents.

National Industrial Conference Board Management Record. Monthly. New York, National Industrial Conference Board.

The Office Executive. Monthly. Willow Grove, Pa., National Office Management Association.

Purchasing. Biweekly. New York, Conover-Mast Publications.
Purchasing Week. Weekly. New York, Purchasing Week.
Supervisory Management. Monthly. New York, American Management Association.

SCIENTIFIC MANAGEMENT

Filipetti, A. *Industrial Management in Transition.* Rev. ed. Homewood, Ill., Irwin,
    1953.
Merrill, H. F. *Classics in Management.* New York, American Management Association, 1960.
Rathe, A. W. ed. *Gantt on Management: Guidelines for Today's Executive.* New
    York, American Management Association. 1961.
Urwick, L. ed. *The Golden Book of Management. A Historical Record of the Life
    and Work of Seventy Pioneers.* London, Newman Neame, Ltd., 1956.

TIME AND MOTION STUDY

Barnes, R. N. *Time and Motion Study.* 4th ed. New York, Wiley, 1958.

ASSOCIATIONS

American Management Association, 1515 Broadway, New York 16, N.Y.
American Society of Mechanical Engineers, 29 West 39th Street, New York 18, N.Y.
National Industrial Conference Board, 460 Park Avenue, New York 22, N.Y.
National Office Management Association, 1927 Old York Road, Willow Grove, Pa.
The Society for the Advancement of Management, 74 Fifth Avenue, New York 11,
    N.Y.

11

PERSONNEL AND
INDUSTRIAL RELATIONS

Despite the advances in science and technology, present-day society has a long way to go in improving human relationships. The relations between management and the working force contain many unsolved problems. Furthermore, the public is beginning to become restive over the inconvenience of long shutdowns of vital industries. Management is interested in increasing the productivity of its employees and in building and maintaining an efficient and loyal organization. The employee desires to improve his financial status, reduce his economic insecurity, and secure satisfaction from his job—either as an expression of his creative spirit or his sense of craftsmanship. The successful businessman is able, at least to a degree, to harmonize these divergent interests by means of an enlightened personnel and an industrial relations program.

Clearcut definitions of personnel administrative and industrial relations which accurately delineate the function of each activity do not exist. Personnel administration is the older of the two and covers a wider field. In the main it is concerned with the selection, training, and promotion of personnel; job analysis and classification plans and procedures; safety and recreational programs; and employee counseling. Frequently the supervision of the company's wage-and-hour policy is also a function of the personnel department.

The rapid growth of industrial relations departments has paralleled quite closely the increasing strength of labor unions and the enactment of comprehensive labor legislation. Many industrial relations departments were first organized by management to meet the skillful bargaining of labor representatives and to insure expert assistance in the interpretation of complicated labor legislation. As collective bargaining's range of interests extended, industrial relations activities began to include recreation and welfare programs, wage and grievance adjustments, as well as dealing with the unions and interpretations of labor legislation. Consequently, a considerable overlapping of the duties of the two departments has resulted. In some concerns the industrial relations department is a section of the personnel department, in others it is coequal and largely independent, and in still others, the industrial relations department has completely absorbed the personnel department.

The vital importance of enlightened personnel relations is generally recognized, regardless of the type of business organization, and this phase of management activity will undoubtedly continue to grow. The systematic study of labor relations has been advanced greatly through the efforts of Clarence J. Hicks, who interested the Rockefeller Foundation in the establishment of industrial relations divisions at leading universities. The study of labor problems, the collection of books, pamphlets, and other material and their arrangement in well-equipped libraries, as well as systematic research in the field of industrial relations procedures, have been the outgrowth of this action of the Rockefeller Foundation. The divisions at Princeton, Stanford, California, and Michigan Universities, Massachusetts and California Institutes of Technology, and Queens College, Ontario, are the oldest and best known.

The Industrial Relations Section of the Department of Economics and Social Institutions at Princeton University has been most active in the publication of checklists of current publications dealing with the broad field of labor. A basic working library is listed in two of their publications: Princeton University, Industrial Relations Section. *The Office Library of an Industrial Relations Executive* (Bibliographical Series No. 87) 6th ed., Princeton, N.J., Industrial Relations Section, Princeton University, 1951. Under broad headings of "General Works," "Specific Personnel Problems and Programs," "Trade Unions and Collective Bargaining," "Labor Legislation and Administration," "Social Insurance," "Additional Sources of Information," the basic books and pamphlets in the field are listed. Each topic is further subdivided into sections which deal with component parts of the main heading. The annotations not only indicate the contents of the publication, but also in many instances, suggest how the information may be utilized.

Trade Union Library (Bibliographical Series, No. 84) 6th ed. Princeton, N.J., Industrial Relations Section, Princeton University, 1955.

Although there is some duplication of references between this bibliography and the preceding one, the emphasis is different and much more material is included on the history, organization, and operation of labor unions. These two publications list the essential materials needed by both sides of the bargaining table.

Two publications keep the information in these two bibliographies current:

Outstanding Books on Industrial Relations. Princeton, N.J., Industrial Relations Section, Princeton University. Annually.

Since 1949, appearing in the March issue of *Selected References,* fifteen or twenty books are listed with pithy annotations.

Selected References. Bimonthly. Princeton, N.J., Industrial Relations Section, Princeton University.

Each issue is concerned with one particular aspect of industrial relations. Books, pamphlets, and magazine articles are analyzed, and references are made to specific chapters and pages. This little periodical can be a tremendous time saver to busy management or labor executives in search of exact information on problems of the moment.

The Industrial Relations Section of Princeton University also publishes, from time to time, specialized bibliographies.

Another general source of information in this field is:

Personnel Abstracts. Quarterly. Arlington, Va., 2873 South Abingdon Street, Nathaniel Stewart.

Articles on personnel topics are regularly abstracted from forty-nine periodicals. Each issue has a selected feature article which is presented more fully than the rest of the abstracts. Abstracts of book reviews are a part of this publication. This helps the busy executive to keep abreast of the new developments in this area.

Mrs. Anne Dole, Assistant Librarian, University of California, Los Angeles, Institute of Industrial Relations Library, has been kind enough to supply the information on the next two references.

Employment Relations Abstracts. Semimonthly. Detroit 1, Mich., 10 West Warren, Information Service, Inc. (Formerly *Labor-Personnel Index.*)

   One hundred and twenty-one business, labor, and academic journals in the fields of economics, sociology, etc., are abstracted as are some current pertinent books. Abstracts consist of title, author, source, and one or two descriptive sentences. Material is arranged under twenty broad categories such as collective bargaining, fringe benefits, and wages. The section contents guide is supplemented by a detailed subject guide which gives the location of material on specific subjects by section and abstract number. Subject guides are cumulated in two semiannual issues and an annual cumulation.

Index to Labor Union Periodicals. Ann Arbor, Mich., University of Michigan, School of Business Administration, Bureau of Industrial Relations. Monthly with annual cumulations.

   The notation usually begins with the headline of the article, followed by two or three brief sentences of description. Fifty major union periodicals are regularly abstracted and these are listed with the official names of the unions publishing them. There is a useful list of labor unions, union councils, and associations which are mentioned in the *Index.*

Both labor and management have turned to statistics to prove points in collective bargaining. They have sought a statistical basis for increased wages on grounds of changes in the cost of living, productivity of labor, regional wage differentials, and business profits. In addition, those who are attempting to arrive at the truth amid a barrage of conflicting statements from both parties are utilizing the same statistical data. Unfortunately, statistics too frequently represent averages or trends and are not entirely applicable to individual concerns. As an example, an industry may show a substantial profit for a given year, but at the same time an individual concern may lose money. A second difficulty in the use of statistics is that an identical group of statistical data is susceptible to different interpretations, depending on the user's viewpoint.

Special Libraries Association. *Source List of Selected Labor Statistics.* New York, Special Libraries Association, 1953.

   The usual thorough job of the members of the Special Libraries Association makes this a helpful "finding tool" for statistical sources. The subject classification makes for easy reference.

The statistics most generally used are those compiled and published by the U.S. Bureau of Labor Statistics and made available in bulletins, periodicals, and press releases. The published data can be located most quickly in *Publications of the Bureau of Labor Statistics,* monthly, Washington, D.C., U.S. Bureau of Labor Statistics. A more comprehensive source is the U.S. Superintendent of Documents' *Price List 33, Labor, Child Labor, Women Workers, Employment, Wages, Workmen's Insurance and Compensation,* Washington, D.C., Government Printing Office, 1916-. In addition to the various bulletins published by the Bureau of Labor Statistics on a particular phase of labor or certain industries, statistics and discussions of the entire field of labor are cumulated in the *Handbook of Labor Statistics.* Current statistics on a comparable basis appear in the *Monthly Labor Review, U.S. Monthly Report on the Labor Force* and *The Labor Market and Employment Security.* These four publications provide a wealth of statistical and descriptive data on labor conditions.

Another statistical compilation assembled chiefly from sources outside the U.S. Bureau of Labor Statistics is published by the National Industrial Conference Board. The latter's work provides a means of comparing and verifying the U.S. Bureau of Labor Statistics' series and conclusions. The cumulated figures and indexes are published in the National Industrial Conference Board's *Economic Almanac.* Detailed information can be found in the National Industrial Conference Board's series entitled *Studies in Personnel Policy, Management Research Memoranda,* and *Studies in Business Policy.* Current data on subjects listed in the publications mentioned above can be found each month in *The Conference Board Management Record.*

The publications of the American Management Association supply a third source of information on current personnel practices. This organization publishes several series of bulletins which represent the thinking and experience of leaders in the labor relations field. The bulletins in the *Personnel Series, Office Management Series,* and *Production Series* are the ones which contain most of the personnel relations studies. Their value lies in their dealing with current problems, and the material is presented in a brief and practical form. Most of these publications are available in the larger libraries; others can be purchased from the American Management Association at a nominal price. The details on the sources of labor statistics are as follows:

U.S. Bureau of Labor Statistics. *Handbook of Labor Statistics* (Bulletin 1016) 1950 edition. Washington, D.C., Government Printing Office, 1950. 2 vols. with 1951 Supplement.

This is the sixth issue of the Handbook which has appeared at irregular intervals since 1926. Most aspects of labor and employment are discussed in the appropriate sections. The usual arrangement is a brief résumé of the current situation supported by statistics covering varying lengths of time. From the businessman's viewpoint the most important sections are the "Cost of Living Indexes" (1913–1949), "Indexes of Employment and Payrolls" (1919–1949), "Statistics of Strikes" (1891–1949), "Productivity of Labor," "Retail Prices" (1913–1949), "Wholesale Prices" (1913–1949), and "Wages, Hours and Productivity" (1909, 1914, 1919, 1923–1949).

Monthly Labor Review. Monthly. Washington, D.C., U.S. Bureau of Labor Statistics.

In "Part 2—Current Labor Statistics" the figures and indexes given are within two or three months of being up-to-date. "Prices and the Cost of Living," "Trends of Employment and Labor Turn-over," and "Trends of Earnings and Hours" are the most important series. The main body of this periodical consists of analyses of various aspects of the present-day labor situation. Each issue contains an excellent bibliography of recent labor literature.

The Labor Market and Employment Security. Monthly, Washington, D.C., U.S. Bureau of Employment Security, U.S. Department of Labor.

Brief comments and statistics on employment, unemployment, and unemployment insurance programs. The totals are given for the country as a whole, by states and by industries.

U.S. Monthly Report on the Labor Force. Monthly. Washington, D.C., U.S. Department of Labor.

Statistics and comment on employment, unemployment, hours and earnings for the country as a whole, by industry and class of work, appear monthly in this publication.

The Conference Board Management Record. Monthly. New York, National Industrial Conference Board.

Each month significant labor trends are discussed in short articles. One page of "Significant Labor Statistics" presents the changes that have occurred in the past few months. Many articles record the experience of a number of firms with various types of labor-contract clauses and personnel administrative practices.

Another source of statistical and other information is the *Labor Fact Book:*

Labor Fact Book, No. 16, N.Y., International Publishers, 1963.

Every other year this work supplies a running account of developments affecting labor. This covers general economic conditions and trends, the social and labor situation, health and industrial injuries including legislation covering these areas, facts on American trade unions, the state of civil liberties and rights. One section is devoted to political affairs, and a concluding chapter surveys Canadian labor developments. No sources of information or statistics are given.

Data on the labor situation are also collected and published by the AF of L–CIO in:

Economic Trends and Outlook. Monthly. Washington, D.C., AF of L-CIO, Economic Policy Committee.

> Short articles on the business scene as it affects labor plus statistics to back up the conclusion make up the bulk of this publication.

Another labor publication which covers a more restricted area is:

Steel Labor. Monthly. Indianapolis, Ind., United Steelworkers Union.

> The policies and thinking of the Steelworkers Union are reflected in this periodical. It also has information trends in the industry and the country, wage policies, and news of union activities and union personnel.

International statistics on labor can be found in the *United Nations Statistical Year Book* and in the statistical publications of the leading industrial countries. However, the International Labour Office, Geneva, brings all these together in its *Year Book of Labour Statistics* and the *International Labour Review, Statistical Supplement,* a monthly publication which carries statistics on unemployment, cost of living, hours of work, and wages.

These publications are essential sources of information for any person desiring an over-all picture of the world labor situation. Although the continuity of some of the series was interrupted by World War II, the data on sixty countries are provided.

International Labour Office Year Book of Labour Statistics. Geneva, International Labour Office. Annually since 1940.

> Statistical tables constitute 95 per cent of this work and are presented in considerable detail. Most of the data is presented on an annual basis from 1929. The initial table indicates the total employable or economically active population. This is followed by figures on employment, unemployment, and hours of work. Wages are broken down into a series of tables which give over-all wage ratio—wages in the major divisions of economic activity such as transportation, mining, manufacturing, et cetera—and finally by specific industries. There is a section on consumer price indexes, family consumption expenditures, sources of family income, and the distribution of the family budget. This series of tables is followed by statistics on social security, industrial injuries, and industrial disputes. In the appendix there are world and national indexes of industrial production, wholesale prices, and exchange rates.

International Labour Review Statistical Supplement. Monthly. Geneva, Switzerland. International Labour Office.

This periodical provides current statistics, usually on a monthly basis for the present year, which are cumulated in the *Year Book*. There is usually a time lag of two or three months.

The parent volume, the *International Labour Review,* contains much useful information.

International Labour Review. Monthly. Geneva, Switzerland, International Labour Office.

Long and well-written articles appear each month on some aspect of labor. These include descriptions of developments in personnel administration, social policies, and legislation, and labor conditions in the countries which are members of International Labour Organization. This is a good source from which to learn of conditions of labor and labor legislation in a particular country. There are excellent bibliographies.

Insomuch as industrial relations are, in the main, an outgrowth from personnel relations, the larger field will be considered first despite the considerable overlapping of material. The tremendous interest in both personnel and industrial relations is not entirely due to the passage of labor legislation and the growing influence of labor unions. Management has become increasingly aware of the fact that the costs of industrial warfare, rapid labor turnover, and low productivity create real losses. Realization of the backward conditions in human relations has resulted in intensive studies of labor conditions and human responses to them. The findings on labor management relationships are being widely published, not only in specialized publications of the field but in practically all trade and business publications.

Three handy reference books on current practices, and descriptions of personnel activities, are:

Aspley, John C. ed. *Handbook of Employee Relations.* Chicago, Dartnell Corporation, 1957.

This book is a successor to the *Industrial Relations Handbook* but it is much broader in scope in that it deals with human relations rather than with those within industry. However, there is an excellent discussion of how to handle labor disputes and negotiations, plus information on fringe benefits, job analysis, promotion, orientation of new employees, and improving supervision. There are sections on labor conditions and unions and how to deal with them in production, department stores, banks, insurance companies, publishing, real estate, chain stores, government, and farming.

Yoder, Dale and others. *Handbook of Personnel Management and Labor Relations.* New York, McGraw-Hill, 1958.

In contrast to most handbooks which are made up of contributions from a large number of individuals, this one is put together by the four authors. They have surveyed the literature and have digested or quoted the descriptions of the best practices. Very helpful is the grouping of the most common questions which arise with the answers, plus illustrative material.

Heyel, Carl, ed. *The Foreman's Handbook.* 2d ed. New York, McGraw-Hill, 1955.

In simple, direct style this presents basic principles of personnel administration for the lowest echelon of management. Businessmen other than foremen might profitably read it to secure a clear understanding of the fundamentals of human relations. This volume is about equally divided between personnel and management procedures. The "bibliographies" at the end of each chapter list standard sources for further information.

Four books on personnel administration written by recognized authorities in this field have been widely accepted as standard works. Each of the authors considers the broad implications of personnel policies.

Scott, W. D., Clothier, R. C., and Spriegel, W. R. *Personnel Management, Principles, Practice and Point of View.* 6th ed. New York, McGraw-Hill, 1961.

After four chapters on the background and evaluation of the functions of personnel management, the authors turn to personnel procedures and the mechanics of the operations of the personnel department. Human relations and psychological approaches are next taken up. The labor movement, wage and salary administration and incentives, safety, labor turnover, and working conditions are other topics discussed. Finally, methods of evaluating the personnel program are brought out. The wealth of charts and forms makes this a reference work. There is an excellent current bibliography.

Yoder, D. *Personnel Management and Industrial Relations.* 5th ed. Englewood Cliffs, N.J., Prentice-Hall, 1962.

This is a thoroughly up-to-date treatment of industrial relations. The subject is discussed in depth with recognition of the importance of human relations. The vital parts of personnel policies are brought out along with testing programs, training, and supervision. The points are well illustrated with examples drawn from business and industry.

Pigors, P. and Myers, C. A. *Personnel Administration.* 4th ed. New York, McGraw-Hill, 1961.

The philosophy, approach, and point of view of executives and administrators is stressed in this book. It does not cover the techniques and organization of the personnel function. This approach makes this book valuable for one who wants to learn the broad principles of supervision.

Watkins, G. S., Dodd, P. A., McNaughton, W. L., and Prasow, P. 2d ed. *The Management of Personnel and Labor Relations.* New York, McGraw-Hill, 1950.

The authors discuss clearly and impartially the practical problems of personnel and labor management and methods of procedure that have been found effective in industry and business. After a section on the background of labor relations and the human and psychological factors involved, the book moves on to the selection and retention of personnel. Another section deals with collective bargaining, and the final chapter relates personnel management in a changing economy.

Personnel administrators have realized that they have much to learn from psychologists. Not only do they rely on psychology for the development and use of tests for employment, for particular types of work, and for evaluating mental and emotional attitudes of employees, but also for improving human relations in general. The following book provides the basic concepts of industrial psychology.

Tiffin, J. *Industrial Psychology.* 4th ed. Englewood Cliffs, N.J., Prentice-Hall, 1958.
The latest findings of research in industrial psychology are included in this book. The large section on tests and methods of testing has been retained. The psychological aspects of efficiency, boredom, fatigue, accidents, training, and general morale, comprise the remaining chapters. Language peculiar to psychology is kept to a minimum, and the illustrations drawn from plant conditions make this book an excellent introduction to this subject.

Another book written by a psychologist puts more emphasis on the more ordinary human virtues of interest and tolerance. This is:

Laird, D. A. and Laird, E. C. *Technique of Handling People.* New York, McGraw-Hill, 1954.
Rather than to put their thoughts in complicated psychological terms, the authors have chosen to stress the attributes of genuine friendliness, interest in the other person, and the ability to listen. Any manager can read this book with profit.

Anyone who is interested in the factors affecting employee morale and attitudes will appreciate the very detailed pioneering study carried out at the Hawthorne Works of the Western Electric Company. An account of this study is given in F. J. Roethlisberger and W. J. Dickson's *Management and the Worker,* Cambridge, Mass., Harvard University Press, 1939.

Two other phases of personnel administration are plant and/or office safety and industrial health hazards. Both are very significant issues in union demands, and in addition businessmen are becoming increasingly aware of the costs of accidents and ill health.

Heinrich, H. W. *Industrial Accident Prevention, Scientific Approach*. 4th ed. New York, McGraw-Hill, 1959.

Not only are the principles of accident prevention clearly expressed, but the why of hazards and methods of correction are given. Useful suggestions for safety programs are also listed. An illuminating feature of this text is the dollars-and-cents cost of individual accidents.

Three periodicals devoted exclusively to personnel administration are:

Personnel Journal. Monthly except during July and August. Swarthmore, Pa., Personnel Journal, Inc.

The oldest journal in the field of personnel practices and labor relations, the articles in this publication discuss current management and employee problems and trends in personnel relations. Brief book reviews, research in personnel relations, new publications in the field, and news of people in personnel work are the concluding features of each issue.

Personnel. Bimonthly. New York, American Management Association, New York, N.Y.

There are high quality articles on personnel management policies, testing, personnel relations, and practically all phases of employer-employee relations. The articles are on practical subjects closely related to business and industry—company plans are described as the results of field research reported. Each issue contains a splendid bibliography of books and pamphlets on personnel work. This magazine is the best in the field from the business reader's viewpoint.

Personnel Management. Biweekly. Washington, D.C., The Bureau of National Affairs.

News of interest to personnel managers which includes recruiting, wage progression, employee benefits, personnel policies, and results of collective bargaining are among the major topics kept current.

Both labor legislation and the aggressiveness of organized labor have forced managements to revamp their labor policies and to learn new procedures in dealing with labor. The heavy demand for information on the subject of industrial relations has, quite naturally, produced a flood of books, pamphlets, and magazine articles. The American Management Association and the National Industrial Conference Board serve as agencies that assemble information on the experience and practice of a large number of companies. The data are then published in their bulletins and periodicals, namely, *Management Record* (National Industrial Conference Board), and *Management Review* (American Management Association). The Industrial Relations Research Association publishes each year in its *Proceedings* studies on various aspects of industrial relations. The various industrial relations sections of universities have published numerous studies on a variety of industrial relations topics. The *Monthly Labor Review* and the bulletins issued by the U.S. Department of Labor also contain much valuable information. In each of these publications the material is presented briefly, is timely, and is based on practical experience.

Additional bibliographies which deal with industrial relations are:

Michigan University, Bureau of Industrial Relations. *A Selected List of Books and Periodicals in the Field of Personnel Administration and Labor Management Relations.* Ann Arbor, Mich., University of Michigan, Bureau of Business Research, 1962.

> Books, pamphlets, and periodical articles are arranged under ten broad subject headings without annotations. There is also a list of periodicals and a directory of publishers with their addresses.

University of California at Los Angeles, Institute of Industrial Relations. *Industrial Human Relations.* 6th rev. ed. Los Angeles, Calif., University of California, Institute of Industrial Relations, 1959.

Blum, A. A. *Annotated Bibliography of Industrial Relations and the Small Firm.* Ithaca, N.Y., New York State School of Industry and Labor Relations, 1960.

> Largely concerned with references to periodical articles, pamphlets, and government reports, this bibliography does include some books. There are many American Management Association and National Industrial Conference Board studies cited. All areas of industrial relations are covered. The annotations are rather brief.

To understand the problems involved in industrial relations, a knowledge of the background of labor developments is essential. Many of the union demands reflect deep-seated grievances of workers and basic union policies. Other factors to be considered are the attempts of workers to combat the evil effects of economic forces such as depressions, technological unemployment, and job insecurity. The economic factors involved in labor relations have been analyzed by L. G. Reynolds:

Reynolds, L. G. *Labor Economics and Labor Relations.* 3d ed. Englewood Cliffs, N.J., Prentice-Hall, 1959.

> The economics of wages and wage change are emphasized by the author. This well-written integrated study is based on the original investigations by the author.

A second book covers about the same topics but emphasizes the human factors involved.

Daugherty, C. R. *Labor Problems in American Industry, 1948–1949.* New York, Houghton Mifflin, 1948.

 The author touches on all the areas of human maladjustment in industry and on these problems presents the diverse viewpoints of industry, labor, and society as a whole. He indicates many of the reasons for these conditions, which causes the thoughtful reader to doubt some of the solutions for labor trouble which are so glibly offered. The chapters on trade unions provide a good résumé of union history.

The most complete study of the economic and social problems of labor is H. A. Millis and R. E. Montgomery's *Economics of Labor,* New York, McGraw-Hill, 1938–1945. These three volumes deal with the subject so thoroughly that they constitute a basic reference work on this subject.

Detailed information on labor unions and labor leaders can be found in the following specialized books:

American Council on Public Affairs. *Handbook of Labor Unions.* Washington, D.C., American Council on Public Affairs, 1944.

 One hundred and eighty-two national and international unions are listed. Data include an outline of the organization of each union and its headquarter's address.

Institute of Labor Studies. *Yearbook of American Labor.* Northampton, Mass., Institute of Labor Studies. Biennially.

 A compilation of important events and activities in the field of labor for the preceding two years.

Labor Research Association. *Labor Fact Book.* New York, Labor Research Association. Biennially.

 A convenient arrangement of facts and analytical material dealing with social, economic, and political conditions affecting labor.

Peterson, F. *American Labor Unions; What They Are and How They Work.* 2d ed. New York, Harper, 1963.

 The internal policies of unions and the basis of collective bargaining procedure of each are described in a clear factual manner. This work gives a clue to trends in union thinking and activities. It is a useful source of general information on unions.

Barbash, J. *The Practice of Unionism.* New York, Harper, 1956.

 This is an account of unionism in operation with illustrations drawn from union sources. It supplies an accurate picture of union philosophy and thinking.

Taft, Philip, *The AF of L in the Time of Gompers.* New York, Harper, 1957. Harvard University Press, 1954.

 This work is a careful examination of some of the aspects of the internal operation of trade unions. Topics covered are radicalism, union financial affairs, distribution of power, factionalism, discipline and appeals within unions, and the need for more democratic procedures.

Two other volumes written by Professor Philip Taft are:

Taft, Philip, *The AF of L in the Time of Gompers,* New York, Harper, 1957.
——— *The AF of L from the Death of Gompers to the Merger.* New York, Harper, 1959.
    These two volumes comprise a detailed and scholarly history of the AF of L. The manner in which policies developed within the Federation and the role in the American labor movement are described in detail. The men who contributed to the building up of the AF of L are fitted into the picture. This is an indispensable reference work on labor history.

The works that have been mentioned in the preceding paragraphs provide background for a general knowledge of the labor situation. When it comes down to the actual collective bargaining, much more exact information is needed. The effects and restrictions of collective bargaining on management are brought out in the next book:

Slichter, S. H. and others. *The Impact of Collective Bargaining on Management.* Washington, D.C., Brookings Institution, 1960.
    As a sequel to Slichter's book, *Union Policies and Industrial Management,* this work attempts to answer the questions: What has been the influence of collective bargaining on management? Why has this influence been what it was? What are the effects of unions on efficiency and production? These questions are answered through detailed analyses of union practices and collective bargaining clauses.

The American Management Association and the National Industrial Conference Board have both issued publications helpful to the negotiator in collective bargaining. The two most applicable are:

American Management Association. *Understanding Collective Bargaining, The Executive's Guide.* New York, American Management Association, 1958.
    A step-by-step discussion of preparation for collective bargaining and the actual process. Points emphasized are: pitfalls and costs of bargaining as they affect the company, preparations for negotiations, union demands, the contract issues, bargaining techniques, areas of controversy, strikes, explaining managements' position, and keeping all informed. Well-written and to the point by men experienced in the field.
National Industrial Conference Board. *Preparing for Collective Bargaining.* New York, National Industrial Conference Board, 1959.
    Information necessary to back up bargaining is emphasized. This includes

internal wage and productivity data, cost of living, et cetera. Some of the broad headings are: "Management and Union Policies," "Arrangements for Bargaining," "How Management Develops Demands and Counter-demands," "Bargaining for Wages," "Bargaining Pay," "Information about Unions," and "Controlling Precedent and Practice." This very practical work is based on the experience of 279 companies.

Two books which explain the principles and procedures of collective bargaining are helpful:

Davey, H. W. *Contemporary Collective Bargaining.* 2d ed. Englewood Cliffs, N.J., Prentice-Hall, 1959.

As a member of arbitration panels for fourteen years, Dr. Davey has had an unusual opportunity to observe collective bargaining at work. After four chapters which set up the background of collective bargaining, the author discusses the structure of the bargaining relationships, preparation for negotiations, the various parts of the negotiations such as, wages, grievances, job security, automation, and fringe benefit trends. There is an extensive current bibliography.

Dunlop, J. T. and Healy, J. J. *Collective Bargaining, Principles and Cases.* Homewood, Ill., Irwin, 1953.

After a brief history of collective bargaining and its legal background, collective bargaining is approached from the labor viewpoint and that of management. Further chapters describe the collective bargaining process, the agreement, and standards for wage determination. The remainder of this book is composed of cases.

Two older works that are still of value are:

Golden, C. S. and Ruttenberg, H. J. *The Dynamics of Industrial Democracy.* New York, Harper, 1942.

The thirty-seven principles of union-management relations cover the area of collective bargaining with a fair degree of completeness, according to the union's point of view. If more representatives of management became thoroughly aware of these points, there would be, possibly, fewer deadlocked negotiations. A discussion of the need for unionization and collective bargaining constitutes the bulk of the book. Although both authors were union officials and present their arguments from the union viewpoint, they offer many suggestions which management could study profitably.

Hill, L. H. and Hook, C. R., Jr. *Management at the Bargaining Table.* New York, McGraw-Hill, 1945.

In essence, this is a guide to the negotiating of a union contract. Typical clauses are examined as to their effects on the rights of management, the union, and all employees. Various implications of sections of the agreement are analyzed and suggestions made on how management can protect itself against agreeing to unsound provisions. The short section on preparing for negotiations and methods of handling negotiations contains many excellent suggestions. This book is a fine introduction to the field of collective bargaining.

A recent study on one of the current problems is:

Norgren, P. H. and others. *Employing the Negro in American Industry.* New York, Industrial Relations Counselors, 1960.
    This is an encouraging report of increasing opportunities for Negro employment. Progress is in evidence by the desire of management to give Negroes equal job opportunities and to make the effort to prepare the way for their employment and advancement. Little difference was found in work habits, output, and absenteeism between white and Negro employees.

A broad study on the trends in our industrial civilization is useful background material.

Kerr, C. and others. *Industrialism and Industrial Man.* Cambridge, Mass., Harvard University Press, 1960.
    This book is a study of the new industrialism which is developing in a variety of forms throughout the world, its impact on the individual, and the forms which organizations of management and workers are taking. There are evidences that a new pluralistic industrial society will emerge which will be more controlled by industrial rules but will no longer be fighting ideological wars. Industrialism in underdeveloped countries will follow neither the Western or Marxian pattern.

The large body of rulings on collective bargaining has tended to accumulate and now tends to acquire the force of law. Participants in the collective bargaining process are therefore advised to be aware of both the trend and the scope of court and National Labor Relations Board rulings. Very often clauses in a contract negotiated earlier with some large firm in an industry provide excellent examples and suggestions for contracts with other firms in the industry.

These day-to-day accounts of happenings in the labor field are best supplied by the various labor services. These not only cover the subject thoroughly, but they also present the information organized for ready reference. The rulings of the National Labor Relations Board, court decisions, arbitration awards, and the salient features of important contracts are all provided for the service subscriber. The services discussed below are leaders in this field:

Prentice-Hall Personnel Policies and Practices. New York, Prentice-Hall. 3 vols. with biweekly supplements.
    This loose-leaf manual of personnel methods, practices, and procedures

aims to help the personnel manager improve the personnel program. The material is drawn from the experience of large and small businesses.

Daily Labor Report on Labor-Management Problems. Washington, D.C., The Bureau of National Affairs, Inc.

This report provides overnight notification on the highlights of developments and trends in the field of labor relations: NLRB decisions, court opinions, wage-and-salary and hours-of-work rulings, management, and union strategy. It also covers Congressional debates and legislative action, key arbitration proceedings, significant bargaining negotiations, addresses by business leaders and policy-making officials. In addition, it reports economic data of importance in the field such as cost-of-living fluctuations, wage rates, price trends, and employment statistics.

Prentice-Hall Labor Guide. New York, Prentice-Hall, Inc. 1 vol. with weekly supplements.

Prepared especially for business executives and their managerial staffs, this volume brings together all the information necessary for successful labor relations in the light of current labor laws. Each federal and state law is explained and guidance is given in all phases of employee relations from hiring to retirement, with emphasis on collective bargaining and contract making. The simple language and warnings of what not to do in dealing with employees appeal to those who have neither the time nor the inclination to delve through complicated statutes and rulings.

Commerce Clearing House Labor Law Course. Chicago, Commerce Clearing House, Inc. 1 vol. up to date of publication.

This training manual is used by those who wish to become acquainted with the background and general principles of today's labor laws. Useful in self-training, this Course, also forms the basis of university and college instruction in labor-management law. Step by step, the explanatory text discusses the principal phases of federal labor laws, with illustrations and actual working examples. Among the subjects covered are labor unions, labor relations, union contracts, arbitration, strikes, wage-hours. Texts of statutes and leading decisions round out the contents.

Prentice-Hall Labor Course. New York, Prentice-Hall, Inc. 1 vol. up to date of publication.

A quick grasp of all the federal and state labor laws that affect employers and employees can be secured with this concise course. Designed for use by business men and students, it covers labor legislation, collective bargaining and arbitration. Both background information and clear explanations of the provisions are given for each of the following laws or groups of laws: Railway Labor Act, National Labor Relations Act as amended by the Taft-Hartley Act, Federal Anti-Injunction Act, Fair Labor Standards Act of 1938, government contracts wage and hour laws, workmen's compensation acts, social security laws, state labor laws, collective bargaining, labor arbitration, and others.

Commerce Clearing House Labor Law Guide—Federal. Chicago, Commerce Clearing House, Inc. 1 vol. with weekly supplements.

This reporter service is designed especially for the man whose interest in labor law is incidental to his regular duties. The subject of labor relations under current federal law is emphasized, sample union contracts and contract clauses are provided to assist in drafting contracts and formulating contract policies; and the application of federal wage and hour laws in the various employment situations is made plain. All types are discussed in everyday working language for ease of understanding and application.

Commerce Clearing House Labor Law Reports. Chicago, Commerce Clearing House, Inc. 5 vols. with weekly supplements.

All the federal and state laws concerned with the settlement of labor disputes and employer-employee relationships are analyzed and discussed in this reporter service. Weekly issues discuss the news of the week and show how the new applies to the old, whereas the loose-leaf volumes analyze minutely and discuss the law of labor relations, wage-hours, and state labor laws.

Labor Relations Reporter. Washington, D.C., The Bureau of National Affairs, Inc. 3 vols. with semiweekly supplements.

This service furnishes semiweekly notification on new developments and trends in labor relations—National Labor Relations Board decisions, court opinions, agency rulings and regulations, legislative action, arbitration awards, significant negotiations, wage-and-hour controls. Material of permanent value is cumulated periodically into bound reference volumes. One set of volumes covers NLRB and court decisions; another covers arbitration; the third covers wage-hour standards and cases. Cumulative digests and indexes afford ready reference to a dozen years of labor-relations precedents by topics.

Prentice-Hall Labor Service. New York, Prentice-Hall, Inc. 3 vols. with weekly supplements.

All federal and state labor laws are treated fully in this comprehensive loose-leaf service. The full text of each federal labor law and digests of the state labor laws are provided. The latest decisions, rulings, and opinions by government agencies and officials are reported with editorial explanations and examples. Vol. 1 deals with the Federal Wage and Hour Act and related laws, Vol. 2 covers the National Labor Relations Act and laws related to it, and Vol. 3 covers the state labor laws. Another volume, American Labor Cases, gives the full text of labor court decisions.

Prentice-Hall Employee Relations Guide and Arbitration. New York, Prentice-Hall, Inc. 1 vol. with biweekly supplements.

The various procedures that have been used for settling grievances are described and explained in this loose-leaf service. The full texts of arbitration awards are reported. Also included are the experiences of hundreds of companies in dealing successfully with infractions of company rules and maintaining smooth-running employee relations. A "who's who" lists the leading labor arbitrators in the country.

Collective Bargaining Negotiations and Contracts. Washington, D.C., The Bureau
of National Affairs. 4 vols. with weekly supplements.

A convenient, up-to-date compilation of facts and information essential
to the conduct of collective bargaining. Two loose-leaf volumes are devoted
to a Contract Clause Finder, in which thousands of actual clauses on hundreds
of topics are organized and indexed by subject matter. The other binders contain the full text of existing union-management agreements in representative
industries, periodic studies of bargaining trends, and reports on bargaining
techniques and strategy written by qualified experts.

Prentice-Hall Union Contracts and Collective Bargaining Service. New York,
Prentice-Hall, Inc. 1 vol. with biweekly supplements.

This loose-leaf service helps employers and unions to meet each other
on even terms at the bargaining table. Examples are given of successful bargaining techniques, tested contract clauses with complete analyses, and full
texts of leading contracts. A check list of the pitfalls to avoid and points to
be covered in a contract is featured.

Prentice-Hall Pension and Profit Sharing Service. New York, Prentice-Hall, Inc.
1 vol. with biweekly supplements.

Matters to be considered in creating a pension, profit-sharing or stock
bonus plan or trust, and in qualifying it for income tax advantages are described and explained fully in this loose-leaf guide. It contains model plans and
agreements, approved clauses, and checklists, and shows how competently
drafted plans save taxes and help prevent labor unrest. Also included are
digests of current court decisions and decisions of administrative boards affecting pensions, profit-sharing and stock-bonus plans and trusts.

Union Labor Report. Washington, D.C., The Bureau of National Affairs, Inc.
2 vols. with biweekly supplements.

This guide to "do's" and "don'ts" in labor relations under current labor
laws is prepared especially for the use of union locals. Material is organized
under topic classifications. Applicable rules are stated in simplified terminology,
and case examples show how the rules work. *Union Labor Report* also provides weekly notification of trends and developments of special interest to
unions plus a weekly charting of facts useful in negotiations.

Commerce Clearing House Workmen's Compensation Law Reports. Chicago,
Commerce Clearing House, Inc. 1 vol. with frequent supplements.

Employers' liability for injuries to his workmen is regulated by the
statutes of the various states. The principal phases of each state's system
are outlined in this reporter service and kept up to date with supplements.
Occupational diseases laws establishing employers liability for sickness of his
employees are also covered, and court decisions interpreting the statutes of each
state on these issues are featured.

More general information on current phases of industrial relations
can be found in the bulletins of the U.S. Department of Labor; the *Studies*

in Personnel Policy, Management Research Memoranda, and *Studies in Business Policy* of the National Industrial Conference Board; and the *Personnel* and *Production* series of the American Management Association. The publications of the various industrial relations sections of universities are another excellent source of up-to-date material.

The magazines that touch on industrial relations are, in general, the same ones which were mentioned earlier on pages under statistical sources or publications which deal with personnel. At the risk of some repetition they will be included here:

Advanced Management. Quarterly. New York, Society for the Advancement of Management.

> Reports of Research studies in personnel management are included as well as accounts of the experience of various companies. Each issue contains articles on labor management that cover both the theoretical as well as the practical phases.

The Conference Board Management Record. Monthly. New York, National Industrial Conference Board.

> The statistics on payrolls, cost of living, employment, and strikes are exceedingly useful. Short articles on current labor topics and a chronology of labor happenings for the month are other features.

DM Digest. Biweekly. New York, Morton Dodge & Co.

> The news contained in the labor press is digested in this publication, thus providing a cross section of labor opinion on current events.

Economic Trends and Outlook. Monthly. Washington, D.C., AF of L-CIO Economic Policy Committee.

> Current economic facts and statistics as interpreted by the AF of L-CIO are provided by this periodical.

Factory. Monthly. New York, McGraw-Hill Publishing Company.

> Articles on labor and personnel relations are interspersed with studies of more efficient factory operations. The section entitled "Significant Labor Developments" supplies a digest of rulings, programs, and articles in the labor field.

Industrial and Labor Relations Review. Quarterly. Ithaca, N.Y., State School of Industrial Relations.

> Each issue carries four or five long articles written by recognized leaders in the field of industrial relations. A wide range of subjects is covered, and the following are typical: competitive unionism in various industries, price behavior and productivity, and labor relations in the United States and abroad. There is a very fine book review section.

Industrial Relations Magazine. Monthly. Chicago, Ill., Dartnell Corp.

> Articles on all aspects of industrial relations and employer-employee relations are provided.

Industrial Relations Research Association Proceedings. Annually. Madison, Wis. Industrial Relations Research Association, Sterling Hall, University of Wisconsin.

Broad subjects such as unemployment, employment of racial minorities, labor history, and management of policies are treated in considerable detail.

Industry and Labor. Monthly. Geneva, Switzerland, International Labour Organization.

Short articles with statistics on social and economic policy, International Labour Organization, manpower, migration, condition of work, social legislation, and workers education, comprise the bulk of this periodical. Useful for information on current social welfare and labor legislation throughout the world.

Information Service Bulletin. Ten issues a year. Northampton, Mass., Institute of Labor Studies.

Significant current material gathered from the labor press is presented in digested form.

International Labour Review. Monthly. Geneva, Switzerland, International Labour Organization.

This magazine is probably the best source for information on labor conditions outside the United States. Articles describe particular situations and labor legislation.

A Journal of Economy and Society. Three times a year. Berkeley, Calif., University of California, Institute of Industrial Relations.

This is a recent scholarly journal dealing with developments of industrial relations. The editorial statement in the first issue declares that industrial relations "will deal with all aspects of the employment relationship in modern industrial society." Symposia on significant issues are the features of the publication. There are no book reviews.

Labor and the Nation. Bimonthly. New York, Inter-Union Institute Inc.

Information of concern to labor, including reports, analyses, and surveys appears in the publication. It features articles by prominent labor leaders expressing the labor viewpoint.

Mill & Factory. Monthly. New York, Conover-Mast Corp.

In addition to articles on numerous industrial topics this periodical contains information and the results of special research on bargaining collectively, health and safety, the labor market, and wages.

Monthly Labor Review. Monthly. Washington, D.C., U.S. Bureau of Labor Statistics.

A most exhaustive treatment of the labor situation is furnished by this magazine: various labor and industrial relations are analyzed and in the second section statistics are accumulated. It also carries the most extensive current bibliography of labor literature.

Personnel. Bimonthly. New York, American Management Association.

Although personnel administration is the dominant feature, each issue contains several articles on industrial relations. Most of the articles are based on actual company experience or research.

CHECKLIST OF INDUSTRIAL RELATIONS AND PERSONNEL ADMINISTRATION

ACCIDENT AND HEALTH

Heinrich, H. W. *Industrial Accident Prevention, Scientific Approach.* 4th ed. New York, McGraw-Hill, 1959.

BIBLIOGRAPHY

Blum, A. A. *Annotated Bibliography of Industrial Relations and the Small Firm.* Ithaca, N.Y., New York State School of Industry and Labor Relations, 1960.
University of California, Los Angeles, Institute of Industrial Relations. *Industrial Human Relations.* 6th rev. ed. Los Angeles, Calif., Institute of Industrial Relations, 1959.
Employment Relations Abstracts. (Formerly *Labor-personnel Index.*) Semimonthly. Detroit 1, Mich., 10 West Warren, Information Service, Inc.
Index to Labor Union Periodicals. Monthly. Ann Arbor, Mich., University of Michigan, School of Business Administration, Bureau of Industrial Relations.
Michigan University, School of Business Administration, Bureau of Industrial Relations. *A Selected List of Books and Periodicals in Personnel and Labor Management Relations.* Ann Arbor, Mich., University of Michigan, Bureau of Business Research, 1962.
Personnel Abstracts. Quarterly. Arlington, Va., 2873 South Abingdon Street, Nathaniel Stewart.
Princeton University. Industrial Relations Section. *The Office Library of an Industrial Relations Executive.* 6th ed. (Bibliographical Series. No. 81.) Princeton, N.J., Industrial Relations Section, Princeton University. 1951.
—— *Outstanding Books on Industrial Relations.* Princeton, N.J., Industrial Relations Section, Princeton University. Annually.
—— *Selected References.* Bimonthly. Princeton, N.J., Industrial Relations Section, Princeton University.
—— *Trade Union Library.* 6th ed. (Bibliographical Series. No. 84.) Princeton, N.J., Industrial Relations Section, Princeton University, 1955.
Special Libraries Association. *Source List of Selected Labor Statistics.* New York, Special Libraries Association, 1953.
U.S. Bureau of Labor Statistics. *Publications of the Bureau of Labor Statistics.* Monthly. Washington, D.C., U.S. Bureau of Labor Statistics.
U.S. Superintendent of Documents. *Labor, Child Labor, Women Workers, Employ-*

ment, Wages, Workmen's Insurance and Compensation. Price List 33. Washington, D.C., Government Printing Office, 1916–.

COLLECTIVE BARGAINING

American Management Association. *Understanding Collective Bargaining.* New York, American Management Association, 1958.

Davey, H. W. *Contemporary Collective Bargaining.* 2d ed. Englewood Cliffs, N.J., Prentice-Hall, 1959.

Dunlop, J. T. and Healy, J. J. *Collective Bargaining, Principles and Cases.* Homewood, Ill., Irwin, 1953.

Golden, C. S. and Ruttenberg, H. J. *The Dynamics of Industrial Democracy.* New York, Harper, 1942.

Hill, L. H. and Hook, C. R., Jr. *Management at the Bargaining Table.* New York, McGraw-Hill, 1945.

National Industrial Conference Board. *Preparing for Collective Bargaining.* New York, National Industrial Conference Board, 1959.

Norgren, P. H. and others. *Employing the Negro in American Industry.* New York, Industrial Relations Counselors, 1960.

Slichter, S. H. and others. *The Impact of Collective Bargaining on Management.* Washington, D.C., Brookings Institution, 1960.

HANDBOOKS

Aspley, J. C. ed. *The Handbook of Employee Relations.* Chicago, Dartnell Corporation, 1957.

Heyel, C. ed. *The Foreman's Handbook.* 3d ed. New York, McGraw-Hill, 1955.

Yoder, D. and others. *Handbook of Personnel Management and Labor Relations.* New York, McGraw-Hill, 1958.

INDUSTRIAL PSYCHOLOGY

Laird, D. A. and Laird, E. C. *Technique of Handling People.* New York, McGraw-Hill, 1954.

Roethlisberger, F. J. and Dickson, W. J. *Management and the Worker.* Cambridge, Mass., Harvard University Press, 1939.

Tiffin, J. *Industrial Psychology.* 4th ed. Englewood Cliffs, N.J., Prentice-Hall, 1958.

LABOR ECONOMICS

Daugherty, C. A. *Labor Problems in American Industry 1948–1949.* New York, Houghton, Mifflin, 1949.

Kerr, C. and others. *Industrialism and Industrial Man.* Cambridge, Mass., Harvard University Press, 1960.

Reynolds, L. G. *Labor Economics and Labor Relations.* 3d ed. Englewood Cliffs, N.J., Prentice-Hall, 1959.

Labor Unions and Labor Leaders

American Council on Public Affairs. *Handbook of Labor Unions*. Washington, D.C., American Council on Public Affairs, 1944.

Barbash, J. *The Practice of Unionism*. New York, Harper, 1956.

Institute of Labor Studies. *Yearbook of American Labor*. Northampton, Mass., Institute of Labor Studies. Biennially.

Labor Research Association. *Labor Fact Book*. New York, Labor Research Association. Biennially.

Peterson, F. *American Labor Unions; What They Are and How They Work*. 2d ed. New York, Harper, 1963.

Taft, Philip. *The AF of L in the Time of Gompers*. New York, Harper, 1957.

—— *The AF of L from the Death of Gompers to the Merger*. New York, Harper, 1959.

—— *The Structure and Government of Labor Unions*. Cambridge, Mass., Harvard University Press, 1956.

Walsh, J. R. *CIO—Industrial Unionism in Action*. New York, W. W. Norton, 1937.

Periodicals

Advanced Management. Quarterly. New York, Society for the Advancement of Management.

The Conference Board Management Record. Monthly. New York, National Industrial Conference Board.

DM Digest. Biweekly. New York, New York, Martin Dodge & Co.

Economic Trends and Outlook. Monthly. Washington, D.C., AF of L-CIO Economic Policy Committee.

Factory Management and Maintenance. Monthly. New York, McGraw-Hill.

Industrial and Labor Relations Review. Quarterly. Ithaca, N.Y., State School of Industrial Relations.

Industrial Relations. Journal of Economy and Society. Three times a year. Berkeley, Calif., University of California, Institute of Industrial Relations.

Industrial Relations Magazine. Monthly. Chicago, Ill., Dartnell Corp.

Industrial Relations Research Association Proceedings. Annually. Madison, Wis. Industrial Relations Research Association, Stanley Hall, University of Wisconsin.

Industry and Labour. Monthly. Geneva, Switzerland. International Labour Organization.

Information Service Bulletin. Ten issues a year. Northampton, Mass., Institute of Labor Studies.

International Labour Review. Monthly. Geneva, Switzerland, International Labour Organization.

Labor and the Nation. Biweekly. New York, Inter-Union Institute.

The Labor Market and Employment Security. Monthly. Washington, D.C., U.S.
   Bureau of Employment Security, U.S. Department of Labor.
Mill & Factory. Monthly. New York, Conover-Mast Corp.
Monthly Labor Review. Monthly. Washington, D.C., U.S. Bureau of Labor Statistics.
Personnel. Bimonthly. New York, American Management Association.
Personnel Journal. Monthly except July and August. Swarthmore, Pa., Personnel
   Journal, Inc.
Personnel Management. Biweekly. Washington, D.C., The Bureau of National
   Affairs.
Steel Labor. Monthly. Indianapolis, Ind., United Steelworkers Union.

PERSONNEL ADMINISTRATION

Pigors, P. and Myers, C. A. *Personnel Administration.* 4th ed. New York, McGraw-
   Hill, 1961.
Scott, W. D., Clothier, R. C. and Spriegal, W. R. *Personnel Management, Princi-
   ples, Practice and Point of View.* 6th ed. New York, McGraw-Hill, 1961.
Watkins, G. S., Dodd, P. A., McNaughton, W. L., and Prasow, P. *The Management
   of Personnel and Labor Relations.* 2d ed. New York, McGraw-Hill, 1950.
Yoder, D. *Personnel Management and Industrial Relations.* 5th ed. Englewood
   Cliffs, N.J., Prentice-Hall, 1962.

SERVICES

Collective Bargaining Negotiations and Contracts. The Bureau of National Affairs,
   Inc., 24th and N. Streets, N.W., Washington, D.C., 4 vols. with weekly sup-
   plements.
Commerce Clearing House Labor Law Course. Commerce Clearing House, Inc.,
   214 W. Michigan Ave., Chicago, Ill., 1 vol. up to date of publication.
Commerce Clearing House Labor Law Guide—Federal. Chicago, Commerce Clear-
   ing House, Inc. 1 vol. with weekly supplements.
Commerce Clearing House Labor Law Reports. Chicago, Commerce Clearing
   House, Inc. 5 vols. with weekly supplements.
Commerce Clearing House Workmen's Compensation Law Reports. Chicago,
   Commerce Clearing House, Inc. 1 vol. with frequent supplements.
Daily Labor Report. Washington, D.C., The Bureau of National Affairs, Inc.
Labor Relations Reporter. Washington, D.C., The Bureau of National Affairs, Inc.
   3 vols. with semiweekly supplements.
Prentice-Hall Employee Relations Guide and Arbitration. New York, Prentice-
   Hall, Inc. 1 vol. with biweekly supplements.
Prentice-Hall Labor Course. New York, Prentice-Hall, Inc. 1 vol. up to date of
   publication.
Prentice-Hall Labor Guide. New York, Prentice-Hall, Inc. 1 vol. with weekly sup-
   plements.

Prentice-Hall Labor Service. New York, Prentice-Hall, Inc. 3 vols. with weekly
supplements.
Prentice-Hall Pension and Profit Sharing Service. New York, Prentice-Hall, Inc.
1 vol. with biweekly supplements.
Prentice-Hall Personnel Policies and Practices. New York, Prentice-Hall, Inc. 3 vols.
with biweekly supplements.
Prentice-Hall Union Contracts and Collective Bargaining Service. New York,
Prentice-Hall, Inc. 1 vol. with biweekly supplements.
Union Labor Report. Washington, D.C., The Bureau of National Affairs, Inc. 2 vols.
with biweekly supplements.

STATISTICS

International Labour Organization. *Yearbook of Labour Statistics.* Geneva, Switzerland, International Labour Organization, 1940–.
National Industrial Conference Board. *The Economic Almanac.* New York, The
Conference Board. Annually.
U.S. Bureau of Labor Statistics. *Handbook of Labor Statistics,* 1950 ed. (Bulletin
1016.) Washington, D.C., Government Printing Office, 1950. 2 vols. with 1951
supplements.

STATISTICS CURRENT

The Conference Board Management Record. Monthly. New York, National In-
dustrial Conference Board.
Economic Trends and Outlook. Monthly. Washington, D.C., AF of L-CIO Economic
Policy Committee.
International Labour Review. Statistical Supplement. Monthly. Geneva, Switzerland,
International Labour Organization.
The Labor Market and Employment Security. Monthly. Washington, D.C., U.S.
Bureau of Employment Security.
Monthly Labor Review. Monthly. Washington, D.C., U.S. Bureau of Labor Statis-
tics.
National Industrial Conference Board. *Management Research Memoranda, Studies
in Personnel Policy, Studies in Business Policy.* New York, National Industrial
Conference Board.
U.S. Monthly Report on the Labor Force. Monthly. Washington, D.C., U.S. Depart-
ment of Labor.

RESEARCH ORGANIZATIONS

American Arbitration Association, 477 Madison Avenue, New York 20, N.Y.
American Management Association, 1515 Broadway, New York, N.Y.
Dartnell Corporation, 4660 Ravenswood Avenue, Chicago 40, Ill.
Industrial Relations Counselors, 1270 Avenue of the Americas, New York 20, N.Y.

Industrial Relations Research Association, Sterling Hall, University of Wisconsin, Madison 6, Wis.

Industrial Relations Sections of the leading universities.

International Labour Organization, 917 15th Street, N.W., Washington, D.C.

Labor Research Organization, 80 East 11th Street, New York 3, N.Y.

National Industrial Conference Board, Inc., 460 Park Avenue, New York 22, N.Y.

National Labor Management Foundation, 737 North Michigan Avenue, Chicago 11, Ill.

U.S. Department of Labor, Bureau of Employment Security, Washington 25, D.C.

U.S. Department of Labor, Bureau of Labor Statistics, Washington 25, D.C.

U.S. Department of Labor, Division of Labor Standards, Washington 25, D.C.

U.S. Department of Labor, Women's Bureau, Washington 25, D.C.

12

MARKETING, SALES MANAGEMENT, AND ADVERTISING

There has been a great deal of effort and research that has gone into marketing. This has been directed toward achieving better results and reducing costs. Much of the effort has been along the lines of mass merchandising through chain stores and discount houses.

The information on marketing has become extensive and much of it has resulted from the activities of bureaus of market research. There have been a number of bibliographies published in this field.

Perhaps the most useful sources of information on marketing is:

Marketing Information Guide. Monthly. Washington, D.C., U.S. Department of Commerce.

This is a well-selected, annotated listing of publications of the U.S. Government, state and local organizations, trade associations, and colleges and universities. The material covered includes books, pamphlets, reports, periodicals, and periodical articles. Special issues of government and other periodicals are noted. This is a most excellent running source of current data on marketing.

Distribution Data Guide. Monthly. Washington, D.C., U.S. Office of Distribution, Business and Defense Services Administration.

This publication differs from the preceding entry in that it provides more references to statistical data. It is an annotated bibliography of selected current reports (government and nongovernment) which supply basic information and statistics on marketing and distribution. Books and pamphlets published by colleges and universities, associations and commercial publishers, along with periodical articles, are covered. The semiannual index makes it easy to locate particular references.

Another current bibliography is:

Marketing Review. Weekly. Toronto 1, Canada, 160 Bay Street, Librex Ltd.
>For marketing and advertising executives, here is a weekly index of articles which appear in general publications and advertising periodicals. It is in two parts—the first deals with subjects of broad interest to most executives in the field; and the second part brings articles on marketing, and problems in marketing specific products.

The American Marketing Association has been in the forefront in pushing market research and upgrading the entire marketing profession. The Association publishes a Bibliographical Series, the latest of which is:

Gunther, E. and Goldstein, F. A. *Current Sources of Marketing Information.* (American Marketing Association Bibliography Series No. 6.) Chicago, American Marketing Association, 1960.
>Books, government reports, and special studies published since 1954 are arranged by subject in an annotated list. There is also a section on periodicals which carry information of interest to students of marketing. The annotations are descriptive; its timeliness makes it helpful to those other than marketing executives.

Two older bibliographies are of value for their completeness and listing of earlier sources.

Rezvan, D. A. *A Comprehensive Classified Marketing Bibliography.* Berkeley, Calif., University of California Press, 1951.
Parts I and II.
>Books, government publications, pamphlets, and periodical articles published through 1949 appear in this bibliography. The entries are arranged under a very detailed classification.

U.S. Bureau of Foreign and Domestic Commerce. *Market Research Sources, 1950. A Guide to Information on Domestic Marketing.* Prepared by Rachel Bretherton. (Domestic Commerce Series No. 20.) Washington, D.C., Government Printing Office, 1950.
>The period covered is from 1940 to 1949; the 1940 edition (Domestic Commerce Series No. 110) contains references for the years 1937 to 1939; the 1938 edition (Domestic Commerce Series No. 55) 1933 to 1937; and the 1936 edition from 1931 to 1935 inclusive. *Market Research Agencies* (Domestic Commerce Series No. 6) includes references prior to 1925. The activities of the federal and state governments are described by department, bureau, and

agency, and useful publications on market research issued during the period covered are listed. A section on colleges and universities engaged in research on topics of value to marketing students is also included. Foundations, book publishers, publishers of trade directories and catalogs, advertising agencies, and broadcasting systems, business services, chambers of commerce, individual firms, newspapers, periodicals, and trade associations are the titles which head other units of this publication. In each case, the surveys, studies, and books published are listed and described. A separate section supplies a checklist of periodicals useful to marketing research workers. The monthly *Marketing Information Guide* put out by the Department of Commerce brings this material up to date.

Market research has expanded into a large scale activity in universities, government agencies and, in the larger advertising firms. As a result of this increased activity in this field there are more bibliographies and directories available. Useful material for locating data and firms can be found in:

Wales, H. G. and Ferber, R. A. *A Basic Bibliography on Marketing Research.* Chicago, American Marketing Association, 1956.

An annotated list of sources of information on marketing research.

Carpenter, R. N. *Guidelist for Marketing Research and Economic Forecasting.* New York, American Management Association, 1961.

A carefully selected, up-to-date compilation of sources with excellent annotations. Many directories, bibliographies, and government sources are listed. Invaluable to persons engaged in marketing and forecasting and highly useful to all businessmen.

U.S. Department of Commerce. *State and Regional Market Indicators, 1939–1945.* (Economic Series No. 60.) Washington, D.C., Government Printing Office, 1947.

This publication indicates the statistics of value to marketing executives, manufacturers, and distributors. Selected indicators on a geographic basis are: population, employment, national income, finance, retail sales, and agriculture. These figures can be updated by the latest census figures.

Market Research Society. *Statistical Sources for Market Research.* London, Market Research Society, 1957.

This publication provides an excellent introduction to the governmental statistics of the United Kingdom.

Clarke, G. T. *Advertising and Marketing. Theses for the Doctorate in United States Colleges and Universities.* New York 21, 655 Madison Ave., Advertising Educational Foundation, 1961.

Three hundred doctoral dissertations from thirty-eight institutions are listed under forty-six subject categories. Dissertations are listed alphabetically by title under subjects. Other data supplied are name of author, degree granting institution, and date.

Bradford, E. S. ed. *Survey and Directory of Marketing Research Agencies in the United States and the World*. New Rochelle, N.Y., 50 Argyle St., The Editor. Biennially. The 1962–1963 edition is the latest.

> This directory gives, by cities, the names and addresses of agencies and individuals engaged in marketing, advertising, and economic research, public opinion polls, community surveys and store locations, personnel research and employee rating, and related lines, with names of officers and an outline of services. A second list groups the names and addresses by the type of research activity in which these persons are engaged. The research bureaus of a limited number of trade associations are also listed.

A current supplement to the previously mentioned bibliographies is "Basic Sources in the Field of Sales and Advertising" which appears as a special section of *Sales Management* at irregular intervals. Although the emphasis is on material dealing with advertising and selling, it also contains many articles on marketing in general and market research.

The improvement in the scope and accuracy of statistics has been most helpful in enabling the retailer and salesmanager to plan his activities more effectively.

The retailer is the last link in the marketing chain before the goods reach the consumer. For this reason retail sales have become a barometer not only for all marketing agencies but for the manufacturer and producer as well. Observing changes in retail sales volume as well as the amount of consumer credit outstanding and the accumulation of retail inventories enables businessmen to gain a rough estimate of business conditions in the immediate future at the consumer's level.

This information is of immediate value to the retailer and the manufacturer. Declining sales and expanding inventories, especially if they occur on a national basis, warn that buying policies or selling policies or perhaps both, should be altered. Unusual circumstances may cause advances or declines in markets, and the alert seller may take advantage of these shifts.

The most complete set of statistics on marketing can be found in government publications. The following governmental and private publications are the principal sources of information:

U.S. Bureau of the Census. *Census of Business:* Vol. I—*Retail Trade;* Vol. II— *Wholesale Trade;* Vol. III—*Service Businesses;* Vol. IV—*Construction;* Vol.

V—*Distribution of Manufacturers;* Vol. VI—*Selected Service Areas.* Washington, D.C., Government Printing Office, 1958.

This extremely detailed study of marketing provides figures on all kinds of establishments and also on a large-city basis. Number of establishments, sales, number of employees, payrolls, and stock at the end of the year are the data supplied. The new Census of Business is in progress in 1963.

U.S. Bureau of the Census. *Statistical Abstract of United States.* Washington, D.C., Government Printing Office. Annually.

The *Census of Business* figures for chain stores and mail order houses and indexes of department store sales are carried forward from the last *Census of Business.*

Federal Reserve Bulletin. Monthly. Washington, D.C., Board of Governors of the Federal Reserve System.

Monthly statistics are published on department store sales and inventories on hand by federal reserve districts and cities. A further breakdown gives total sales and stocks by major departments. Other statistics deal with consumer credit, accounts receivable, and collections. This publication contains the most complete current information. In addition, each of the twelve Federal Reserve Banks publish monthly bulletins which comment on the retail trade situation in their districts.

Survey of Current Business. Monthly. Washington, D.C., U.S. Office of Business Economics.

The same statistics as in the preceding publication are given, plus additional figures on advertising and the wholesale trades.

Dun's Review and Modern Industry. Monthly. New York, Dun & Bradstreet, Inc.

Wholesale prices are carried on a daily basis in this publication. Particularly valuable to those engaged in marketing is "The Failure Record." In addition to the number of failures and liabilities involved, failures are listed by industries. All of this information is compiled into a "Failure Index." Other useful features are "The Trend of Business" and "Regional Trade Barometers."

National Retail Merchants Association. Controllers Congress. *Departmental Merchandising and Operating Results of Departmentalized Stores.* New York, National Retail Merchants Association. Annually.

Expenses, sales, departmental merchandising, and inventory statistics are compiled for over 8,300 departments. These data and the compilation which follows are prepared by the Harvard Graduate School of Business Administration.

National Retail Merchants Association. Controllers Congress. *Operating Results of Department and Specialty Stores.* New York, National Retail Merchants Association. Annually.

A detailed statistical analysis of store operating income and expense.

The shifts in population and industry since World War II plus the growth of new metropolitan areas has changed the sales map of the United States. The editors of *Sales Management* magazine have been able to provide current information on retail sales, population, and buying power in the "Survey of Buying Power," which appears annually as a supplement to *Sales Management*.

Sales Management Survey of Buying Power. New York, Sales Management, Inc. Annually.

> Although the figures contained in this survey are labeled estimates, they represent the most current figures available and reflect shifts in population and industry. Population, retail sales (both totals and grouped by food, general merchandise, and drug stores), wholesale sales, effective buying income, and gross farm income, are among the various statistics provided. Regional and state summaries and figures by counties and larger cities further amplify the data. The percentages of national and state totals of population, sales, and effective buying income enable the seller to select concentrated, desirable markets. This survey provides both an excellent starting point for individual surveys and a yardstick with which to measure marketing efforts of the individual concerns; estimates are given for the preceding year.

Marketing research has more nearly come of age with the development of more precise methods and the contributions which have been made by psychologists. There is much more material available both in books and periodical literature. The books which are mentioned here will provide basic information for those interested in undertaking marketing research:

Brown, L. O. *Marketing and Distribution Research*. 3d ed. New York, Ronald, 1955.

> In this very comprehensive treatment of the fundamentals of marketing and distribution research, mechanics and methods of marketing research are described very thoroughly. The author first outlines the methods which may be used in market research, and then describes various kinds of analyses and investigations. Very complete discussions of the project, the preparation of questionnaires, testing and analyzing the results, and the usefulness and limitations of various methods of marketing research complete the contents of this book. The text is extremely helpful for any person who is planning on making a market survey or analysis.

Boyd, H. W. and Westfall, R. *Marketing Research*. Homewood, Ill., Irwin, 1956.

> The authors describe and define marketing research and then go on to outline the procedures and application. The motivations which make people buy and express preferences for one product over another are dealt with in

some detail. Research methods as applied to various products, to advertising, and sales control, are described. Sampling techniques and methods of collection and interpreting data are illustrated.

Lorie, J. H. and Roberts, H. L. *Basic Methods of Marketing Research*. New York, McGraw-Hill, 1951.

The methods, procedures, and organization of marketing research are thoroughly developed. These include the application of the scientific method, sampling, evaluation of data interviewing, and processing of marketing research data.

Luck, D. C. and Wales, H. G. *Marketing Research*. Englewood Cliffs, N.J., Prentice-Hall, 1952.

An introductory book with sound suggestions as to how to obtain data, its use and application, and suggestions as to the interpretation of the findings. There is a good bibliography of publications up to the date of issue.

Two books deal with consumer motivation, an aspect of marketing research which is becoming increasingly important. These are:

Clark, L. H. and Carney, J. B., eds. *Consumer Behavior*. New York, Harper, 1958.

This study, in some depth, is concerned with what motivates the consumer to buy or not buy. The theory of consumer behavior is tested against consumer reactions to certain products. The "Review of Recent Research on Human Behavior" is a useful bibliography on this subject.

Newman, J. A. *Motivation Research and Marketing Management*. Cambridge, Mass., Harvard University, Division of Research, 1957.

The concepts of motivation research and its relationship to marketing are defined. Instances of actual research are illustrated by cases. The concluding section is an evaluation of the usefulness of motivation research to the marketing management.

A useful publication which defines marketing terms is:

American Marketing Association Committee on Definitions. *Marketing Definitions; A Glossary of Marketing Terms*. Chicago, American Marketing Association, 1960.

This is an up-to-date set of definitions of the most commonly used terms in marketing.

Another of the useful compilations that the marketing executive can keep at hand for ready reference is:

Nystrom, P. H. ed. *Marketing Handbook*. New York, Ronald, 1948.

This is another working-tool for the marketing executive which supplies brief but authoritative information on types of marketing and channels of distribution. Others of the thirty topics covered are sales promotion, training salesmen, distribution costs.

General works on marketing which have become standard texts in the field are:

Beckman, T. N. *Marketing*. 7th ed. New York, Ronald, 1962.
> The author treats the subject broadly. The consumer, principles of retailing, wholesaling, marketing functions, policies, and costs are the major topics treated. In this latest edition there is more emphasis on the managerial aspects of marketing. The presentation in clear short paragraphs of the many phases of marketing, plus ample illustrations and explanations of the advantages and disadvantages of each, make this book readable and informative. A short, selected bibliography suggests to the reader some of the more important current books on marketing.

Phillips, A. F. and Duncan, D. J. *Marketing Principles and Methods*. 3d ed. Homewood, Ill., Irwin, 1960.
> An excellent presentation of the principles of marketing is followed by chapters developing their application to specific marketing operations. The tables and statistics are brought up-to-date with the 1960 census data. New chapters on product development, selection of channels of distribution, and the physical supplies needed in marketing supply additional information.

Converse, P. D., Huegy, H. W. and Mitchell, R. *Elements of Marketing*. 6th ed. Englewood Cliffs, N.J., Prentice-Hall, 1958.
> Practical marketing decisions based on the application of marketing principles and policies are emphasized. The marketing process is described in terms of functions, commodities, and institutions. There is also an explanatory section on merchandising and government regulations. Readers will find the definitions and explanations at the beginning of each chapter and the bibliographies at the end very helpful.

Two other books which treat of marketing from a somewhat different approach or more restricted area of marketing are:

McCarthy, E. J. *Basic Marketing*. Homewood, Ill., Irwin, 1960.
> The author looks at the various phases of marketing through the eyes of the manager of the marketing department or store. The reconciling of consumer behavior and company policies is a thread which runs consistently through this book. There are many suggestions as to how the effectiveness of the marketing program can be evaluated.

Corey, E. R. *Development of Markets for New Materials*. Cambridge, Mass., Harvard University, Division of Research, 1956.
> The introduction of a product unknown to the consumers is difficult. The customer must be informed as to the usages of the new product and be

convinced that it has superior characteristics to materials currently in use. This book provides a logical step-by-step discussion of the introduction, marketing development, and sales promotion of aluminum, fibrous glass, and plastics. Many good ideas for similar campaigns can be derived from this presentation.

Much current information on marketing trends, general market conditions, and new developments can be found in general business periodicals, and trade publications. These articles are catalogued in the *Business Periodicals Index*. Publications which regularly carry articles on marketing are *Business Week*, McGraw-Hill Publishing Company, New York, N.Y.; *Dun's Review*, Dun & Bradstreet, Inc., New York, N.Y.; *Journal of Business*, University of Chicago, Chicago, Ill.; and the bulletins of the twelve Federal Reserve Banks. Three other publications stress advertising and sales management, but they also contain discussions of the broader aspects of marketing. These are *Sales Management*, Sales Management, Inc., New York, N.Y.; *Printers' Ink*, Printers' Ink Publishing Company, Inc., New York, N.Y.; and *Advertising Age*, Advertising Publications, Inc., Chicago, Ill.

The following journal contains a great variety of articles on marketing:

The Journal of Marketing. Quarterly. Menasha, Wis., The American Marketing Association.

This is probably the most scholarly of the journals dealing with marketing because many of the contributors are teachers or researchers in the field of marketing. The articles are presented in an objective and scientific manner, and the book reviews supply an excellent evaluation of the more important current marketing publications.

As the marketing field has broadened, become more complex, and more product competition has developed, more books have been published on special aspects of marketing. The individual who has an adequate understanding of marketing principles will find these works of assistance in learning special techniques and in solving specific problems. The following are representative studies in the topics indicated:

Shepherd, G. S. *Marketing Farm Products: Economic Analysis.* 3d ed. Ames, Iowa, Iowa State College, 1955.

Because the production, processing, and distribution of food is the largest business activity in the country, its marketing problems are extremely important. The author discusses distribution methods, pricing, and marketing costs from the farmer's viewpoint. The effects of the various government programs are brought out. The up-to-date tables and charts, and discussion of the various government plans for aiding and regulating farm markets, make this a worthwhile reference book.

Staudt, T. A. and Lazer, W. *A Basic Bibliography on Industrial Marketing*. (American Marketing Association Bibliography Series, No. 4.) Chicago, American Marketing Association, 1958.

Almost 1,700 concise annotated references to periodical articles provide a very thorough coverage of all phases of industrial marketing.

Phillips, C. F. ed. *Marketing by Manufacturers*. Homewood, Ill., Irwin, 1948.

The various authors represent a blend of the thinking and experience of the leading market teachers and individuals concerned with marketing in large manufacturing concerns. The aim of the book is to assist manufacturers with their marketing problems and to provide students with an understanding of the requirements and difficulties involved in marketing manufactured goods. Parts I and II define and explain the general policies governing the market for industrial goods. The remaining sections consider the preparation and pricing of the product, organizing the sales force, distribution and financing, and foreign sales. This is a good treatment of a type of selling that has heretofore received inadequate attention.

Industrial Marketing. Market Data Book. Chicago, Advertising Publications. Annually.

The up-to-date descriptive information and current statistics make this publication valuable to businessmen outside the field of industrial marketing. Data are supplied on agriculture, forestry and fisheries, mining, construction, manufacturing industries, transportation, electric and gas utilities, finance, insurance and real estate, and service industries. Publishers of trade publications and associations in each field are listed. For the benefit of advertisers, page size, layout requirements, and costs are given.

Industrial Marketing. Monthly. Chicago, Ill., Advertising Publications, Inc.

This periodical is largely given over to articles on sales and advertising for industrial marketers. It also has articles on general business trends and developments and governmental activities affecting business.

Retailing is by far the largest segment of marketing, insomuch as the retailers are in direct contact with the consumer. Since World War II retailing has changed radically with the rapid growth of chains, supermarkets, discount houses, and now, automatic merchandising. Consequently, retailing problems and procedures are well represented in marketing literature.

The bibliographies on marketing described earlier in this chapter supply sources of information on retailing, especially, *Marketing Informa-*

tion Guide, Marketing Review, and *Distribution Data Guide.* The *Survey of Buying Power* published as a part of *Sales Management* is also useful to the retailer.

A still useful listing of information as to where to locate helpful material and to get assistance is:

U.S. Bureau of Foreign and Domestic Commerce, *Guide to Information on Government Retailing,* by J. H. Rhoads. Washington, D.C., Government Printing Office, 1949.

>   Agencies which aid the retailer and those that regulate retail trade are listed. There is a bibliography of selected government publications and periodicals. The excellent subject index makes it easy to locate the agency and publication which can be helpful in solving problems of finance, record keeping, and statistics. This publication is helpful to the small retailer. *Marketing Information Guide* updates this information.

The following books provide the retailer with the background and principles of his business:

Duncan, D. J. and Phillips, C. F. *Retailing Principles and Methods.* 5th ed. Homewood, Ill., Irwin, 1959.

>   The needs of both the student of retailing and the small and medium-sized retailer have been considered in the writing of this book. The authors emphasize that if the retail merchant is to succeed, he must have more than a superficial knowledge of the habits and tastes of his customers and of general business conditions. All the elements of a retail store operation from the choosing of a location to insurance on the stock are analyzed thoughtfully. The chapters on merchandise control and retail pricing explain clearly the fundamentals of these important elements of retail management. Chapters have been added to the earlier edition on supermarkets and discount selling.

Wingate, J. W. and Schaller, E. D. *Techniques of Retail Merchandising.* 2d ed. Englewood Cliffs, N.J., Prentice-Hall, 1950.

>   This book is an intensive study of the statistics and controls of mercantile activities. The authors start with a discussion of profits, describing the basic elements which contribute to successful operation and the analysis of accounting records to show profit trends. Succeeding chapters take up the important items which make for profitable merchandising, namely, pricing, inventories, and planning and control of costs and inventories. There is much practical information as to how to establish policies and set up controls and other phases of retail store operation.

Davidson, W. R. and Brown, P. L. *Retailing Management.* New York, Ronald, 1953.

>   The requisites for starting a retail store are presented in detail. These are proper location, layout, building and equipment, organization and personnel,

merchandise control, pricing, sales promotion, and accounting and expense management.

A very practical book on retailing which has gone through three editions is:

Wingate, I. B., Gillespie, K. R. and Addison, B. G. *Know Your Merchandise.* 3d ed. New York, McGraw-Hill, 1963.

> Written for the salesperson, this book is designed to increase his efficiency and knowledge. However, it can be read profitably by retail managers and customers as well. Short definitions of the materials which go into merchandise with descriptions of their uses and wearing qualities, make this a most practical book. The accounts of manufacturing processes add interest. At the end of each chapter the "Highlights of This Chapter" distil the salient points. The "Terms for Reference" in each chapter provide explanations of the terms which all salespeople use but often with little comprehension of what they mean. The buying, selling, and executive staff could read this book and profit from it.

Often the difference between a profit and a loss can be traced to buying wisely.

Wingate, J. W. and Brisco, N. A. *Buying for Retail Stores.* 3d ed. Englewood Cliffs, N.J., Prentice-Hall, 1953.

> This work very thoroughly covers buying activities. Buying to specifications, informative labels, and government regulations are treated fully. Yardsticks for the buyer include (1) organization of his job and department, and (2) how, what, and where to buy. The chapter on "Buying as a Career" indicates the possibilities of this vocation.

The U. S. Department of Commerce, Business and Defense Services Administration publish many pamphlets and reports helpful to the small retailer. They cover the general principles of retailing and information on specific types of retail businesses.

In addition to the sources of statistics mentioned earlier in this chapter, the U. S. Department of Commerce, Bureau of the Census, publishes several helpful compilations of statistics:

U.S. Bureau of the Census. *Monthly Retail Trade Report.* Monthly. Washington, D.C., U.S. Bureau of the Census.

> This report includes dollar sales, unadjusted and adjusted for seasonal and trading day differences of all retail stores, of retail stores of eleven or more establishments, and those of one to ten establishments. The breakdown is by kind of business, estimated sales for the month of larger grocery chains. The data are by census regions and for selected metropolitan areas.

———— *Monthly Retail Trade Report: Independent Retail Stores.* Monthly. Washington, D.C., U.S. Bureau of the Census.

Similar data as above are supplied for nonchain stores.

———— *Sales of Retail Chain Stores and Mail Order Houses.* Monthly. Washington, D.C., U.S. Bureau of the Census.

Data are selected and presented on the same basis as that in the *Monthly Retail Trade Report.*

———— *Monthly Wholesale Trade Report. Sales and Inventories.* Monthly. Washington, D.C., U.S. Bureau of the Census.

The report provides data on sales and inventory trends, stock sales, ratios of merchant wholesalers by kinds of business for the United States and census regions. Forty-five different kinds of business are covered.

As mentioned earlier, general business magazines carry many articles and much news related directly to retailing. *Business Week* and the *Survey of Current Business* should be read regularly. The advertising magazines also touch on various phases of retailing; *Printers' Ink* and *Sales Management* are particularly useful. Periodicals that are specifically identified with the retail field are:

Bulletin of the National Retail Merchants Association. Monthly. New York, National Retail Merchants Association.

Trends in all branches in the industry are discussed. Features include statistical studies of costs and other phases of retailing affecting the industry.

Department Store Economist. Monthly. Philadelphia, Pa., Chilton Publications.

Written for the store executive, this periodical contains many suggestions for sales promotions and merchandising ideas.

Distribution Age. Monthly. Philadelphia, Pa., Chilton Publications.

This publication serves the transportation, warehousing, containerization, and materials handling industries. In addition to suggestions as to how to improve operations, it contains news of the industry.

Journal of Retailing. Quarterly. New York, New York University School of Retailing.

The articles analyze the broader aspects of retailing and developments within the field.

Merchandising has developed into a variety of organizations and one of the first to appear was the chain store. Two publications provide current information on this aspect of business activity.

Chain Store Business Guide, Inc. *Chain Store Guides.* New York, Chain Store Business Guides, Inc. Annually.

These directories list stores with addresses, names of buyers and number of stores in each chain. Five guides are published, namely: *Directory of Drug*

Chains; Grocery and Supermarket Chains; Hardware and Auto Supply Chains; 5¢ to $1.00 Variety and Department Store Chains; and, *Independent 5¢ to $1.00 Variety Stores.*

Chain Store Age. Monthly. New York, Chain Store Age.

The nine editions of this publication supply news and ideas for the chain store business. This information includes merchandising, sales promotion, stock control, warehousing, store equipment, management, and display.

A second development in merchandising has been the variety chain and the following are helpful sources:

Variety Store Merchandiser. *Directory of the Variety Market.* New York, Variety Store Merchandiser. Annually.

Manufacturers of variety store merchandise and equipment are listed along with sales representatives, jobbers, and brand names.

Variety Store Merchandiser. Monthly. New York, Merchandiser Publishing Company.

The developments and trends in variety merchandising, including those of individual companies, are discussed. Statistics on sales and profits and ideas for store and executive development are other features.

Another rapidly growing segment of the retail field is the supermarket. The following provide information in this area.

Supermarket Institute Inc. *Index of Supermarket Articles, 1961.* Chicago, Supermarket Institute Inc., 1962.

Published annually for the past six years, this index covers over 500 articles in *Chain Store Age, Food Merchandising, Food Topics, Progressive Grocer, Supermarket Merchandising* and *Supermarket News.* Usually the entry is by title only. However, when the title is not self-explanatory, a brief résumé of the article is given.

Supermarket News. Weekly. New York, Fairchild Publishing Company.

News of the industry, promotion, and products, are the major sections of the publication. The first issue in July contains a study of supermarket profits.

An outgrowth of the supermarket has been the shopping center where a number of stores are clustered in one area.

Kelley, E. J. *Shopping Centers: Locating Controlled Regional Centers.* Saugatuck, Conn., The Enos Foundation for Highway Traffic, 1956.

The theory and practice of the location of shopping centers is clearly presented in this book. Detailed examples of the factors which go into the location of shopping centers—such as buying power, the number of adjacent population, accessibility, and the distance from which customers are drawn, are illustrated by a description of the process of locating six shopping centers on the East Coast. A summing up of principles and an excellent bibliography comprise the rest of this work. This is an indispensable book for anyone planning a development or leasing a business in a shopping center.

National Research Bureau, Inc., Merchandising Division. *Directory of Shopping Centers in the United States and Canada.* 1963 ed. Chicago, National Research Bureau, 1962.

The arrangement is by city under state or province. Information supplied indicates the location, developer-owner, rental agency, size of physical plant and cost, parking facilities, and availability of space.

In recent years, more and more laws have been passed to regulate the sale and marketing of products. The purity of products, prices, discounts and other factors affecting marketing under both state and federal laws. The easiest way to keep up-to-date on these regulations is to refer to one of the following services:

Prentice-Hall Trade Regulation Edition of the Labor Guide. New York, Prentice-Hall, Inc. 1 vol., with biweekly supplements.

For concise information on the regulation of unfair competition, price discrimination, and other practices prohibited by law this service is particularly helpful. It explains the Federal Trade Commission Act, the Robinson-Patman Act and the various State fair trade laws. It also contains the labor guide information described in the Prentice-Hall Labor Guide (see page 192).

Commerce Clearing House Regulation Reports. Chicago, Commerce Clearing House, Inc. 4 vols., with current issues.

All the antitrust and trade laws affecting the operation of business today are discussed in the reporter service. Active competition has brought more interest in price discrimination and price maintenance laws along with the continuing necessity to follow similar state laws. How the Federal Trade Commission assures free and clean competition is followed closely with full reports on details of current interest.

Commerce Clearing House Food, Drug, Cosmetic Law Reports. Chicago, Commerce Clearing House, Inc. 2 vols., with frequent supplements.

In order to protect the consumer, the manufacturer of foods, drugs and cosmetics is quite closely regulated. Rulings on purity, packaging, and labeling of products are of special interest to producers and distributors in these fields and to their advisors as well. The federal law is analyzed and annotated with all interpretive rulings, and the basic rules respecting the liability of sellers for product defects are discussed in detail.

Sales management and advertising are essential phases of present-day marketing techniques. Every person in the field soon realizes that few goods are bought—most of them must be sold. Customers must be told what is available, and then be persuaded to buy.

Extended research in the techniques of sales management and into consumer motivation has produced an expanding and more solid literature in this field. Reference is again made to "Basic Sources in the Field of Sales and Advertising" which appears periodically in *Sales Management*. Other bibliographies are:

National Sales Executives Inc. *Sources of Information for Sales Executives and Specialists in Marketing*. Rev. ed. New York, National Sales Executives, Inc., 1954.

> This subject listing of books and periodical articles falls under the headings of "Sales Organization," "Sales Executives," "Sales Planning and Policies," "Motivation," "Salesmanship," "Compensation," "Unionization," "Research Advertising," "Trade Associations," "Reference Books," and, lastly, a list of publishers.

Scan. Monthly. Chicago, Advertising Checking Bureau.

> Articles of particular interest to sales executives are digested from the leading marketing magazines regularly. Trade and general magazines are scanned for articles on selling and salesmanship.

Other useful works on sales management are:

Aspley, J. C. ed. *The Sales Managers' Handbook*. 8th ed. Chicago, Dartnell Corporation, 1959.

> Each revision has seen a reworking and updating of material to keep this handbook abreast of recent changes and news conditions of selling. Over the years this book has become an indispensable reference work which puts at the reader's disposal a wealth of information on selling and selling methods. Methods of selling and marketing research are described in the earlier chapters, but the bulk of the handbook emphasizes sales organization and how salesmen can be properly trained and directed. It contains a prescription for every ill that plagues a sales manager. The explanations of the various trade practices are most valuable.

Aspley, J. C. ed. *The Sales Promotion Handbook*. Chicago, Dartnell Corporation, 1954.

> This book outlines various methods of organizing and developing sales campaigns. There are many successful sales techniques which are illustrated by descriptions of campaigns which have proven their worth.

Canfield, B. R. *Sales Administration, Principles and Problems*. 4th ed. Englewood Cliffs, N.J., Prentice-Hall, 1961.

> The author uses a practical approach whereby sales management principles are clearly related to problems that arise. The latter are abundantly illustrated

with actual business cases. Research, operation of the sales department, and
sales policies and controls are the topics covered.

Maynard, H. H. and Davis, J. H. *Sales Management*. 3d ed. New York, Ronald,
1957.

In addition to the discussion of the principles and techniques of sales
management which were the concern of the authors in earlier editions. The
emphasis here is placed on the making of decisions and the influencing of
general business policies by the sales manager.

The majority of the periodicals in the field of sales management and
selling tend to be largely promotional and inspirational. Two publications,
however, have a more objective approach and contain a core of factual
articles: *Sales Management* and *Printers' Ink*.

Sales Management. Semimonthly. New York, Sales Management, Inc.

Each issue carries at least one serious study of sales management or selling
or a broad gauge article on the general aspects of marketing. Furthermore,
statistics are compiled for various markets and products and are cumulated
in the annual "Survey of Buying Power" issues. Trends of business and selling
are summarized, and numerous accounts of individual sales campaigns, sales
programs, selling pointers, methods and media are included. There is a short
book review section in each issue. This periodical appeals to the general business
executive, the salesman, the advertising man, and to the sales manager. It is
probably the best in this field.

Sales Management. *Survey of Buying Power*. New York, Sales Management, Inc.
Annually.

Buying power is defined and the uses of the *Survey* are explained in the
first part of this publication. The population, effective buying income, case
income and the percentage of buyings in each income group are the statistics
provided. These statistics cover the United States and Canada and are arranged
by state, counties, cities and metropolitan area. These statistics are available on
IBM cards.

Printers' Ink. Weekly. New York, Printers' Ink Publishing Company.

Space in *Printers' Ink* is about equally divided among articles on marketing and sales and advertising. Sales campaigns, marketing problems and conditions, selling techniques, and advertising methods and media are the featured
topics. Statistics on sales, marketing conditions and advertising appear frequently. This is the best source of current statistics on advertising.

Distribution of goods rests on three legs: (1) the population, buying,
stocking, and displaying of the product; (2) selling to the individual by
solicitation; (3) publicizing the product.

The growth of research and more precise methods has added a much more solid literature to the field of advertising. Nevertheless, so much of advertising is based on human nature that it is most difficult to make a general evaluation—each campaign must be judged on its own merits.

Books about advertising and selling flow from the presses in a steady stream, and they vary greatly in the quality and usefulness of content. The books mentioned here by no means exhaust the good publications in this field. For those who wish to make a serious study of advertising, the following bibliographies and general works will serve as a guide:

Advertising Federation of America. Bureau of Research and Education. *Books for the Advertising and Marketing Man.* Rev. ed. New York, Advertising Federation of America, 1957. Supplement, 1958.

    The advertising and related fields are covered very thoroughly. The very detailed classification is an aid to the specialist in locating what has been published in his own lines. An author index and a separate publishers' index provide easy reference to any work. No attempt is made to evaluate the works included.

Advertising Research Foundation Inc. *Bibliography of Theory and Research Techniques in the Field of Human Motivation.* New York, Advertising Research Foundation, Inc., 1956.

    A very thorough coverage of books and periodicals dealing with what induces human beings to act.

Barton, R. ed. *Advertising Handbook.* Englewood Cliffs, N.J., Prentice-Hall, 1950.

    The operation of the advertising department, how to select, evaluate, and utilize various media and how to organize an advertising campaign are some of the most useful features of this book. Suggestions as to how to check upon the costs of advertising are useful. Ready reference to material on layout of the advertising department and a glossary of advertising terms are additional features of this handbook.

Caples, J. *Tested Advertising Methods.* Rev. ed. New York, Harper, 1961.

    Thirty years of successful advertising experience have been distilled into this book. The essentials of advertising are discussed along with the "do's" and "don'ts" of advertising. Tests are described for headline writing, evaluating advertising, and getting the right appeal. This is a very practical book.

Sandage, C. H. *Advertising Theory and Practice.* 5th ed. Homewood, Ill., Irwin, 1958.

    Built on the excellent presentation of the subject in earlier editions, this book has been thoroughly updated. The author takes cognizance of the part of advertising in market research, the greater need for research in consumer behavior, the building of brand images, the impact of television and radio's changing structure. These features are in addition to chapters on methods of testing the effectiveness of advertising, and the practical section on writing and placement of advertising. Finally, the author deals with the general principles for the organization and operation of advertising departments and agencies. References at the end of each chapter permit the reader to pursue his study more fully.

Brown, L. O., Lessler, R. S. and Weilbacher, W. M. *Advertising Media.* New York, Ronald, 1957.

The selection, evaluation, and utilization of advertising media are the major objectives of this book. It is written for the businessman whose work involves the use of advertising media, the media specialist, and the college student. This is an unusually detailed study.

Another good book on advertising is H. W. Hepner, *Modern Advertising Practice and Principles,* 3d ed., New York, McGraw-Hill, 1956.

Both the advertiser and the advertising man are interested in the coverage and rates of various advertising media. The following publications are the accepted sources for this information:

N. W. Ayer & Son's Directory of Newspapers and Periodicals. Philadelphia, N. W. Ayer & Son. Annually.

A very complete compilation of newspapers published in the United States, Canada, Newfoundland, Bermuda, and the West Indies. The arrangement is alphabetical under each state and city. Frequency of publication, special feature, circulation, size of page and column width, subscription price, politics, and names of the editor and publisher are given. Farm, religious, trade and technical publications, both monthly and weekly, are in separate lists. Many good state maps are reproduced along with information on each city's location, transportation, banking, and manufacturing facilities. No one connected with advertising should be without this book.

Standard Rate and Data Service. Monthly. Chicago, Ill., Standard Rate and Data Service, Inc.

This service, published in four sections, is the best source on rates and advertising facilities. The sections are (1) newspapers, (2) business papers, (3) magazines, farm publications, religious papers, and transportation advertising, and (4) radio advertising rates and data. Rates for various types of advertising, as well as contract, copy and mechanical requirements, and discounts are supplied. Population figures, names of officers who are concerned with advertising, and advertising representatives for each kind of advertising complete the features of this service.

Radio News Bureau. *Television Factbook.* Washington, D.C., Radio News Bureau. Semiannually with weekly addenda supplements.

The very complete coverage of this publication covers a directory of TV stations, rate digests, sales and transfers of stations, ownership, program sources, NARTB-TV Code of Practices, new station and channel applications, manufacturing directory, trade statistics, and market data. This is a very complete source of information on the TV industry.

National Register Publishing Company, Inc. *Standard Advertising Register*. New York, National Register Publishing Company, Inc. Annually with monthly supplements.

Information is supplied on 14,000 national advertisers as to the names of the personnel in their advertising departments, the agency handling the account, media used, and products advertised. Similar data are supplied on advertising agencies. This information is also available in a geographical edition and a product edition.

Two directories, one of which cover somewhat the same ground as the above, are useful to those in the business of advertising. These are:

McKittrick Directory of Advertisers. New York, George McKittrick & Company. Annually.

Listed under a subject breakdown are the name and address of the company, type of business, officers (including the advertising manager), the agency handling the account, and the media used. A trade name index and an alphabetical index is included.

B. Klein and Company. *Guide to American Directories for Company Mailing Lists*. New York, B. Klein and Company, 1960.

Twenty-three hundred sources of up-to-date mailing lists are supplied. Specific types of business, industries and professions are listed along with state, county, city, and foreign directories.

No student of advertising can ignore the excellent studies that appear in *Sales Management,* especially in the "Survey of Buying Power" issue. Other periodicals which keep the advertising man supplied with current information are the following:

Printers' Ink. Weekly. New York, Printers' Ink Publishing Company.

The "National Advertising Index" is a regular feature of *Printers' Ink*. Studies and statistics on sales and advertising appear regularly. Longer articles on sales management, advertising campaigns, and the development of advertising techniques are supplemented by short accounts of what is doing in advertising and among advertising personalities. One of the oldest and most factual periodicals in the field.

Advertising Age. Weekly. Chicago, Ill., Advertising Publications, Inc.

A few long articles on marketing and advertising are interspersed with scores of short news items on all phases of advertising and selling.

Journal of Advertising Research. Quarterly. New York, Advertising Research Foundation.

Results of objective and impartial research on all phases of advertising are published in this journal. It also carries the results of tests and methods to measure the effectiveness of advertising and supports efforts to establish research standards.

In addition to the sources mentioned in this chapter, it is often helpful to contact the proper trade association for additional data.

CHECKLIST FOR MARKETING, SALES MANAGEMENT AND ADVERTISING SOURCES

ADVERTISING

Advertising Federation of American Bureau of Research and Education. *Books for the Advertising and Marketing Man.* Rev. ed. New York, Advertising Federation of America, 1957. Supplement 1958.

Advertising Research Foundation, Inc. *Bibliography of Theory and Research Techniques in the Field of Human Motivation.* New York, Advertising Research Foundation, Inc., 1956.

Barton, R. *Advertising Handbook.* Englewood Cliffs, N.J., Prentice-Hall, 1950.

Brown, L. O., Lessler, R. S. and Weilbacher, W. M. *Advertising Media.* New York, Harper, 1961.

Hepner, H. W. *Modern Advertising. Practice and Principles.* 3d ed. New York, McGraw-Hill, 1956.

Sandage, C. H. *Advertising Theory and Practice.* 5th ed. Homewood, Ill., Irwin, 1958.

ADVERTISING—PERIODICALS

Advertising Age. Weekly. Chicago, Ill., Advertising Publications, Inc.

Journal of Advertising Research. Quarterly. New York, Advertising Research Foundation.

Printers' Ink. Weekly. New York, Printers' Ink Publishing Company.

ADVERTISING—SOURCES OF INFORMATION

N. W. Ayer & Son's Directory of Newspapers and Periodicals. Philadelphia, N. W. Ayers & Son. Annually.

B. Klein and Company. *Guide to American Directories for Company Mailing Lists.* New York, B. Klein and Company, 1960.

McKittrick Directory of Advertisers. New York, George McKittrick & Company. Annually.

National Register Publishing Company, Inc. *Standard Advertising Register.* New York, National Register Publishing Company, Inc. Annually with monthly supplements.

Radio News Bureau. *Television Factbook*. Washington, D.C., Radio News Bureau. Semiannually with weekly addenda supplements.

Standard Rate and Data Service. Monthly. Chicago, Ill., Standard Rate and Data Service.

MARKETING RESEARCH

Boyd, H. W. and Westfall, R. *Marketing Research*. Homewood, Ill., Irwin, 1956.

Brown, L. O. *Marketing and Distribution Research*. 3d ed. New York, Ronald, 1955.

Lorie, J. H. and Robert, H. L. *Basic Methods of Marketing Research*. New York, McGraw-Hill, 1951.

Luck, D. C. and Wales, H. G. *Marketing Research*. Englewood Cliffs, N.J., Prentice-Hall, 1952.

Newman, J. W. *Motivation Research and Marketing Management*. Cambridge, Mass., Harvard University Division of Research, 1957.

MARKET RESEARCH SOURCES

Bradford, E. S. ed. *Directory of Market Research Agencies in the United States and the World*. New Rochelle, New York, 50 Argyle St. The Editor. Biennially.

Carpenter R. N. *Guide List for Marketing Research and Economic Forecasting*. New York, American Management Association, 1961.

Clarke, G. T. *Advertising and Marketing Theses for the Doctorate in United States Colleges and Universities*. New York, Advertising Educational Foundation, 1961.

Market Research Society. *Statistical Sources for Market Research*. London, Market Research Society, 1957.

U.S. Department of Commerce. *State and Regional Market Indicators, 1939–1945*. (Economic Series, No. 60.) Washington, D.C., Government Printing Office, 1947.

Wales, H. G. and Ferber, R. A. *A Basic Bibliography on Marketing Research*. Chicago, American Marketing Association, 1956.

MARKETING—GENERAL AND PRINCIPLES

American Marketing Association. Committee on Definitions. *Marketing Definitions; A Glossary of Marketing Terms*. Chicago, American Marketing Association, 1960.

Beckman, T. N. *Marketing*. 7th ed. New York, Ronald, 1962.

Converse, P. D., Huegy, H. W. and Mitchell, R. *Elements of Marketing*. 6th ed. Englewood Cliffs, N.J., Prentice-Hall, 1958.

Corey, E. R. *Development of Markets for New Products*. Cambridge Mass., Harvard University, Division of Research, 1956.

McCarthy, E. J. *Basic Marketing*. Homewood, Ill., Irwin, 1960.

Nystrom, P. H. ed. *Marketing Handbook.* New York, Ronald, 1948.
Phillips, C. F. and Duncan, D. J. *Marketing Principles and Methods.* 3d ed. Homewood, Ill., Irwin, 1960.

MARKETING—PERIODICALS

Business Week. Weekly. New York, McGraw-Hill.
Dun's Review and Modern Industry. Monthly. New York, Dun & Bradstreet, Inc.
The Journal of Business. Quarterly. Chicago, Ill., University of Chicago.
The Journal of Marketing. Quarterly. Menasha, Wis., American Marketing Association.

MARKETING SERVICES

Commerce Clearing House Food Drug Cosmetic Law Reports. Chicago, Commerce Clearing House, Inc. 2 vols. with frequent supplements.
Commerce Clearing House Regulation Reports. Chicago, Commerce Clearing House, Inc. 4 vols. with current issues.
Prentice-Hall Trade Regulation Edition of the Labor Guide. New York, Prentice-Hall, Inc. 1 vol. with biweekly supplements.

MARKETING SOURCES

Distribution Data Guide. Monthly. Washington, D.C., U.S. Office of Distribution, Business and Defense Services Administration.
Gunther, E. and Goldstein, F. A. *Current Sources of Marketing Information.* (American Marketing Association Bibliography Series, No. 6.) Chicago, American Marketing Association, 1960.
Marketing Information Guide. Monthly. Washington, D.C., U.S. Department of Commerce.
Marketing Review. Weekly. Toronto, Canada, Librex Ltd.
Rezvan, D. A. *A Comprehensive Classified Marketing Bibliography.* Berkeley, Calif., University of California Press, 1951. Parts I and II.
Sales Management. "Basic Sources in the Field of Sales and Advertising." Irregular.
U.S. Bureau of Foreign Domestic Commerce. *Market Research Sources, 1950. A Guide to Information on Domestic Marketing.* Prepared by Rachel Bretherton, Washington, D.C., Government Printing Office, 1950.

MARKETING—SPECIALIZED

Industrial Marketing Market Data Book. Chicago. Advertising Publications. Annually.
Phillips, C. F. *Marketing by Manufacturers.* Homewood, Ill., Irwin, 1948.
Shepherd, G. S. *Marketing Farm Products.* 3d ed. Ames, Iowa, Iowa State College, 1955.

Staudt, T. A. and Lazer, W. A. *A Basic Bibliography on Industrial Marketing.* (American Marketing Association Bibliography Series, No. 4.) Chicago, American Marketing Association, 1958.

MARKETING—SPECIALIZED, PERIODICAL

Industrial Marketing. Monthly. Chicago, Ill., Advertising Publications, Inc.

RETAILING

Chain Store Business Guide, Inc. *Chain Store Guides.* New York, Chain Store Business Guides, Inc. Annually.

Davidson, W. R. and Brown, P. L. *Retailing Management.* New York, Ronald, 1953.

Duncan, D. J. and Phillips, C. F. *Retailing Principles and Methods.* 5th ed. Homewood, Ill., Irwin, 1959.

Kelley, E. J. *Shopping Centers: Locating Controlled Regional Centers.* Saugatuck, Conn., The Enos Foundation, Inc., 1956.

National Research Bureau, Inc., Merchandising Division. *Directory of Shopping Centers in the United States and Canada.* 1963 ed. National Research Bureau Inc., 1962.

Supermarket Institute, Inc. *Index of Supermarket Articles, 1961.* Chicago, Supermarket Institute, 1962.

U.S. Bureau of Foreign and Domestic Commerce. *Guide to Government Information on Retailing,* by J. H. Rhoads. Washington, D.C., Government Printing Office, 1949.

Variety Store Merchandiser. *Directory of the Variety Market.* New York, Variety Store Merchandiser. Annually.

Wingate, I. B., Gillespie, K. R. and Addison, B. G. *Know Your Merchandise.* 3d ed. New York, McGraw-Hill, 1963.

Wingate, J. W. and Brisco, N. A. *Buying for Retail Stores.* 3d ed. Englewood Cliffs, N.J., Prentice-Hall, 1953.

Wingate, J. W. and Schaller, E. D. *Techniques of Retail Merchandising.* 2d ed. Englewood Cliffs, N.J., Prentice-Hall, 1950.

RETAILING PERIODICALS

Bulletin of the National Retail Merchants' Association. Monthly. New York, National Retail Merchants Association.

Chain Store Age. Monthly. New York, Chain Store Age.

Department Store Economist. Monthly. Philadelphia, Pa., Chilton Publications.

Distribution Age. Monthly. Philadelphia, Pa., Chilton Publications.

Journal of Retailing. Quarterly. New York, New York University School of Retailing.

Supermarket News. Weekly. New York, Fairchild Publishing Company.

Variety Store Merchandiser. Monthly. New York, Merchandiser Publishing Company.

SALES MANAGEMENT

Aspley, J. C., ed. *The Sales Managers' Handbook*. 8th ed. Chicago, Dartnell
  Corporation, 1959.
—— *The Sales Promotion Handbook*. Chicago, Dartnell Corporation, 1954.
Canfield, B. R. *Sales Administration, Principles and Practices*. 4th ed. Englewood
  Cliffs, N.J., Prentice-Hall, 1961.
Maynard, H. H. and Davis, J. H. *Sales Management*. 3d ed. New York, Ronald,
  1957.
National Sales Executives, Inc. *Sources of Information for Sales Executives and
  Specialists in Marketing*. Rev. ed. New York, National Sales Executives, Inc.,
  1954.
Sales Management. "Basic Sources in the Field of Sales and Advertising." Appears
  irregularly.

SALES MANAGEMENT—PERIODICALS

Printers' Ink. Weekly. New York, Printers' Ink Publishing Company.
Sales Management. Semimonthly. New York, Sales Management, Inc.
Scan. Monthly. Chicago, Ill., Advertising Checking Bureau.

STATISTICS

Dun's Review and Modern Industry. Monthly. New York, Dun & Bradstreet, Inc.
Federal Reserve Bulletin. Monthly. Washington, D.C., Board of Governors of the
  Federal Reserve System.
Industrial Marketing Market Data Book. Chicago, Advertising Publications. An-
  nually.
National Retail Merchants Association. Controllers Congress. *Departmental Mer-
  chandising and Operating Results of Departmentalized Stores*. New York,
  National Retail Merchants Association. Annually.
National Retail Merchants Association. Controllers Congress. *Operating Results
  of Departments and Specialty Stores*. New York, National Retail Merchants
  Association. Annually.
Printers' Ink. Weekly. New York, Printers' Ink Publishing Company.
Sales Management Survey of Buying Power. New York, Sales Management. An-
  nually.
Survey of Current Business. Monthly. Washington, D.C., U.S. Office of Business
  Economics.
U.S. Bureau of the Census. *Census of Business*. Vol. I—*Retail Trade;* Vol. II—
  Wholesale Trade; Vol. III—*Service Businesses;* Vol. IV—*Construction;* Vol.
  V—*Distribution of Manufacturers;* Vol. VI—*Selected Service Areas*. Washington,
  D.C., Government Printing Office, 1958.

U.S. Bureau of the Census. *Monthly Retail Trade Report*. Monthly. Washington, D.C., U.S. Bureau of the Census.

—— *Monthly Retail Trade Report: Independent Retail Stores*. Monthly. Washington, D.C., U.S. Bureau of the Census.

—— *Monthly Wholesale Trade Report: Sales and Inventories*. Monthly. Washington, D.C., U.S. Bureau of the Census.

—— *Sales of Retail Chain Stores and Mail Order Houses*. Monthly. Washington, D.C., U.S. Bureau of the Census.

—— *Statistical Abstract of the United States*. Washington, D.C., Government Printing Office. Annually.

Associations—Advertising

Advertising Educational Foundation, 655 Madison Avenue, New York 21, N.Y.

Advertising Federation of America, 250 West 57th Street, New York 19, N.Y.

Advertising Research Foundation, 3 East 54th Street, New York 22, N.Y.

American Association of Advertising Agencies, 420 Lexington Avenue, New York, N.Y.

Association of Industrial Advertisers, 271 Madison Avenue, New York 6, N.Y.

Association of National Advertisers, 155 East 57th Street, New York 17, N.Y.

Audit Bureau of Circulations, 123 North Worker Drive, Chicago 6, Ill.

Direct Mail Advertising Association, 3 East 57th Street, New York 22, N.Y.

International Advertising Association, Hotel Roosevelt, New York 17, N.Y.

Mail Advertising Service International, 18120 James Couzens Highway, Detroit 35, Mich.

Outdoor Advertising Association of America, 24 West Erie Street, Chicago 10, Ill.

Premium Advertising Association of America, 527 Lexington Avenue, New York 17, N.Y.

Radio Advertising Bureau, 460 Park Avenue, New York 2, N.Y.

Television Bureau of Advertising, 1 Rockefeller Center, New York 22, N.Y.

Associations—Marketing and Selling

American Institute of Coöperation, 1616 H. Street, N.W., Washington, D.C.

American Institute of Food Distribution, 420 Lexington Avenue, New York 17, N.Y.

American Marketing Association, 27 East Monroe Street, Chicago 3, Ill.

Institute of Distribution, 1441 Broadway, New York 18, N.Y.

National Association of Marketing Officials, 342 North State Capitol, Madison 2, Wis.

National Association of Purchasing Agents, 11 Park Place, New York 7, N.Y.

National Association of Retail Druggists, 205 West Worker Drive, Chicago 6, Ill.

National Association of Retail Grocers, 360 North Michigan Avenue, Chicago 1, Ill.

National Association of Textile and Apparel Wholesalers, 10 East 40th Street,
    New York 16, N.Y.
National Retail Merchants Association, 100 West 31st Street, New York 1, N.Y.
National Sales Executives, 135 East 57th Street, New York 22, N.Y.
National Wholesale Druggists Association, 60 East 42d Street, New York 17, N.Y.
Supermarket Institute, 500 North Dearborn Street, Chicago 10, Ill.

13

PUBLIC RELATIONS

Public relations, in a sense, are an outgrowth of the advertising department. However, the director of public relations has as his objectives the projection of a favorable image of the company and its officials to the community, the trade, and the employees, and to advise the officers of the company in order to forestall actions which will bring unfavorable reactions in these areas. The bigness of corporations with tens of thousands of employees has both a large impact on the community and at the same time isolates the corporation from the community. This poses a problem of communication with both the community and the employees.

The public relations department must be alert to many facets of the company's activities. It must work closely with top management in order to be abreast of company policy. The sales department should keep public relations informed of new products and new sales and advertising campaigns and should coöperate with the personnel department in a two-way exchange of information.

It is only in recent years that the public relations department has assumed an identity separate from the advertising department. Not only does this department stand distinct but there is an increasing recognition of the important contributions it can make to the successful operation of the company.

There are two handbooks which provide the public relations staff

with practical guides to the operation of the department and its operations.
These are:

Aspley, J. C. and Van Houten, L. L. eds. *The Dartnell Public Relations Handbook*.
    3d ed. Chicago, Dartnell Corporation, 1961.
    The editors' approach is practical and to the point. They supply suggestions
    on all phases of public relations activities which include policy and strategy,
    organization of the department, and coördination with other departments.
    This is followed by descriptions and suggestions as to all kinds of publicity
    devices, and how to work with groups. These latter include relations with the
    community, employees families, the press, and with government. The many
    helpful approaches suggested are illustrated by descriptions of successful cam-
    paigns for better understanding. The handbook ends with a description of
    equipment and budget needed for the department and methods of evaluating
    public relations activities.
Stephenson, H. *Handbook of Public Relations*. New York, McGraw-Hill, 1960.
    This handbook differs from the preceding in that it deals less with theory
    and policies by moving directly in relations with various groups. Separate
    chapters deal with relations with the community, trade and professional associ-
    ations, and other areas and groups upon which company operations may
    impinge. Methods and media of public relations are discussed fully. The last
    chapter contains a code of ethics for the public relations fraternity.

Public relations personnel often do not appear in directories of company officials and their own "Who's Who" is useful in locating these
individuals.

Who's Who in Public Relations, 1961–1962. Meriden, N.H., Public Relations Publi-
    cations, Inc., 1962.
    The usual who's who arrangement with name and address of the indi-
    vidual and his company affiliation plus a brief description of his education,
    work experience, and hobbies. The coverage is world-wide.

The pioneer text on public relations is:

Harlow, R. F. and Black, M. M. *Practical Public Relations*. New York, Harper, 1952.
    The practical aspect of public relations is emphasized throughout this
    book. The authors bring home to the reader that there is no magic formula
    for a successful public relations operation. A carefully worked out program
    must be developed, and this must be followed over a period of time. The
    objectives to be achieved must be kept clearly in mind, and consideration must
    be given to the reactions of the groups which are to be influenced.
Bernays, E. L. ed. *Engineering of Consent*. Norman, Okla., University of Oklahoma
    Press, 1955.
    Edited by one of the pioneers in public relations, the authors stress the

adherence to a well-thought-out plan. Objectives must be kept in mind and the public relations campaign move toward them step by step. There is an excellent chapter on strategies to be employed in various situations. Many themes and symbols are suggested to appeal to various human motivations. This book contains much of the philosophy of public relations.

Two other books on this subject are, Cutlip, S. M. and Center, A. H., *Effective Public Relations,* 2d ed., Englewood Cliffs, N.J., Prentice-Hall, 1958 and Bristol, L. A., ed. *Developing the Corporate Image,* New York, Scribner's, 1960.

Since psychology plays an important part in public relations the following work will be useful to the public relations personnel:

Beach, L. R. and Clark, E. L. *Psychology in Business.* New York, McGraw-Hill, 1959.
    The three-pronged approach of the authors covers the psychological background which is basic for relations with customers, with company personnel, and to project the image of the product.

As corporations grow larger and tend to decentralize, the impact on the community becomes greater and more apparent. H. R. Bowen has pointed up these effects for the public relations man and the businessman in general in:

Bowen, H. R. *Social Responsibilities of the Businessman.* New York, Harper, 1953.
    By pointing out the effects of the business activities of large corporations on the community and the individual, the author highlights the ethical and moral problems involved. This is a book which should provoke thought on the part of the businessman.

Three books cover various aspects of the activities which frequently are part of the duties of the public relations staff. These are:

Hodges, W. *The Company and the Community.* New York, Harper, 1959.
    Largely through case studies one can gain ideas as to various ways in which a company can improve its relationships with the community. There are a number of practical and helpful suggestions given.
Held, W. J. *The Technique for Proper Giving.* New York, McGraw-Hill, 1959.
    Large corporations are considered a fair target for all sorts of fund-raising activities. The matter of giving becomes complicated when a firm's plants are spread across the country. This book outlines how the company can give on a basis which is fair both to the community and itself. By so doing and explaining its policy fully, giving can make a contribution to a successful public relations program.

Peel, J. D. *Anniversary Celebrations Made Easy.* New York, Chilton, 1959.
> Anniversary celebrations can be a source of cementing relations with the community and the employees. However, if carelessly planned and not carefully carried out, an anniversary celebration can be damaging to a company's relations. This is a sourcebook of public relations ideas for company anniversaries and the machinery to put them in action.

As yet there have not been periodicals published exclusively in the field of public relations. This may be because so many of the management personnel, sales, and general business journals frequently carry articles on public relations. There are two magazines given over to public relations and these are:

Public Relations Journal. Monthly. New York, Public Relations Society of America.
> The broad aspects and policies of publications are discussed along with problems and suggestions as to their solutions. These are illustrated by actual cases.

Public Relations News. Weekly. New York, Griswold News Service.
> Short articles on happenings in the world of public relations and news of people active in the field comprise the bulk of this publication.

CHECKLIST OF PUBLIC RELATIONS SOURCES

Aspley, J. C. and Van Houten, L. L. eds. *The Dartnell Public Relations Handbook.* 3d ed. Chicago, Dartnell Corporation, 1961.

Beach, L. R. and Clark, E. L. *Psychology in Business.* New York, McGraw-Hill, 1959.

Bernays, E. L. ed. *Engineering of Consent.* Norman, Okla., University of Oklahoma Press, 1955.

Bowen, H. R. *The Social Responsibilities of the Businessman.* New York, Harper, 1953.

Bristol, L. H. ed. *Developing the Corporate Image.* New York, Scribner's, 1960.

Cutlip, S. M. and Center, A. H. *Effective Public Relations.* 2d ed. Englewood Cliffs, N.J., Prentice-Hall, 1958.

Cutlip, S. M., comp. *Public Relations Bibliography, Reference and Film Guide.* Madison, Wis., University of Wisconsin Press, 1957.

Harlow, R. F. and Block, M. M. *Practical Public Relations.* New York, Harper, 1952.

Held, W. J. *The Technique for Proper Giving.* New York, McGraw-Hill, 1959.

Hodges, W. *The Company and the Community.* New York, Harper, 1959.

Lerley, P., ed. *Handbook of Public Relations.* 2d ed. Englewood Cliffs, N.J., Prentice-Hall, 1960.

Melander, W. A. *Selected and Annotated Bibliography of Public Relations.* Rev. ed.
    Austin, Texas, University of Texas, Bureau of Business Research, 1961.
Peel, J. D. *Anniversary Celebrations Made Easy.* New York, Chilton, 1959.
Stephenson, H. *Handbook of Public Relations.* New York, McGraw-Hill, 1960.
Who's Who in Public Relations, 1961–1962. Meriden, N.H., Public Relations Publi-
    cations, Inc., 1962.

PERIODICALS

Public Relations Journal. Monthly. New York, Public Relations Society of America.
Public Relations News. Weekly. New York, Griswold News Service.

ASSOCIATION

Public Relations Society of America, 375 Park Avenue, New York 22, N.Y.

14

BASIC INDUSTRIES

As business has become increasingly competitive, a manufacturer needs to know the following types of information; (1) statistics of his own particular industry, (2) sources of equipment and supplies, (3) prices, (4) new developments, and (5) general conditions within his particular field of activity. He will acquire much of this information from day-to-day operations, but if a new line is to be manufactured, a different process is to be utilized, or the type of raw material radically changed, he will need to consult sources of specialized information.

Businessmen must be conversant with the price and inventory situation within their own industries, particularly in times of rapid change. Substitute products and competition between units and products of the same industry must be watched carefully. For example, a manufacturer may find that he can substitute aluminum for copper, thereby materially speeding up production, cutting costs, and retaining his markets. However, before making the switch he must weigh the costs of a change-over in methods and equipment as well as analyze the sources of supply, the adequacy of the raw materials supply, price trends, and demands.

Two recent publications by the Special Libraries Association are helpful in locating factual material. Of these, Special Libraries Association, *Guide to Special Issues and Indexes of Periodicals*. New York, Special Libraries Association, 1962, has been described in Chapter 5 but will be mentioned again here as a handy tool for locating statistics and specialized data in the trade press. The other work is somewhat more specialized:

Wasserman, Paul, comp. *Sources of Commodity Prices.* New York, Special Libraries Association, 1959.
> This painstaking work attempts to cover all the sources of commodity prices on the U.S. national market and the local markets as well. Some world-wide and international sources are included. The periodicals listed are those which provide regular or seasonal price information.

A very complete retroactive study of commodity prices can be found in Potter and Christy:

Potter, N. and Christy, F. T. J. *Trends in Natural Resource Commodities.* Baltimore, Published for the Resources for the Future by the Johns Hopkins Press, 1962.
> Tables of statistics from 1870 to 1957 provide data on price, output, consumption, employment in relation to the national products of the United States. Statistics have been gathered from a number of sources and converted to a common base. The highlights of the data are given in 324 tables which are summarized in the concluding chapter.

The annual *Industrial Marketing, Market Data Book Number,* published in Chicago by Advertising Publications, includes statistics of varying degrees of up-to-dateness. However, the trade magazines, associations, directories, and trade catalogs listed supply additional statistical and technical information. The coverage of both statistics and magazines is not complete, but it does have the benefit of annual revisions.

The publication which has the greatest amount of current statistical data on consumption, sales, inventories, and, to a lesser extent, prices, is the *Survey of Current Business,* issued each month by the U.S. Bureau of Foreign and Domestic Commerce. The statistics for the preceding year are cumulated in the February number. Similar statistical data cumulated over a period of years is supplied by the U.S. Bureau of Census, *Statistical Abstract of the United States,* Washington, D.C., Government Printing Office, 1879-. The value of this work to the manufacturer is its indication of trends—both in output and prices over a long period, thus providing some knowledge of supply sources and competition in specific geographic areas for various types of manufacturing. Because the statistics cover war and postwar periods, the manufacturer gains some insight into the future of his industry.

Another publication of the Bureau of the Census is the *Current Industry Reports:*

Current Industry Reports. Frequency varies, some are monthly, others quarterly or annually. Washington, D.C., U.S. Bureau of the Census.

These reports continue the *Facts for Industry* series. Statistics on sales, current production, shipments, inventories, and other business activity indicators are given for seventy-nine commodities. Brief comments add further information.

The U.S. Business and Defense Services Administration in its *Industry Reports* provides somewhat more detailed information on selected industries. These reports give a brief résumé of the industry, short accounts of developments in the industry at home and abroad, and statistics on production, consumption, products, and trade. The following industries are covered by the indicated titles:

Industry Reports—Chemical and Rubber. Monthly.
Industry Reports—Containers and Packaging. Quarterly.
Industry Reports—Copper. Quarterly.
Motor Truck Production Report. Monthly.
Pulp, Paper and Board. Quarterly.

The raw materials of commerce and industry are described, and figures on production, consumption, and prices are given for a wide variety of products in the following publication.

Commodity Year Book. New York, Commodity Research Bureau, Inc., 1948–.

The commodities of commerce are briefly described as are the areas of production. Points covered are the physical characteristics of the commodity, methods of production, principal uses, marketing methods, comparative recent prices, and principal types and grades. In a number of instances price trends over many years are given. Special features include "The Commodity Price Trend," "Commodity Spreads and Straddles," "The Long Term Outlook for Petroleum," "Weights and Measures," and, "Conversion Factors." A good quick reference for data on commodities.

Daily prices on a large number of commodities are available in the *Journal of Commerce,* Journal of Commerce Corporation, New York, N.Y. Daily quotations on ferrous and nonferrous metals can be obtained from *American Metal Market* published by American Metal Market, New York, N.Y. Statistics on prices, consumption, production, and stocks have been published annually in *Metal Statistics,* New York, American

Metal Market. These statistics are carried back for varying periods of years but show monthly averages of prices and annual production for the past ten years.

The leading trade journals usually carry statistics, including price quotations of raw and semifinished commodoties utilized by the industries they serve. New developments, new processes and equipment, directories of suppliers, and discussion of trends in a given industry comprise the bulk of the information supplied by trade periodicals. Many of the better journals issue annual review numbers in which the news and statistics for the past year are cumulated.

The Special Libraries Association, *Guide to Special Issues and Indexes of Periodicals,* New York, Special Libraries Association, 1962 and Paul Wasserman, compiler, *Sources of Commodity Prices,* New York, Special Libraries Association, 1959 make it easy to locate trade publications in a particular line of business. The annual publication, *Industrial Marketing, Market Data Book Number,* Advertising Publications, Chicago, provides a current listing of trade magazines. The *Business Periodicals Index* and *Applied Science and Technology Index* and the *Public Affairs Information Service Bulletin* also help the individual to locate a particular article in a trade publication. As a rule, these latter three indexes do not indicate statistical material or price quotations.

To recapitulate briefly; the first place to consult in a search for current statistics and prices is the *Survey of Current Business.* Should this prove unproductive, check both the current and annual review numbers of the leading trade journals in the industry under review. The appropriate journals can best be located by consulting the references previously cited.

Two other publications, though concerned chiefly with the financial aspects of industry, contain much information on the current status and immediate future of particular industries. For the manufacturer, the data on the state of industries, price structure, the market, and general financial conditions within the industry are the most useful. These two publications are: *Standard and Poor's Industry Surveys,* Standard and Poor's Corporation, New York, and *Moody's Investors Service, Manuals of Security Rating, Industrial Securities,* Moody's Investors Service, New York.

In addition to his knowledge of prices, sources of raw materials, and the general status of the industry, the manufacturer may need to know who makes what and where. Such facts are essential when locating equipment makers for his own plant, investigating the competitive strength of a rival plant, or developing sales prospects for his own products.

An excellent up-to-date list of directories is Chamber of Commerce of the U.S., *Guide to Listings of Manufacturers,* Washington, D.C., Chamber of Commerce of the U.S., 1961. Not only are the usual commercial directories covered and those dealing with specific industries, but also annual directories published by periodicals.

The *Industrial Marketing, Market Data Book Number,* Advertising Publications, Chicago, contains a list of directories and trade catalogs published in the preceding year. Directories are also included in the *Public Affairs Information Service, Annual Cumulative Bulletin,* Public Affairs Information Service, New York, N.Y.

Other general directories helpful in locating manufacturers of a wide range of products are:

Thomas' Register of American Manufacturers. Annually. New York, Thomas Publishing Co.

 In section one, manufacturers are classified under kind of product. The products are listed alphabetically, and under each product the names of the manufacturers are arranged by states. Street address and capital rating are given. A second alphabetical listing by company indicates the product manufactured. Trade names appear in a third section.

MacRae's Blue Book and Hendrick's Commercial Register. Annually. Chicago, MacRae's Blue Book Company.

 Manufacturers and products are listed by product and alphabetically. In many instances, distributors are included under the manufacturer's name.

Kelly's Directory of Merchants, Manufacturers and Shippers. Annually. London, Kelly's Directory, Ltd.

 The British Isles are covered comprehensively in four sections. These are followed by a section on British Commonwealth Overseas and a final section on the other countries of the world. The information supplied is the name, type of business, and address. There are indexes to towns and countries, trades, and importers and exporters. The fore-edge index to sections is an interesting feature.

The manufacturer, purchasing agent, engineer, or executive who wants to secure basic data quickly on any kind of industrial material can locate it in:

Brady, G. S. *Materials Handbook*. 8th ed. New York, McGraw-Hill, 1956.

    This work contains brief data on hundreds of materials. The material is
defined, its uses catalogued, where it is obtained, the trade names under which
it is produced, and the manufacturers or suppliers. The second part has useful
tables and definition of terms, data on location of natural products, and
government agencies concerned with the technical aspects of materials.

Many trade publications and, in some instances trade associations,
publish yearbooks or annual review numbers. These works vary in content, but almost all supply the names and addresses of manufacturers
within the industry. Usually the suppliers of raw materials and equipment and, quite frequently, the jobbers who handle the finished product
are also given. The better type of yearbook includes descriptions and
catalogs of equipment specifications for products and processes, and
statistical information on the industry. Trade journals or association an-
nuals are sometimes the only source for the names of the executives of
the smaller firms.

Two widely used general catalogs which list all types of general
equipment—valves, boilers, and other more or less standard devices used
in all types of manufacturing plants—are described below:

Mechanical Catalog. New York, The American Society of Mechanical Engineers.
Annually.

    Mechanical equipment is arranged under headings classified as to type.
Each item is described, illustrated, and in many instances, dimensions and
specifications are given. A second section contains a directory of manufacturers.

Sweet's Catalog Service. *Sweet's Catalog File*. New York, Sweet's Catalog Divison
of F. W. Dodge Corp. Annually.

    This service consists of six separately bound files of manufacturers' cata-
logs. Though designed primarily for industrial engineers and contractors, the
information provided is useful to manufacturers who desire to locate sources
of mechanical equipment.

Prices are not given in these catalogs, therefore quotations must be
obtained direct from the manufacturer or his local agent.

When a new process or type of machine is being developed, there
is always the problem of patent rights to be considered. The enormous
number of patents which have been issued make it impossible for the
individual to be certain that either he is adequately protected or that
he is not infringing on another's rights. Just as it is unwise for the
average individual to act as his own lawyer, so it is inadvisable for him

to be his own patent searcher. Putting the matter into the hands of a competent patent attorney is much wiser. The latter will arrange for a patent search and handle the purely legal aspects of the case. Local bar associations are prepared to supply the names of competent patent attorneys.

There are firms of patent searchers located in Washington, D.C., who may be employed to locate any patents that may possibly conflict with a proposed development. The use of a patent attorney and patent searching organization quickly runs into money, but it is far cheaper than to bring an invention through the costly stages of development and then be forced to fight a suit for infringement.

Any firm engaged in intensive research and development work may place a standing order with the United States Patent Office to receive notification of all patents in its special field. As this file accumulates, it reduces materially the necessity for paying for extensive searches.

In locating statistics and general trend data on an industry, it is always advisable to consult the rather general publications first. These furnish large amounts of information within the covers of one publication and tend to relate it to general conditions. A useful method of approach follows:

1. Refer to the *Survey of Current Business* and *Standard and Poor's Industry Surveys.*

2. Consult the annual review or statistical number of one of the leading trade publications or trade associations of the industry concerned.

3. Finally, to obtain the latest information on trends and price quotations, refer to the daily *Journal of Commerce* and the latest issue of the appropriate trade publication. The leading trade publications of the major industries are listed in this chapter, pages 243–268. A similar procedure should be followed when trying to locate firms and information on equipment.

1. Consult *Thomas Register of American Manufacturers,* The American Society of Mechanical Engineers' *Mechanical Catalog,* and *Sweets' Catalog File.*

2. If the information supplied is inadequate, then turn to catalogs and directories issued by trade associations and trade journal publishers.

Information on new methods and processes through the operation and development of new equipment and current news of the industry, usually may be found in the appropriate trade periodical. Much time can be saved if articles on the desired subject are first located through *Business Periodicals Index, Applied Science and Technology Index,* and *Public Affairs Information Service Bulletin* because these services give the exact issue and page of the article.

If no data on the subject can be found, an inquiry addressed to the appropriate trade association may turn up either the required data or clues to other information sources. The U.S. Business and Defense Services Administration, a part of the U.S. Department of Commerce, is preparing a new edition of the basic directory, *National Associations of the United States* which will provide data on some 4,000 Associations. In the meantime, the same section of the Department of Commerce has issued:

Directory of National Associations of Businessmen.
> Over 2,000 national associations are listed with name, address, year of founding, executive officer, number of members and number of staff.

The Gale Research Co. *Encyclopedia of American Associations,* Detroit, Michigan, The Gale Research Company, 1961, includes business associations along with almost every type of association imaginable.

A recent book which describes the broad outlines of the development of the economy is:

Kindelberger, C. P. *Economic Development.* New York, McGraw-Hill, 1958.
> The use and accumulation of capital, labor, technology, changes, methods of development, planning, foreign trade, population, and, interregional and international development, are discussed by the author. He compares the developed and underdeveloped countries.

Two books can be consulted for histories of the major industries in the United States.

Glover, J. G. and Cornell, W. B. *The Development of American Industries.* 3d ed. Englewood Cliffs, N.J., Prentice-Hall, 1959.
> Brief histories of the leading industries are given and a chapter is devoted to the work of trade associations. The coverage consists of early history, including discoveries and operations, growth of the industry and the leaders in its field; the geographic location of important industrial centers; raw materials used; manufacturing methods; important products, including their value, volume, chief uses and by-products; methods of marketing, both domestic and foreign; methods of financing and capital invested; labor—the number and

trades of people employed, health and safety conditions, etc.; internal organization of a typical company in the industry; and possible future developments.

Clarke, V. S. *History of Manufacturers in the United States.* New York, McGraw-
Hill, 1929. 3 vols.

This economic history of the manufacturing industry interprets in broad
outlines the development, the organization, and the economic interactions of
manufacturing industry activities in the United States from their feeble beginnings three centuries ago down to 1928.

In the remainder of this chapter, sources of information are given
on the following specific industries: building and building materials,
chemical process industries, coal, electrical equipment, food, lumber,
metal producing and working industries, paper, petroleum, rubber, shoe
and leather, and textile. Only the publications that cover the greatest
amount of information and statistics concerning a particular industry are
included. Many of the periodicals mentioned issue annual review numbers
which summarize activities of the preceding year and furnish a current
directory of equipment and materials suppliers.

BUILDERS AND BUILDING MATERIALS

Since World War II there has been an improvement in the statistical
information available on the building industry. The coverage is more
complete and there is more detailed information available.

The *Construction Review* published monthly by the U.S. Business
and Defense Services Administration brings together all governmental
statistics on construction. Regular features are "Construction at a Glance,"
"The Economy at a Glance," "Construction Comments," and one longer
article on some phase of construction. There are statistics on total construction, housing building permits issued, contracts and awards, costs
and prices of construction materials, and construction employment. The
statistics are on a monthly basis with five year annual averages or cumulations and there are price indexes for building materials and over-all costs.

The United States Housing and Home Finance Agency in its monthly
Housing Statistics publishes a large amount of material on residential
housing which includes the number of housing starts by states and areas
and much statistical data on financing.

The *Survey of Current Business* carries in each monthly issue the
dollar volume of construction awards, broken down by type of construc-

tion. It also publishes the leading indexes on building activity and costs as compiled by the Federal Reserve Board, the United States Department of Labor, Housing and Home Finance Agency, Federal Home Loan Bank Administration, Oberthaw, American Appraisal Company, Associated General Contractors, E. H. Boeckh and Associates, and the Engineering News Record. Number of building projects, floor area, and valuation statistics prepared by the F. W. Dodge Corporation and the *Engineering News Records* valuation of engineering construction awards also appear in the *Survey*. Additional information on building costs, mortgage lending, and total construction is published in the *Federal Home Loan Bank Review*. *The Monthly Labor Review* also supplies figures on construction and labor costs, wages in the building industry, and total construction by types.

Among the private statistical sources, the *Dodge Statistical Research Service*, published by the F. W. Dodge Corporation, is the most comprehensive. This service has been expanded to include the western states as well as the thirty-seven states east of the Rocky Mountains. Actual figures on the number of building projects, floor area of each, and valuation are subdivided into the following groups: residential, nonresidential, public works and utilities, private and public building, and types of building in eighty metropolitan areas. Subscribers receive service once a month; cumulative comparison with the corresponding period of preceding years is also provided. A *Daily Report* service is also available to subscribers which lists building and engineering projects. Except for data on heavy engineering awards, Dodge's service is the best for the areas it covers.

Engineering News Record provides the most complete data on heavy engineering contracts—highway, dam, reclamation, and public work projects. Information is also supplied on contracts to be awarded. The annual *Engineering News Record Construction Costs* provides an unusually good cumulation of data on all building costs. Monthly wage rates in twenty-six categories for sixty-five cities and nationwide averages, tabulated annually, carry these rates back to 1913. Very complete figures on material costs are included. Other data supplied are tables of special costs in various cities, financing costs, and the "Boeckh Construction Costs in Twenty-One Cities." The February issue of the *Engineering News Record* contains the "Annual Report and Forecast."

Other types of information on the building and construction industry can be located in the following publications:

Contractors Register. Annually. New York, Sub-Contractors Register, Inc.

This standard reference book, known in the trade as the "Blue Book" of the building industry, contains a classified list of general contractors, subcontractors, architects, engineers, material and equipment, dealers, and manufacturers. It covers individuals and firms located in New York, New Jersey, Connecticut, Philadelphia, Boston, Washington, D.C., and adjacent territories.

Domestic Engineering Catalog Directory and Air Conditioning Blue Book, 1960– 1961. Champaign, Ill., Domestic Engineering Co., 1961.

This volume includes: (1) An indexed compilation of manufacturers' catalogs, with product information in concise practical form; (2) a classified directory of every known industry product and every known manufacturer of the product; (3) a list of every known trade name (over 7,500) used in the plumbing, heating, refrigerating, insulating, and air conditioning industries, with the name of the manufacturer using the trade name; (4) the names and addresses of virtually every known manufacturer in the plumbing, heating, refrigerating, insulating, and air conditioning industries, listed alphabetically; and (5) basic technical information (hundreds of charts, tables, standard rules, layout diagram, and explanatory material) to aid the designers and installers of plumbing, heating, refrigerating, and air conditioning systems and accessories.

Heating, Ventilating and Air Conditioning Guide. Annually. New York, American Society of Heating and Air Conditioning Engineers, Inc.

Design and layout of heating, ventilating, and engineering systems are the major portion of this work. Description of equipment is also included.

Kelly, B. *Design and Production of Houses.* New York, McGraw-Hill, 1959.

This is a book useful to the contractor who is planning tract developments, but there is also information here for the small builder as well.

American Builder. Monthly. New York, Simmons-Boardman Publishing Corporation.

Three regional editions are published—New York, Midwest, and West Coast. Practical and technical illustrated articles on home building and light-load-bearing commercial construction are the principal topics of this publication.

Practical Builder. Monthly. Chicago, Ill., Industrial Publications, Inc.

Practical, instructive articles and ideas of value to the building contractor are presented. Regular features include a how-to-do-it department, buyers' directory, and building newsletter.

Architectural Forum. Monthly. New York, Time, Inc.

Contains complete building-industry news coverage, including the latest and most progressive ideas in design, product development, and construction techniques. Every phase of the building project, from conception to occupancy is covered—design, land development, engineering, construction, financing, merchandising, sales, and management.

Architectural Record. Monthly. New York, F. W. Dodge Corporation.

   The purpose of this professional and technical publication for the architect and construction engineer is to keep its readers informed on all important phases of the building industry.

Civil Engineering. Monthly. New York, The American Society of Civil Engineers.

   Complete news coverage and reporting on all activities of the civil engineering profession is provided by this magazine.

Progressive Architecture. Monthly. New York, Reinhold Publishing Corporation.

   This technical magazine is for the members of the architectural profession.

   Current and reference information on the industries that supply information on industries furnishing materials to the building trades, may be found in the periodicals listed below. The lumber and metals industry, also important suppliers to the construction industry, are mentioned separately, pages 259–260.

Sweet's File, Architectural. Rev. annually. New York, Compiled and distributed by Sweet's Catalog Service, a division of F. W. Dodge Corporation.

   A bound file of manufacturers' catalogs used as a source of buying information by important specifiers and buyers of building materials, equipment, and services.

Sweet's File for Builders. Rev. annually. New York, Sweet's Catalog Service, division of F. W. Dodge Corporation.

   A bound file of manufacturers' catalogs used as a source of buying information by builders of houses and light-construction units.

American Lumberman and Building Products Merchandiser. Fortnightly. Chicago, H. A. Vance.

   A nation-wide news roundup of the building industry and trade developments is featured in each issue. It is the advertising medium of the light-construction industry.

The Timberman. Monthly. Portland, Ore. The Timberman.

Ceramic Data Book. Annually. Chicago, Industrial Publications, Inc.

   This book contains catalogs on equipment and materials and a fairly comprehensive buyers' directory. A substantial amount of data on processes and equipment, design, etc., relative to the glass, enamel, pottery, refractories, and structural clay-products industries is also provided.

What's New in Building Products. Bimonthly. New York, Thomas Publishing Co.

   Essentially a product information service, this publication concentrates on new developments in, and applications of, products, materials, and equipment. Architects, builders, contractors, materials dealers, realtors, and engineers, are its most regular readers.

Building Supply News. Monthly. Chicago, Industrial Publications, Inc.

   The principal trade paper of the building materials trade. Each issue contains where-to-buy information about building supplies and materials; it is the advertising medium for dealers, wholesalers, jobbers, and building materials manufacturers. The annual *Dealers' Directory Issue* contains a most complete list of dealers' names and addresses of dealers together with the commodities they offer.

Stone. Monthly. Dobbs Ferry, New York, Stone Publishing Co.

A publication that seeks to promote better architecture and building construction through the use of natural stone, such as limestone, marble, sandstone, granite, and other materials of quarry and mine.

Pit and Quarry. Monthly. Chicago, Complete Service Publishing Co.

Trade news, articles and information for producers and manufacturers of cement, crushed stone, gypsum, lime, sand, gravel, and other nonmetallic minerals are furnished.

Pit and Quarry Handbook. Annually. Chicago, Complete Service Publishing Co.

A technical reference manual with twenty-four specialized sections for producers and manufacturers of cement, crushed stone, gypsum, lime, sand, gravel, and other nonmetallic minerals. Useful features are a Buyers' Guide Section, a Directory of the Industry (with classified index of all plants and executive personnel), an Equipment Index, and a Trade Names Index.

The Plasterers and Cement Mason. Monthly. Washington, D.C., Operative Plasterers and Cement Masons of the U.S. and Canada.

This journal is the official organ of the Operative Plasterers and Cement Masons of the U.S. and Canada. It carries news items about the trade and reports activities of the union.

Ceramic Age. Monthly. Cleveland, Ohio, Ceramics Publications, Inc.

This trade journal covers pottery, enamel, glass, refractories, structural clay products, and raw materials. It also includes news of the industry, technical data, trade notes, and where-to-buy section on materials and equipment.

Ceramic Industry. Monthly. Chicago, Ill., Industrial Publications, Inc.

News of the glass, enamel, and pottery industries is reported. Features include coverage of new developments, products, personnel, equipment, methods, and materials.

Brick and Clay Record. Monthly. Chicago, Ill., Industrial Publications, Inc.

This is the leading clay journal of the world. It contains news, information and articles about masonry building, refractories, brick, structural tile, sewer pipe, and drain-tile manufacturing industries.

Bricklayer, Mason and Plasterer. Monthly. Washington, D.C., Bricklayers, Masons, and Plasterers International Union of America.

This publication is the official trade journal of the Bricklayers, Masons, and Plasterers. International Union of America. Trade news and information about union activities are featured.

American Glass Review. Weekly. Pittsburgh, Commoner Publishing Company.

This is a news magazine that covers glass products production, activities of manufacturers, materials' supply, new patents, and products. Would-be purchasers advertise their needs for specific glass products in a special "Information Please" column. The personnel changes in various companies are noted, and announcements of manufacturers' and suppliers' new catalogs and bulletins are given.

Roofing Year Book, Buyers' Directory and Reference Manual. Chicago, Shelter Publications.

Purchasers of materials used in roofing, siding, waterproofing, and insulation work will find this manual a handy reference source.

United Roofer Magazine. Monthly. Chicago, United Roofing Contractors Association.

Feature articles in this publication deal with the manufacture, application, and sale of roofing and siding products and insulation. An information and research bureau for the benefit of its subscribers answers thousands of queries each year on the manufacture, distribution, sale, application, and estimating of roofing, siding, and insulation products.

Steel Construction Digest. Quarterly. New York, American Institute of Steel Construction.

All the news and goings-on in the steel construction industry are reported in this magazine.

Rock Products. Monthly. Chicago, MacLean-Hunter Publishing Corporation.

This publication is the rock products industry's recognized authority. It reports the latest news about the industry, new machinery developments, labor relations trends, operating problems, and results of association meetings in related fields.

Wood Construction and Building Materialist. Monthly. Xenia, Ohio, The Wood Construction Publishing Co., Inc.

News and information about building materials and the construction industry are reported by this magazine which covers America's richest building market every month.

The Carpenter. Monthly. Indianapolis, United Brotherhood of Carpenters and Joiners of America.

This publication, the official journal of the United Brotherhood of Carpenters and Joiners of America, contains news items about the trade and reports on union activities.

Domestic Engineering. Monthly. Chicago, Domestic Engineering Co.

News, articles, and information about plumbing and heating contractors, air conditioning, and materials and supplies are featured in this trade paper.

Fuel Oil and Oil Heat. Monthly. New York, Heating Publishers, Inc.

This magazine contains news, articles, and information about the oil heat, fuel oil, and air conditioning industries.

Heating, Piping and Air Conditioning. Monthly. Chicago, Keeney Publishing Co.

The design, installation, and maintenance of heating, piping, and air conditioning equipment make up the contents.

Air Conditioning, Heating and Refrigeration News. Weekly. Detroit, Mich., Air
Conditioning, Heating and Refrigeration News.

Sales and technical news of all phases of the industry are covered.

Master Plumber and Heating Contractor. Monthly. Brooklyn, N.Y. The Master
Plumber.

This trade paper contains general news and information about the plumbing, heating, and oil burner industries.

American Artisan. Monthly. Chicago, Keeney Publishing Co.

This trade journal deals with residential air conditioning, warm-air heating, and sheet-metal contracting.

BUILDING CONSTRUCTION ASSOCIATIONS

The American Institute of Architects, 1735 New York Ave., N.W., Washington,
6, D.C.

American Society of Heating and Air Conditioning Engineers, 62 Worth Street,
New York, N.Y.

Associated General Contractors of America, 20th and E. Street, N.W., Washington
6, D.C.

General Contractors Association, 341 Madison Avenue, New York 17, N.Y.

Each of the industries supplying building materials has its own association.

CHEMICAL PROCESS INDUSTRIES

Chemical Engineering. Monthly. New York, McGraw-Hill Publishing Co.

Each month the outlook for general business plus the trends affecting the
chemical industries is described. Figures on production, consumption, and
foreign markets are among the data supplied. The remainder of each issue
is devoted to discussions of new products, processes, equipment, and news
of men and companies in the chemical industries both in the United States
and abroad. Digests of recent chemical papers and reviews of chemical literature are also included. Annual numbers review achievements and trends of the
preceding year.

Chemical Engineering Catalog. Annually. New York, Reinhold Publishing Corp.

This book lists all types of chemical engineering equipment from manufacturers' catalogs.

Chemical Week. Weekly. New York, McGraw-Hill Publishing Co.

Although this periodical is largely concerned with processes and operations, it does include a market newsletter and a "Business Bench-marks"
section.

Chemical Week Buyers' Guide. Annually. New York, McGraw-Hill Publishing Co.

Suppliers of chemicals and chemical equipment are listed.

Drug and Cosmetic Industry. Monthly. New York, Drug Markets, Inc.

New products, merchandising, technological developments and a listing of trade publications and books make up the contents of this periodical. The coverage is thorough.

Industrial and Engineering Chemistry. Monthly. Washington, D.C., American Chemical Society.

This publication supplies statistics on the chemical industry, information on new products, plant operations, and techniques. The section on new books reviews recent monographs.

Modern Plastics. Monthly. New York, Briskin Publications, Inc.

News on the production, marketing and use of plastics is provided by this magazine. One section is a digest of significant articles published elsewhere.

Oil, Paint, and Drug Reporter. Weekly. New York, Schnell Publishing Co.

Prices, new developments, and processes in this sector of the chemical industry comprise the bulk of this periodical. Titles of sections; "Association News," "Government News," "Industry News," "International News," "Personnel News," and "Market Reports" indicate the contents. The information is cumulated in an annual review and directory number. This is probably the best source for prices.

Polk's Directory of the Chemical and Oil Industries. Annually. Detroit, Mich., R. L. Polk & Co.

A complete listing of the top personnel of the most important chemical plants and oil refineries in the United States and Canada appears in this directory. Personnel included are the president, engineers, superintendents, purchasing agents, and chief chemists and laboratory staff. The location of all plants and offices is given. The companies are grouped alphabetically by states, and there is also an alphabetical index by company.

Soap and Chemical Specialties. Monthly. New York, Chemical Specialties Manufacturers Association.

News of the soap and allied industries, plus articles on promotion, production, packaging, and products, is the make-up of this periodical. There are few statistics.

Haynes, W. *This Chemical Age: The Miracle of Manmade Chemicals*. New York, Knopf, 1942.

This is a readable account of the development of synthetic products.

Modern Plastics Encyclopedia. Annually. New York, Plastics Catalog Corp.

Each year this publication brings together data on the plastics industry. This includes information on the properties, methods of utilization, a description of moulding, forming, and other treatments of individual kinds of plastics, and their application. An index by product, and a directory of firms producing and processing plastics, with product produced and trade name, complete this directory.

Perry, J. H. ed. *Chemical Business Handbook*. New York, McGraw-Hill, 1954.

The aspects of finance, cost control, production, marketing, et cetera, peculiar to the chemical industry are presented in some detail. A helpful feature is the "Reference Index to Chemical and Related Market Research Data" and "Reference Index to Non-Chemical and Related Market Research Data." The first of these relies entirely on government publications and the second on trade associations and government reports.

Shreve, R. N. *The Chemical Process Industries.* New York, McGraw-Hill, 1945.
    This describes the various industries using chemical processes and their products.

Stanford Research Institute. *Chemical Economics Handbook.* Menlo Park, Calif., Stanford Research Institute. Annually.
    The editor provides data and charts on costs of production for every phase and branch of the chemical industry.

CHEMICAL ASSOCIATIONS

American Ceramic Society, 4055 N. High Street, Columbus 14, Ohio.

American Chemical Society, 1155 16th Street, N.W., Washington 6, D.C.

Association of American Soap & Glycerine Producers, 295 Madison Avenue, New York 17, N.Y.

Chemical Market Research Association, 100 Church Street, New York 7, N.Y.

Chemical Specialties Manufacturing Association, 50 E. 41st Street, New York 17, N.Y.

Essential Oil Association, 2 Lexington Avenue, New York 10, N.Y.

Manufacturing Chemists' Association, 1825 Connecticut Avenue, N.W., Washington 6, D.C.

National Paint, Varnish and Lacquers Association, 1500 Rhode Island Avenue, N.W., Washington 5, D.C.

Plant Food Institute, 1700 K Street, N.W., Washington 6, D.C. (Formerly National Fertilizer Association.)

Plastic Products Manufacturers Association and Plastic Soft Materials Manufacturers Association, 1133 Broadway, New York 10, N.Y.

Society of the Plastics Industry, 250 Park Avenue, New York 17, N.Y.

Synthetic Organic Chemical Manufacturers Association, 41 E. 42d Street, New York 17, N.Y.

COAL INDUSTRIES

Yingst, P. O. *Annotated Bibliography on Coal.* Golden, Colo., Colorado School of Mines, 1958.
    Although largely concerned with the geology and chemical qualities of coal, this bibliography does have some references to production and utilization of coal.

Keystone Coal Buyers Manual Including Directory of Mines. New York, McGraw-Hill 1960.

This handbook contains a directory of coal sales organizations, listed alphabetically; a map of the coal fields of the United States; a directory of coal trade names; a directory of mechanical cleaning plants; description of coal seams, including average or range analyses; mines directories, listed by states, with 1944 coal production maps for each State section; alphabetical index of producing companies and mines showing state in which the mine is located.

MacQuown's Coal Directory and Buyers' Guide. Annually. Pittsburgh, Pa., National Coal Publications.

This directory lists coal selling companies, alphabetically arranged by states and cities, with the names of officials and addresses of sales offices and mines. Bituminous and anthracite coal operating companies are listed alphabetically by states and counties, together with the name of operating company, location of general office, name of officials, name of mine, railroad service, shipping points, etc. A section is devoted to coal trade names and another to coke plants.

MacQuown's Directory and Handbook of Anthracite. Annually. Pittsburgh, Pa., National Coal Publications.

Complete data, alphabetically arranged, are provided on anthracite selling and producing companies, collieries, mines and trade names. A map of the anthracite fields, showing regions and counties, with the location of collieries, mines and railroads is a useful feature. It also lists equipment approved by the Anthracite Industries Laboratory and includes authoritative articles on important phases of the industry.

MacQuown's Directory of Coal Operating Companies. Annually. Pittsburgh, Pa., National Coal Publications.

The operating companies of both bituminous and anthracite mines are listed alphabetically by states. The names and addresses of officials, mine names, location, railroad, shipping point, etc., and addresses of selling companies for each mine are also given in this very complete directory. Indexes of purchasing offices, of operating and producing mines, grouped alphabetically by states and cities, and including the names of purchasing agents are another special feature.

MacQuown's Directory of Coal Docks on the Great Lakes. Annually. Pittsburgh, Pa., National Coal Publications.

All coal docks on the Great Lakes and St. Lawrence River, both in the U.S. and Canada, are listed. Maps showing the specific location, description of each dock, name, tonnage, etc. are provided. Other features are a table of freight rates (fuel and cargo); an alphabetical list of self-unloading vessels operating on the Great Lakes; an alphabetical list of companies operating bulk freighters; charts; statistics and maps relating to shipments to and from

Great Lakes ports; statistical data on coal-handling vessels; and special informative articles.

MacQuown's "B & O" Coals. Periodically. Pittsburgh, Pa., National Coal Publications.

This publication contains accurate, complete, and up-to-date information on coal mines and coke ovens served by, and coal handling facilities of, the Baltimore & Ohio Railroad and the Alton Railroad. Fourteen maps show location of each mine and accompanying tables, give the name of the operator and the mine, shipping point, tonnage, sales agent, etc.

The Mining Catalogs. Annually. New York, McGraw-Hill.

This completely indexed collection of manufacturers' catalogs covering the machinery, equipment, supplies, and services important to the mining industries is a standard reference.

Statistics on the coal mining industry are published by the following sources:

U.S. Bureau of Mines, Department of the Interior, Washington, D.C.

1. *Annual Statistics:* Anthracite and bituminous production, distribution, consumption, and stocks of coal; annual accident figures.

2. *Monthly Statistics:* Distribution of coal shipments; preliminary estimates of production of coal, anthracite and beehive coke production; coal mine fatalities; coke report; international coal trade report.

3. *Weekly Statistics:* Coal report.

U.S. Bureau of the Census, Department of Commerce, Washington, D.C., *Census of Mineral Industries, 1958.*

Available reports on anthracite and bituminous coal cover the number of operating companies, number of mines, number of preparation plants, employment, principal expenses, buildings, machinery and equipment, etc. Also tables of bituminous coal output by counties.

U.S. Bureau of Labor Statistics, Department of Labor, Washington, D.C.

Employment statistics on the number of workers, hours worked, hourly and weekly earnings are released monthly. Statistics on retail and wholesale prices are issued monthly.

Saward's Annual. N.Y., Estate of Frederick W. Saward.

This statistical review of the coal trade, contains figures (1) on U.S. coal production by states for the previous five years, (2) on fuel consumption in the principal markets, (3) on weekly and monthly production by districts, and (4) on data on prices of coal in different markets, trade news of the year (about people and companies), and a list of trade associations.

Current Coal Trends. Monthly. Washington, D.C., Department of Economics, National Coal Association.

Statistics on production, consumption, prices, employment and competing fuels are supplied on a current basis.

Perry, Josephine. *The Coal Industry.* New York, Longmans, Green & Co., 1944.
    This book tells briefly the story of the coal industry. The author outlines some of the facts about coal itself, and its formation; describes the mining methods and processing for the market. The potentialities of coal in this age of industrial chemistry as well as the part it already plays in the economic importance of our country are discussed.

Coal Age. Monthly. New York, McGraw-Hill Publishing Co. Inc.
    News of coal mining and feature articles on methods and operations are provided in this magazine. Labor relations, personnel, marketing problems, new equipment and trade literature and equipment maintenance are also covered.

The Black Diamond. Biweekly. Chicago, Black Diamond Company.
    This news report of coal mining and retailing activities covers the problems and prospects of the industry, and gives special attention to labor matters, legislative trends, and automatic heating.

The Coal Dealer. Monthly. Minneapolis, Northwestern Publishing Co.
    General news and information about the retail coal trade, modern heating equipment and accessories, principles of combustion as applied to various types of heating equipment, home construction and design as they affect heating satisfaction, and the advantages of uniform and constant heating are among the topics covered. Coal convention dates and the activities of retail coal associations are also reported.

The Coal Herald-Stoker and Air Conditioner. Monthly. Boston, The Coal Herald, Inc.
    News and information about coal and coal dealers, stokers, air conditioning, and coal and heating equipment markets are presented in this magazine.

Coal Mining. Monthly. Pittsburgh, Pa., Modern Mining Publishing Co.
    Reports news and contains general information about the coal industry, and mining machinery and equipment.

Mechanization. Monthly. Washington, D.C., Mechanization, Inc.
    The coverage includes news and articles about the methods and equipment for the coal industry and a regularly featured section on equipment catalogs that lists the latest equipment offered by manufacturers.

The Retail Coalman. Monthly. Chicago, Retail Coalman, Inc.
    A trade journal devoted exclusively to the retail coal business.

Mining World. Monthly. San Francisco, American Trade Journals, Inc.
    News of the metal mining industries in the United States is grouped by geographical regions and reported on. Feature articles cover actual operations, new projects, improved methods and equipment.

Mining Congress Journal. Monthly. Washington, D.C., American Mining Congress.
    Contains news, articles, and information about the mining industry. Reports the work and activities of the American Mining Congress, labor relations in coal mining, effect of labor laws on the mining industry, and discusses im-

proved mining methods and equipment. A special feature is the manufacturers' forum that lists manufacturers' catalogs, bulletins, and descriptions of new mining machinery and equipment offered to the industry.

Mining and Metallurgy. Monthly. New York, American Institute of Mining and Metallurgy.

Reports news of mining industry, calendar of coming meetings of the American Institute of Mining and Metallurgy, results of such meetings, and activities of the Institute. Contains sections on personnel service, what's new in the industry, opportunities, new technical books. A professional directory is also included.

The Mining and Contracting Review. Semimonthly. Salt Lake City, Utah, Salt Lake Mining Review, Inc.

This periodical provides a review of the metal mining and coal mining industry in the West plus general news of interest to miners and contractors.

Saward's Journal. Weekly. New York, Estate of Frederick W. Saward.

General news coverage, articles, and information about the coal industry are furnished in this leading coal trade newspaper.

Coal Associations

Anthracite. Anthracite Industry Council and Anthracite Information Bureau, 342 Madison Avenue, New York 17, N.Y.

Anthracite Institute, 237 Old River Road, Wilkes-Barre, Pa.

Bituminous. National Coal Association, 1130 17th Street, N.W., Washington 6, D.C.

Southern Coal Producers Association, 1725 K Street, N.W., Washington 6, D.C.

A list of local bituminous coal operators' Associations throughout the United States may be obtained from the National Coal Association.

ELECTRICAL EQUIPMENT INDUSTRIES

The American Television Directory. Annual. New York, American Television Society, Inc.

The official yearbook of the American Television Society, Inc. Important and interesting articles about television, its development, future and progress are published. Each issue contains a "television vocabulary," chronology of television progress, bibliography, and list of publications reporting on television.

1947-48 Directory of Verified Electrical Wholesale Distributors. New York, Electrical Wholesaling.

Contains names and addresses of electrical supply wholesalers.

Electronics Buyers' Guide. Annual. New York, McGraw-Hill Publishing Co.

Section one, Reference Data, contains important technical articles about electronics, a directory of consulting electronic engineers, a list of recent books on electronics, a list of colleges that give courses in electronics, and a trade and technical association directory. Section two, Directory, includes an alphabetical listing of products, a list of registered trade names, and an index of manufacturers.

American Standard Definitions of Electrical Terms. New York, American Institute of Electrical Engineers, 1941.

Electrical World. Weekly. New York, McGraw-Hill Publishing Co.

General news and articles about the electrical industry. Statistical information is provided annually in one January issue (3rd week).

Edison Electric Institute Bulletin. Monthly. New York, Edison Electric Institute.

Contains statistics of the electrical utility industry.

Electric Light and Power. Monthly. Chicago, Electrical Publications, Inc.

News and information regarding generating and distributing equipment are furnished.

Electrical Construction and Maintenance. Monthly. New York, McGraw-Hill Publishing Co.

A publication for electrical contractors, electrical engineers, and inspectors. Its topic is the installation and maintenance of electrical equipment.

Electrical Equipment. Monthly. New York, Sutton Publishing Co.

This publication contains news, articles, and information on new developments in electrical products, parts, and materials. A products index is included.

Electrical Manufacturing. Monthly. New York, Gage Publishing Company.

Features articles and information on engineering design, production of electrically energized machines, and appliances and equipment. Reports news on products and materials, new literature, and industry highlights. Includes both a calendar of trade associations and a buying guide.

Electrical Merchandising. Semimonthly. New York, McGraw-Hill Publishing Co.

A buyers' directory is included in each issue. The January issue features statistical tables on the production and sales of appliances.

Electrical South. Monthly. Atlanta, Ga., W. R. C. Smith Publishing Company.

Articles of special interest to southern electrical power companies, electrical contractors, and wholesalers are featured.

Electrical West. Monthly. Los Angeles, McGraw-Hill Company of California.

News and articles about the electrical industry on the West Coast. The February issue features statistics on the West Coast electrical industry and the April issue contains a manufacturers' directory, with a list of western branch offices and representatives.

Electrified Industry. Monthly. Chicago, B. J. Martin and Company.

The main topic of this technical electrical trade magazine is electricity in industrial plants.

Electronics. Monthly. New York, McGraw-Hill Publishing Co.

Technical articles on the electronics industry are featured, and a directory of electronics and allied products with the names and addresses of supplies is included. The June 15 issue contains a Buyers' Guide and Material Section.

Electronic Industries and Electronic Instrumentation. Monthly. New York, Caldwell-Clements, Inc.

Articles on the design, application, and operation of electronic equipment in the industrial production and control field are featured.

New England Electrical News. Monthly. Boston, New England Electrical News Publishing Company.

News and informative articles of interest to contractors, electrical inspectors, and manufacturers' representatives are provided.

Qualified Contractor. Monthly. Washington 6, D.C., National Electrical Contractors Association.

This official publication of the NECA reports the program and activities of the association.

Radio and Television Retailing. Monthly. New York, Caldwell-Clements, Inc.

Special articles and timely news on the radio and television fields are featured. The January issue contains statistics on the radio and appliance industries.

Electrical Equipment Associations

Air Conditioning & Refrigeration Institute, 1346 Connecticut Avenue, N.W., Washington 6, D.C.

Commercial Refrigerator Manufacturers Association, 111 West Washington Street, Chicago 2, Ill.

Electronic Industries Association, 1721 De Sales Street, N.W., Washington 6, D.C.

International Association of Electrical Leagues, 155 E. 44th St., New York 17, N.Y.

National Electrical Contractors Association, 1200 18th Street, N.W., Washington 6, D.C.

National Electrical Manufacturers Association, 155 E. 44th Street, New York 17, N.Y.

National Electronics Distributors Association, 343 South Dearborn Street, Chicago 4, Ill.

Vacuum Cleaner Manufacturers Association, 2775 South Moreland Boulevard, Cleveland 20, Ohio.

Professional Societies

American Institute of Electrical Engineers, 33 West 39th Street, New York 18, N.Y.

American Society of Heating and Air Conditioning Engineers, 62 Worth Street, New York, N.Y

American Society of Mechanical Engineers, 29 West 39th Street, New York, N.Y.

American Society of Refrigerating Engineers, 234 Fifth Avenue, New York 1, N.Y.

Electrochemical Society, Inc., 1860 Broadway, New York 23, N.Y.

Illuminating Engineering Society, 1860 Broadway, New York 23, N.Y.

Institute of Radio Engineers, Inc. 1 East 79th Street, New York 21, N.Y.

FOOD INDUSTRIES

American Miller and Processor. Monthly. Chicago, Ill., National Miller Publications.
> This is a leading journal in the grain processing and related industries.

Bakers' Helper. Fortnightly. Chicago, Ill., Bakers' Helper Co.
> Technical information, trends in the baking industry, and a directory of suppliers of raw material and equipment are the salient features of this magazine.

Food Engineering. Monthly. Philadelphia, Pa., Chilton Publishing Co.
> The management in the food industries is served by this magazine through articles on the manufacturing, packaging, and marketing of food products. New processes, equipment, patents, and new construction are the principal section. Current news appears in the "Trends and Forecasts" and the "Washington Report."

Food Industries. Monthly. New York, McGraw-Hill.
> Information on all phases of the food industries is supplied by this publication. New processes, equipment, activities of particular companies, trends of business, patents, and new construction are the principal sections. An equipment catalog and reference service are included.

Food Products Directory. Annual. San Francisco, Canner and Packer.
> This directory of firms in all phases of the food industry includes not only canners, packers, and manufacturers of food products but also processors of dried fruits; importers, exporters, and shippers; and wineries and breweries.

The Manufacturing Confectioner. Monthly. Chicago, Ill., Manufacturing Confectioner Publishing Co.
> The Annual Bluebook number provides a directory of equipment and raw materials suppliers.

May, Earl C. *The Canning Clan.* New York, Macmillan, 1937.
> This very readable account of the development of the industry includes descriptions of the early problems and processes and the men who were active in building up the industry.

National Provisioner. Weekly. Chicago, Ill., National Provisioner, Inc.
> News, statistics, trends, equipment, and processes of the meat-packing and related industries are featured in this periodical. The *Meat Packers Annual Guide,* a directory of all sections of the industry, is also published.

United Nations. Food and Agriculture Organization. *Monthly Bulletin of Agricultural Economics and Statistics.* Monthly. Rome, Italy, United Nations, Food and Agriculture Organization.
> Data on prices, competitive position of products, production and trade in agricultural commodities throughout the world are supplied.

U.S. Department of Agriculture. *Agricultural Statistics.* Washington, D.C., U.S. Department of Agriculture. Annual.

Here are statistics on all farm and forestry products.

Canner / Packer. Monthly. San Francisco 5, Calif., Miller Freeman Publications of California.

The national coverage of this magazine is complete. It is an excellent source of information of stocks, production, carry-over, prices, and general developments in canned, dried, and frozen foods industries. The annual yearbook number provides the valuable cumulation of this information.

FOOD ASSOCIATIONS

American Bakers Association, 20 N. Wacker Drive, Chicago 6, Ill.

American Meat Institute, 59 E. Van Buren Street, Chicago 5, Ill.

Can Manufacturers Institute, 821 15th Street, N.W., Washington 5, D.C.

Canners League of California, 215 Market Street, San Francisco, Calif.

Canning Machinery and Supplies Association, 4630 Montgomery Avenue, Washington 14, D.C.

Dried Fruit Association of California, P.O. Box 618, San Jose, Calif.

National Association of Frozen Food Packers, 919 18th Street, N.W., Washington 6, D.C.

National Canners Association, 1133 20th Street, N.W., Washington 6, D.C.

National Meat Canner Association, 59 E. Van Buren Street, Chicago 5, Ill.

LUMBER

Lumbermen's National Red Book Service Reference Book. Semiannually with twice weekly supplements. Chicago, Ill., Lumbermen's Credit Association.

This is a combination directory and credit rating book. The names, addresses, and financial status of manufacturers, including furniture factories and other woodworking establishments, and retailers of all types of lumber and lumber products are given for the United States and parts of Canada.

The Timberman. Monthly. Portland, Ore., Miller Freeman Publications.

This periodical carries articles on logging, transportation, forestry, and woods management. Log prices are also a feature of this publication.

West Coast Lumberman. Monthly. Seattle, Wash., Miller Freeman Publications.

New developments in lumbering techniques, methods of sawmill operation, new equipment, statistics, and personalities in the lumber industries in the eleven western states, are recorded in this magazine.

West Coast Lumberman and Directory of the Western Timber Industries. Annual. Seattle, Wash., Miller Freeman Publications.

The directory is a very complete coverage of sawmills and logging camps, shingle mills, plywood and veneer specialties, box factories, wholesalers and exporters, and woodworking plants. A short buyers' guide section lists suppliers of equipment. The capacity, type, and quantity of equipment and principal officers are given for the larger mills.

For additional reference see the Building and Material section pages 245-249.

LUMBER ASSOCIATIONS

National Lumber Manufacturers Association, 1319 18th Street, N.W., Washington, D.C.

West Coast Lumbermen's Association and West Coast Lumber Inspection Bureau, 1410 S.W. Morrison Street, Portland 5, Ore.

METAL PRODUCING AND WORKING INDUSTRIES

American Bureau of Metal Statistics. *Year Book of the American Bureau of Metal Statistics.* New York, American Bureau of Metal Statistics. Annual.

Production, consumption, stocks (inventories), and some prices are supplied on nonferrous metals, both domestic and foreign, for at least a ten-year period. Figures on production of the larger mining and smelting companies are an added feature.

American Iron and Steel Institute. *Annual Statistical Report.* New York, American Iron and Steel Institute. Annual.

This publication contains very complete statistics of production, shipments, and prices on all phases of the steel and its auxilary industries.

American Machinist. Forthnightly. New York, McGraw-Hill Publishing Co.

Each issue contains information on the administration, engineering, assembly and inspection, material cutting and forming, and tooling aspects of metalworking. Other features include special discussions of metalworking techniques, reports on labor conditions, news of the trade, and short descriptions of new techniques and equipment. The annual review number presents an appraisal of the metalworking industry with a statistical summary and a catalog of metalworking equipment, parts, and materials. This magazine is probably the best source of current information on the metalworking industry.

American Metal Market. *Metal Statistics.* New York, American Metal Market, Inc. Annual.

Data on prices, production, and stocks (inventories) of practically all the commercial metals and metal products have been cumulated for a period of years in this publication. Furthermore, both American and foreign statistics are presented, thus making it a splendid source of information for one interested in price and production data for several years past. The annual also contains a buyers' directory to metal manufacturers and brokers.

Engineering and Mining Journal. Monthly. New York, McGraw-Hill Publishing Company.

The "Outlook" is a brief account each month of trends in the industry plus statistics on production and prices. Other articles on production, labor, and management techniques provide additional information on the minerals industries. The June issue is entitled the "Mining Guidebook" and deals in detail with some issue of general interest to the industry and also includes a buyers' guide.

E & M.J. Metal and Mineral Markets. Weekly. New York, McGraw-Hill Publishing Co.

Prices and developments in the metal and mineral industries markets comprise the bulk of this publication. There are also brief news items on governmental and company activities.

Iron Age. Weekly. New York, Chilton Co., Inc.

Trade news, both domestic and foreign, technical descriptions of equipment and layouts, personalities in the industry, and brief information on production and prices are the major sections of this periodical. The annual review number summarizes activities in all phases of the metal-producing and working industries with the addition of extensive statistical material.

The Mineral Industry. New York, McGraw-Hill Publishing Company. Annual.

Data on production, prices, uses, and methods of production on all the commercially important minerals are provided on both United States and foreign mineral industries.

U.S. Bureau of Mines. *Minerals Yearbook.* Washington, D.C., Government Printing Office. Annual.

Brief accounts cover the statistics and prices, and describe methods of production for all minerals produced in the United States. The data are supplied on a national and state basis, some reference is made to foreign production and competition, and information on petroleum and cement is also included.

Metals Associations

Aluminum Association, 420 Lexington Avenue, New York 17, N.Y.

American Iron and Steel Institute, 150 E. 42d Street, New York 17, N.Y.

American Machine Tool Distributors Association, 1500 Massachusetts Avenue, N.W., Washington 5, D.C.

American Tin Trade Association, 26 Broadway, New York 17, N.Y.

Copper and Brass Research Association, 420 Lexington Avenue, New York 17, N.Y.

Gray Iron Founders Society, 210 National City-E 6th Building, Cleveland 14, Ohio.

Lead Industries Association, 292 Madison Avenue, New York 17, N.Y.

Machinery and Allied Products Institute, 1200 18th Street, N.W., Washington 6, D.C.

National Machine Tool Builders Association, 2139 Wisconsin Avenue, N.W., Washington, D.C.

National Metal Trades Association, 222 W. Adams Street, Chicago 6, Ill.

U.S. Copper Association, 50 Broadway, New York 17, N.Y.

PAPER

American Paper Merchant Source of Supply Directory. Annual. Chicago, Howard
Publishing Company.

Dealers in various kinds of paper and paper products are classified according to the lines they handle. Officers of each firm and lines handled are
listed under each firm name.

Lockwood's Directory of the Paper and Allied Trades. Annual. New York, Lockwood Trade Journal Company.

Paper and pulp mills in the United States and Canada are listed by geographical areas with additional information on capacity, products, type of
machinery used, and officers. Lists of concerns in related lines of activity are
also included.

Paper and Pulp Mill Catalogue. Annual. Chicago, Fritz Publications, Inc.

Manufacturers and suppliers of machinery, equipment, and supplies utilized by pulp and paper manufacturers are classified in this directory.

Paper Trade Journal. Weekly. New York, Lockwood Trade Journal Co., Incorporated.

General news of the industry, descriptions of design and operation of new
equipment, market quotations on both raw materials and finished products,
and explanations of technical products are among the more important items
appearing in this publication. The annual review number summarizes the
year both editorially and statistically.

Paperboard Packaging. Monthly with weekly supplement, *Official Board Markets.*
Chicago, Ill., Board Products Publishing Company.

The very large technical section has much information on processes, equipment, and plant layouts. There are also charts of prices and trends in the industry. The weekly supplement supplies current prices.

Stephenson, J. N. Editor-in-chief. *Pulp and Paper Manufacture.* New York, McGraw-
Hill, 1950–.

Although this publication is largely concerned with the technical phases
of pulp and paper manufacturing, there are a number of statistics on the
industry.

PAPER ASSOCIATIONS

American Paper and Pulp Association, 122 E. 42d Street, New York 17, N.Y.

Paper Bag Institute, 41 E. 42d Street, New York 17, N.Y.

Specialty Paper and Board Affiliates, 122 E. 42d Street, New York 17, N.Y.

Technical Association of the Pulp and Paper Industry, 360 Lexington Avenue,
New York 17, N.Y.

United States Pulp Producers Association, 122 E. 42d Street, New York 17, N.Y.

PETROLEUM

American Petroleum Institute. *Petroleum Facts and Figures*. New York, American
Petroleum Institute, 1959.

This publication supplies statistics on all phases of the petroleum industry,
both domestic and foreign. Among the topics covered are the utilization, production, refining, transportation, marketing, and prices of petroleum and petroleum products. Published every two or three years, this is a most useful
cumulation of statistics.

Fanning, L. M. *Rise of American Oil*. New York, Harper, 1948.

The development of the American oil industry, both at home and abroad,
is described in nontechnical language.

The Independent Petroleum Association of America Monthly. Monthly. Tulsa,
Oklahoma, The Independent Petroleum Association of America.

Surveys of the industry, statistics, and news of the smaller oil producers
can be found in this magazine.

National Industrial Conference Board. *The Petroleum Almanac*. New York, National Industrial Conference Board, 1946.

The Almanac is an extremely detailed compilation of statistics on all
phases of the petroleum industry. Production, transportation, refining, marketing and distribution, financial data, labor, government regulations, prices, data
on world petroleum, and a glossary of terms, are the major topics. Some of
the statistics date back to the beginning of the industry; in most instances they
cover a considerable number of years. In part these statistics are brought up to
date in the National Industrial Board *Economic Almanac* and the American
Petroleum Institute, *Petroleum Facts and Figures*.

Oil and Gas Journal. Weekly. Tulsa, Oklahoma, Petroleum Publishing Company.

Each of the sections—new developments in the industry, news from the
field, engineering and operating techniques, and petroleum technology—enables
the reader to keep currently informed on these topics. Information on all oil
fields, both foreign and domestic, is provided. Special quarterly issues report
on the annual meeting of the American Petroleum Institute, and on pipelines
and international oil activities. The annual number cumulates statistics and
reviews the industry for the past year.

The Petroleum Register. Annual. New York, Mona Palmer.

This work is both a combination buyers' guide to oil well and refinery
equipment, dealers, and manufacturers, and a directory of producers, refiners,
transporters (pipelines etc). Individuals active in various branches of the industry are also listed. The fact that the capitalization figure and names of
officers of small companies are included makes the publication particularly
valuable. Foreign companies and a trade name section are also included. The
statistical section supplies condensed tables on production, consumption, prices,

etc., for at least five years. The work is the most comprehensive and useful directory published on the industry.

Petroleum World. Monthly. Los Angeles, Calif., Palmer Publications.

The California Petroleum industry is treated in detail including current production, number of wells drilled and production of each operator, prices by fields, and oil in storage. Total production for each California field since its discovery is given in the annual review number and a résumé of developments in techniques and equipment during the past year also is provided.

Rocq, M. M. Compiler. *U.S. Sources of Petroleum and Natural Gas Statistics.* New York, Special Libraries Association, 1961.

This very detailed analysis of 231 publications covers every phase of the petroleum industry. The alphabetical subject listing indicates the geographical area covered by the statistics, and the publication is referred to by its number in the list of magazines covered. Frequency of publication is also indicated. Probably the best source available for locating statistics on petroleum.

Swanson, E. B. *A Century of Oil and Gas in Books: A Descriptive Bibliography.* New York, Appleton-Crofts-Century, 1960.

This very detailed annotated bibliography is arranged by subject. It is a good source for locating material on the history, development, and economics of the petroleum industry. A helpful feature is the list of petroleum journals, along with the names of the libraries having the most complete files.

U.S. Bureau of Mines. *Mineral Industry Surveys—World Petroleum, Statistics.* Weekly. Washington, D.C., U.S. Bureau of Mines.

This publication carries statistics on production, imports and exports of petroleum, and petroleum products; also consumption along with brief comments on significant trends and events.

PETROLEUM ASSOCIATIONS

American Petroleum Institute, 1271 Avenue of the Americas, New York 20, N.Y.
California Oil and Gas Association, 609 South Grand Avenue, Los Angeles, Calif.
Mid-Continent Oil and Gas Association, 608 Tulsa Building, Tulsa, Oklahoma.
National Oil Marketers Association, National Press Building, Washington 4, D.C.
National Petroleum Association, 927 Munsey Building, Washington, 4, D.C.
National Gasoline Association of America, 421 Kennedy Building, Tulsa 3, Oklahoma.

RUBBER

Rubber Red Book. Biennially. New York, Palmerton Publishing Company, Inc.

This comprehensive directory of the rubber industry contains the following lists; (1) rubber manufacturers in the United States, arranged alphabetically, geographically, and by products; (2) rubber manufacturers in Canada; (3) machinery and equipment arranged by type, together with their manufacturers (including addresses); (4) rubber products accessories and fittings with names and addresses of suppliers; (5) rubber chemicals and compounding materials, including trade and brand names and suppliers' names and addresses; (6) fabrics and textiles, arranged by type, with their suppliers and their addresses; (7) natural rubbers and related materials, with suppliers and their addresses; (8) synthetic rubbers and other rubber-like materials; (9) reclaimed rubber, with manufacturers and addresses, brand names, and trade designations; (10) rubber dealers; (11) latex rubber products, compounds and materials; (12) rubber derivatives; (13) miscellaneous rubber products and services; (14) consulting technologists; (15) branch offices and sales agents; (16) trade and technical organizations; (17) a "Who's Who in the rubber industry"; (18) a list of technical journals.

The Rubber Manufacturers Association, Inc., New York, N.Y., issues monthly statistics on United States rubber consumption, tire production, shipments, and inventories.

India Rubber World. Monthly. New York, Bill Brothers Publications, Inc.

News, articles, and information about the rubber and allied industries are provided including such regular features as plastics technology; scientific and technical activities, patents; trade-marks; new machines and appliances; new publications, book reviews, and a bibliography; available trade lists; foreign trade opportunities, market reviews; and pertinent rubber statistics.

The Rubber Age. Monthly. New York, Palmerton Publishing Company, Inc.

One of the world's outstanding rubber journals. Feature items cover such topics as the activities of rubber products manufacturers, the utilization of new methods and new equipment and news of the rubber and cotton markets. Book reviews and statistics on natural rubber and fabricated products are also included.

Rubber Statistical Bulletin. Monthly. London, Secretariat of the International Rubber Study Group.

Very detailed statistics on production, stocks, consumption, and utilization of both natural and synthetic rubber appear in this publication. There are no prices given.

Tire Review. Monthly. Akron, O., The India Rubber Review Company.

This trade journal for the tire and battery men provides news and special features on the tire and allied industries.

Tires. Monthly. New York, Bill Brothers Publications, Inc.

News, features, and statistics about the tire industry are directed especially toward tire dealers.

RUBBER ASSOCIATIONS

Rubber Manufacturers Association, 444 Madison Avenue, New York 22, N.Y.
Rubber Trade Association of New York, 15 William Street, New York 5, N.Y.

SHOE AND LEATHER INDUSTRY

Hide and Leather and Shoes Blue Book of the Shoe and Leather Industry. Annual. Chicago, Hide and Leather Publishing Co.

A complete and conveniently arranged Directory and Reference Guide of the manufacturers and wholesalers of shoes, leather, and allied products and services, with statistical and miscellaneous information concerning these industries in the United States. It consists of nine parts: (1) General Index of Listings; (2) Shoes; (3) Shoe Manufacturers' Materials, Supplies, Machinery and Equipment; (4) Leather; (5) Tanners' Materials, Supplies, Machinery and Equipment; (6) Leather Goods; (7) Hides and Skins; (8) Statistics, Trade Contracts, Tariff Regulations, Trade Associations, Books, Schools, Government Buying Agencies; (9) Trade-Marks.

Shoe and Leather Reporter Annual. Boston, Shoe and Leather Reporter.

This official directory of the shoe, leather and allied industries includes an alphabetical list of every product and trade organization; a "Where to Buy" section; an alphabetical index of all shoe manufacturers, leather manufacturers, and shoe wholesalers; a list of the best-rated shoe retailers in the country; and statistical information about the industry

Shoediction. New York, National Shoe Manufacturers Association, 1947.

A booklet containing definitions and information about 867 words, terms, phrases, services, and references pertaining to shoes and the shoe industry.

American Shoemaking. Weekly. Boston, Shoe Trades Publishing Co.

Reports the news and publishes comments, articles, and information on the shoemaking industry. Has a section listing "Trade Wants."

Boot and Shoe Recorder. Weekly. New York, Chilton Company, Inc.

This weekly, the national trade paper of the shoe industry, reports news and information about the retail shoe trade, manufacturing and markets, sales and supplies, and trends.

Coast Shoe Reporter. Monthly. San Francisco, William J. Ahern.

The official organ of the California Shoe Retailers Association, the Pacific Northwest Shoe Retailers Association, and the West Coast Shoe Travelers Associates. It features news, and special articles about the West Coast retail shoe industry.

Creative Footwear. Monthly. Boston, Creative Footwear, Inc.

Fashion, style trends, and the role of the shoe industry are featured. A calendar of coming meetings of shoe and leather associations is provided and meetings highlights are reported.

Leather and Shoes. Weekly. Chicago, Hide and Leather Publishing Co.

News and articles on hides and skins, tanning, leather markets, shoes, and market trends are presented.

Shoe and Leather Reporter. Weekly. Boston, Shoe and Leather Reporter Co.

This trade journal contains news, style trends, technical and general information, and current prices for leather manufacturers, wholesale dealers, and buyers. The content is also helpful for those engaged in shoe manufacturing, wholesaling, and directly allied trades.

Shoe and Leather Associations

Last Manufacturers Association, 80 Federal Street, Boston 10, Mass.

Leather Industries of America, 411 Fifth Avenue, New York 16, N.Y.

Luggage and Leather Goods Manufacturers of America, 220 Fifth Avenue, New York 1, N.Y.

National Association of Slipper and Playshoe Manufacturers, 295 Madison Avenue, New York 17, N.Y.

National Association of Shoe Wholesalers, 210 Lincoln Street, Boston 11, Mass.

National Hide Association, 130 North Wells Street, Chicago 6, Ill.

National Industrial Leather Association, P.O. Box 667, Pompano Beach, Fla.

National Shoe Institute, 50 Rockefeller Plaza, New York 20, N.Y.

National Shoe Manufacturers Association, 342 Madison Avenue, New York 17, N.Y.

National Shoe Retailers Association, 274 Madison Avenue, New York 17, N.Y.

New England Shoe and Leather Association, 210 Lincoln Street, Boston 11, Mass.

Tanners Council of America, 411 Fifth Avenue, New York 16, N.Y.

TEXTILES

American Wool and Cotton Reporter. Weekly. Boston, Frank P. Bennett & Co.

Technical news and statistics of the cotton and woolen industry are featured in this periodical. The annual "Official Statistics Section of Textile Corporations" supplies data on capitalization, officers, kind and size of equipment, type of production and capacity, and number of employees in textile mills. In many instances company earnings and dividends are given. A buyers' guide of both textile products and supplies and equipment is also a regular feature. The annual number is an exceedingly helpful source of information on smaller companies that are not listed in the financial manuals mentioned on pages 97–98.

National Association of Wool Manufacturers. *Bulletin.* Annual. New York, National Association of Wool Manufacturers.

Detailed statistics on all aspects of the woolen industry are supplied by this bulletin. The long series of both foreign and domestic wool prices are helpful.

Rayon Organon. Monthly. New York, Textile Economics Bureau.

News of the industry, descriptions of new processes and equipment, and statistics dealing with output, prices, and consumption are the major features of this publication. The special annual supplement provides statistics on all aspects of the textile industry with emphasis on the rayon industry.

Skinner's Cotton Trade Directory of the World. Annual. New York, Skinner & Co., Ltd.

>   Cotton statistics, names and addresses of cotton exporters, merchants, spinners, manufacturers, yarn and piece goods finishers, producers and converters of silk and rayon, British hosiery and knit goods manufacturers, and textile associations are some of the more important types of information to be found in this publication.

The Textile Colorist. Monthly. New York, Textile Colorist, Inc.

>   This highly specialized publication is devoted entirely to the chemical departments of textile and allied industries and is designed to fill the needs of the dyer, bleacher, finisher, and textile printer. It renders practical help by suggesting ways of improving processes and overcoming difficulties that present themselves in everyday operations. Regular contributors from nearly every foreign textile country offer valuable information which would be unobtainable otherwise.

Textile Hi-Lights. Quarterly. New York, American Cotton Manufacturers Institute.

>   Comment and statistics on the consumption and prices of cotton, silk, and rayon are carried in this publication along with detailed data on production, profits, employment, wages, and prices for all types of products of the cotton industry.

Textile World. Monthly. New York, McGraw-Hill Publishing Company.

>   This magazine supplies data on new processes, equipment, trends in factory construction and layout. Economic changes, trends, and news of persons active in the textile industry are also presented. The "Annual Review and Forecast" number cumulates statistics for the year.

TEXTILE ASSOCIATIONS

American Cotton Manufacturers Institute, Johnston Building, Charlotte 2, N.C.

American Rayon Institute, 350 Fifth Avenue, New York 1, N.Y.

Man-Made Fiber Producers Association, 350 Fifth Avenue, New York 1, N.Y.

National Association of Finishers of Textile Fabrics, 350 Fifth Avenue, New York 1, N.Y.

National Association of Hosiery Manufacturers, 468 Fourth Avenue, New York 1, N.Y.

National Association of Wool Manufacturers, 386 Park Avenue South, New York 16, N.Y.

National Cotton Council of America, 1918 Parkway, Memphis 12, Tenn.

National Knitted Outerwear Association, 386 Park Avenue South, New York 16, N.Y.

Northern Textile Association, 80 Federal Street, Boston 10, Mass.

Silk and Rayon Manufacturers Association, Fabian Building, Patterson 1, N.J.

Southern Textile Association, 218 West Morehead Street, Charlotte 6, N.C.

Textile Research Institute, P.O. Box 625, Princeton, N.J.

15

FOREIGN TRADE

Postwar developments have had a very great influence on the attitude of American businessmen toward foreign trade. The growth and size of American industry have made foreign markets more important.

The emergence of former colonial areas as independent countries have changed trends in foreign trade and opened up new opportunities along with putting different restrictions on trade. The European common market has both increased foreign trade opportunities and raised new and formidable competition. A rehabilitated Japan has developed a modern industry capable of producing quality products. Thus the American businessman is confronted with both an opportunity and a threat in entering foreign trade.

The many restrictions placed on foreign trade plus the growth of local markets have led to a steady stream of investments in foreign countries. This has taken the form of the building of branch plants abroad, or joint enterprises with firms and individuals within the foreign countries. But this, at times, has created management and other problems. However, the American businessman is a far more sophisticated foreign trader than he was prior to World War II. He is better trained, has more available information, and recognizes the importance of foreign markets in relation to his business.

The businessman who contemplates entering foreign trade is immediately faced with an entirely different set of conditions from those which affect his domestic business operations. He encounters problems of distance, time, language difficulties and a maze of government regulations, both foreign and domestic. In perhaps no other field is a businessman so dependent on published information as in importing and exporting.

He must know the general business conditions abroad and be conversant with the business customs, transportation schedules, packaging requirements, and customs regulations of each country with which he does business. Monetary standards and their fluctuations create further difficulties for him.

One of the first concerns of our federal government was foreign trade. Its publications on the subject extend over the longest period, are the most voluminous, and constitute the basic sources of information. The Department of Commerce publishes the bulk of foreign trade material, but the Tariff Commission, Treasury Department, and other federal agencies make contributions on practically every aspect of the subject. Not all references to sources of information on foreign trade are included in this chapter; consequently, the reader should consult page 18 for a general explanation on how to locate material published by the federal government.

The needs of persons engaged in foreign trade and those planning to enter the field were the criteria for selecting the reference sources given in this chapter. With two exceptions, packing for foreign shipment and marine insurance, all phases of foreign trade activities have been covered. Since many other activities touch on foreign trade in a general way, several cross references have been made to other parts of this book in order to give full coverage of valuable sources and to avoid unnecessary repetition here.

This chapter deals with the specialized and technical aspects of foreign trade. Because of the enormous number of publications available, only the most useful sources have been enumerated. The bibliographies, especially those in the *Foreign Commerce Handbook* mentioned below, provide a more comprehensive listing of information sources for further research.

The writer has endeavored to classify the various sources by kinds and types of information desired on each phase of importing and exporting activity. Certain text books and periodicals that provide general coverage of the subject have been presented as separate classifications. However, a book, periodical, or other publication that treats only one aspect of foreign trade is included under a topic heading and not relisted with Books or Periodicals.

BIBLIOGRAPHIES

Chamber of Commerce of the United States. *Foreign Commerce Handbook: Basic Information and Guide to Sources.* 14th ed. Washington, D.C., Chamber of Commerce of the United States, 1960.

    This manual is an invaluable guide to sources of essential information on foreign trade. Brief statements outline the functions of governmental and nongovernmental organizations best qualified to render service to exporters and importers. The comprehensive annotated bibliography on foreign commerce is arranged under the following headings: bibliographical sources; reference works; books and pamphlets; economic geographies; atlases; periodicals (reviews, weekly news magazines, newsletters, and daily papers); and trade journals of three varieties—(1) general publications intended primarily for United States foreign traders, (2) general publications intended primarily for foreign markets, and (3) export publications in special fields. Other features are the names and addresses of American Chambers of Commerce abroad, of foreign embassies and legations in the United States, and, foreign Chambers of Commerce in the United States.

Chamber of Commerce of the United States. *Guide to Foreign Information Services.* Washington, D.C., Chamber of Commerce of the United States, 1961.

    Information is supplied on specific countries which includes addresses of foreign embassies in the United States, selected organizations and services relating to various areas of the world, and a bibliography of additional sources.

The International Executive. Quarterly. New York, Foundation for the Advancement of International Business Administration.

    Articles from over 200 periodicals are summarized along with reviews of current books. The selection is of material for the international executive. One of the strong sections is the reference guide to books and articles.

U.S. Department of Commerce. Bureau of Foreign Commerce. *Sources of Information on Foreign Trade Practice.* Washington, D.C., U.S. Department of Commerce, 1959. Also obtainable from Department of Commerce Field Offices.

    An extensive reading list of governmental and nongovernmental publications dealing with foreign trade comprises the bulk of this publication. Directories of foreign traders are listed as are the titles of magazines and journals that have a large foreign circulation.

U.S. Department of Commerce. Bureau of Foreign Commerce. *Guide for the Newcomer to World Trade.* Washington, D.C., U.S. Bureau of Foreign Commerce, 1957.

A clearly expressed but brief outline of the differences between foreign and domestic trade. The facilities upon which the foreign trader can draw and the agencies available to help the foreign trader are listed. Although the list of sources of foreign trade information is not intended to be comprehensive, it is a carefully selected arrangement of books, studies and other publications that are essential in gaining a fundamental knowledge of the techniques of trading abroad.

U.S. Department of Commerce. Bureau of International Commerce. *International Business Publications Checklist*. Washington, D.C., Bureau of International Commerce. Irregular.

Although this checklist is largely given over to listing publications of the U.S. Department of Commerce, it does include publications of other governmental and nongovernmental agencies which publish material on international trade.

U.S. Department of Commerce. *Low Cost Marketing Aids for Higher Export Profits, Services Available through Department of Commerce Field Offices*. Washington, D.C., U.S. Department of Commerce, 1962.

Here is a description of the various kinds of services which are available to assist foreign traders.

U.S. Department of Commerce. Business and Defense Services Administration. *Publications*. Monthly. Washington, D.C., U.S. Department of Commerce.

A number of the publications of this office carry information on world trade conditions affecting various commodities.

U.S. Tariff Commission. *Publications of the U.S. Tariff Commission*. Washington, D.C., U.S. Tariff Commission.

U.S. Congress. House. 87th Congress. House Document 598. *Free Trade, Tariff Legislation and Common Markets for the Western Hemisphere, Collection of Excerpts and Selected References*. Prepared by the Economics Division, Legislative Reference Service, Library of Congress. Washington, D.C., Superintendent of Documents, 1962.

This is a thoroughgoing study of Western Hemisphere trade and sources of information dealing with this subject.

Chamber of Commerce of the United States. *List of Publications of the Chamber of Commerce of the United States*. Annual. Washington, D.C., Chamber of Commerce of the United States.

This compilation includes a list of their publications on the general subject of foreign trade.

COMPENDIUMS

The exporter must know the regulations of the country to which he is shipping, otherwise his consignment may suffer costly delays or be returned because of improper packing. Naturally, he wants to ship via the shortest route and the most economical transportation method.

His need for a great amount of varied data, both general and specific, has resulted in the publication of three source books; two of them supply detailed information on many phases of foreign trade, and a third provides both information and suggestions as to how to utilize it.

Exporters' Encyclopaedia. Annual. New York, Thomas Ashwell & Co., Inc.

This standard handbook, revised annually and kept up to date by supplementary bulletins, gives full information on shipments to the principal countries of the world. It includes: (1) an index of ports and trade centers of the world; (2) an index by countries with information on their consular regulations, ports and trade centers, shipping routes, mail, radio and cable, telephone, exchange restrictions, money, weights, holidays, etc.; (3) a résumé of radio and cable rates, parcel post, regular and air mail, and air express regulations and rates to all parts of the world; (4) general reference tables covering weights, measures, time charts, political and geographic groups; (5) a section on foreign trade organizations in the United States; (6) lists of government agencies, consulates abroad, chambers of commerce, clubs, associations, and organizations; (7) general information about the laws and regulations affecting export trade, insurance, export terms and practice, trade-marks, etc.; (8) a description of export and shipping practices in the principal foreign countries, including customs treatment of weights, packing hints, and shipper's export declaration; (9) information about the United States' licensing system, freight forwarders, and the Webb-Pomerene law; (10) lists of steamship companies, ports of the United States, and freight forwarders in the principal United States cities.

Another useful one-volume source of information for importers and exporters is:

Custom House Guide. Annually with monthly supplements. New York, Import Publications, Inc.

The following information is listed for each port of entry: customs house brokers, freight forwarders, steamship lines and agents, stevedores, United States Customs bonded truckmen, United States Customs bonded warehouses, general warehouses, foreign consuls, chambers of commerce, port authorities; Canadian customs brokers, freight forwarders and customs bonded warehouses; foreign forwarding agents, and customs headquarters of foreign countries. It also contains the United States Customs Tariff Act with amendments, reciprocal trade agreements, the customs regulations of 1944, and parts of the Internal Revenue Code.

The following books are exceedingly helpful both for the novice in the field of foreign trade and the experienced businessman:

Henius, Frank. *Dictionary of Foreign Trade.* New York, Prentice-Hall, 1947.

This work not only explains the language of foreign trade but also reproduces documents that can be understood only by an actual reading of their contents. The Dictionary consists of four parts: (1) a table of some 3,000 English, French, Spanish, and German foreign trade abbreviations including commercial, banking, shipping, and similar terms; (2) a dictionary of more than 6,000 terms with specific how-to-do-it information on international trade practices and procedures—buying, selling, shipping, insurance, importing, exporting, chartering, forwarding, invoicing, commission, collections, customs, banking, credits, finance, communications, and many other vital foreign trade subjects; (3) a complete table of weights and measures that includes a detailed comparison of the metric-system standards with our own, plus instant conversion tables; (4) a collection of about 300 documents used currently in foreign trade, arranged alphabetically by subject.

International Trade Reporter. Loose-leaf service published by The Bureau of National Affairs, Inc., Washington, D.C.

This service provides comprehensive, well-organized information that is vital and useful. Weekly notification of trade developments and trends supplements the three loose-leaf binders that are arranged and indexed by subject matter. The service furnishes working data on export-and-import controls imposed by the United States and overseas market, tariff and tax requirements, forms of export organization, sales policies and contracts, market exploration, patents and trade-marks, transport facilities, communication, packaging and shipping, handling of overseas distributorships and other subjects.

DIRECTORIES-EXPORTERS, IMPORTERS
(DOMESTIC AND FOREIGN) AND PRODUCTS

Directories are the number one source of information for the foreign trader. Because he frequently operates as a broker, a knowledge of who buys and sells what becomes his stock in trade. The directories described here have been compiled especially to serve the foreign trade field. The suggestions given in Chapter 3 for locating pertinent information on firms and individuals should also be consulted, as well as the various directories indicated in Chapter 13, Basic Industries.

U.S. Department of Commerce. Bureau of Foreign Commerce. *Guide to Foreign Business Directories.* Washington, D.C., U.S. Bureau of Foreign Commerce, 1955.

A descriptive list of directories arranged by country, which provides information on foreign exporters, suppliers, individual business and professional men, and government officials. A very useful system of cross references indicates where material on smaller areas or dependencies may be located in larger works.

Angel, J.L. Compiler. *1961–62 Directory of American Firms Operating Abroad.* New York, World Trade Academy Press, Inc., 1962.

    More than 3,300 American business firms in foreign countries operating over 8,500 business enterprises are listed. This directory is in two parts. The first part is a list of companies under each country, and the second is an alphabetical arrangement by company. The full name and address of the company, the name of the president and the officer responsible for foreign operations, and the type of operation or products handled in the area are given.

American Register of Exporters and Importers. Annual. New York, American Register of Exporters and Importers, Inc.

    Approximately 5,000 active American export and import concerns are listed here. The information given includes names of buyers, personnel, banking connections, cable addresses, products handled, export and import markets, trade-marks, and brands. Product indexes are given in Spanish, French, and English.

Kellys' Directory of Merchants, Manufacturers and Shippers of the World—A Guide to the Export, Import, Shipping and Manufacturing Industries. 2 vols. London, Kellys' Directory, Ltd., 1886–. (See page 239 for description.)

Hitchcock's Export Sales Catalogs. Biennially. Chicago, Ill., 542 S. Dearborn St., Hitchcock Publishing Co.

    Foreign buyers and American agents who are commissioned to buy for foreign firms will find this publication useful in locating a manufacturer, dealer, or merchant because it lists the products of various manufacturers.

The directories described on page 239, *Thomas' Register of American Manufacturers* and *MacRae's Blue Book and Hendrick's Commercial Register,* also list sources of supply as do the directory references in Chapter 14, *Basic Industries.*

Buyers for Export in New York City. Annual. New York, 20 Vesey St., Thos. Ashwell and Company, Inc.

    This directory contains lists and useful information on export merchants, export commission houses, export manufacturers' agents, and resident purchasing agents for foreign companies. A supplementary list of combination export managers with the manufacturers they serve is also included.

Phelon's New York City Export Buyers List. Annual. New York, 32 Union Square, J. S. Phelon & Co.

    The export houses in New York City engaged in buying merchandise for foreign countries are listed, together with the class of merchandise bought, countries to which it is exported, and foreign firms.

Latin American Sales Index. Annual with supplements. New York, 290 Broadway, Dun & Bradstreet, Inc.

    More than 160,000 manufacturers, wholesalers, retailers, sales agents, and service organizations in the twenty-nine markets of Central and South America,

Mexico, and the West Indies appear in this publication. Capital employed in the business, kind of business, and credit rating are supplied for each one. It also lists 3,810 towns with population figures, banking connections, the nearest ports, and the economic classification of these communities. The supplements provide current statistics and information on new enterprises. This volume is extremely valuable for market research, market analyses, and direct mail advertising campaigns.

U.S. Department of Commerce. Bureau of Foreign Commerce. *A Directory of Foreign Organizations for Trade and Investment Promotion.* Washington, D.C., Superintendent of Documents, 1961.

Only organizations which have demonstrated a willingness to supply information to American inquirers are included. Government and private agencies which have proven able to supply information are included. English translations of the names of the organizations are given. Name and address of the organization, type of information supplied, and any periodicals published by it comprise each entry. The inclusion of organizations in the newer nations is especially useful.

Market Guide for Latin America. Annual with monthly supplements. New York, 253 Broadway, American Foreign Underwriters Corp.

Credit and capital ratings are supplied for 110,000 importers, exporters, and purchasing organizations in South and Central America and the Caribbean.

Market Guide for the Pacific Area. Annual with monthly supplements. New York, 253 Broadway, American Foreign Underwriters Corp.

This list of the principal business firms, importers, exporters, and purchasing organizations in Hawaii, the Philippines, American Samoa, Tahiti, Taiwan, and Korea gives the credit and capital ratings and also includes the banking facilities in these areas.

Trade Index of U.S. Manufacturers. Annual with supplements. New York, 290 Broadway, Dun & Bradstreet, Inc.

An index of over 3,000 United States manufacturers interested in import and export trade is supplied. More than 10,000 items are listed in a 22-section "Trade Index" that represents the prime industries and trading groups in the United States. One section, "Exporters and Importers," comprises some 300 nonmanufacturing representative companies that specialize in export and import trade. Whenever possible, the name of the export executive or department is included. *The Index,* prepared in English, Spanish, and Portuguese, is distributed to 40,000 leading buyers in Latin America, to acquaint them with American manufacturers and their export products.

U.S.—Far Eastern Trade Directory. Annual. New York, 154 Nassau St., 908 Tribune Bldg., U.S.—Far Eastern Trade Directory Co.

The names and addresses of United States import-export firms are arranged in this directory by states and cities. United States export manufacturers are grouped according to commodity, and their products are listed. Alphabetical lists of United States insurance companies, mail order houses, advertising agencies, steamship and airline companies are also included.

Marconi's International Register of Telegraphic and Trade Addresses. Annual. New York, 280 Broadway, Telegraphic Cable and Radio Registrations, Inc.

The cable and telegraphic addresses of registered firms are listed for all countries. A classification by trades is given.

U.S. Department of Commerce. Bureau of International Commerce. *Trade Lists.* Irregular. Washington, D.C., U.S. Department of Commerce.

In these lists the foreign firms and individuals (agents, distributors or dealers, exporters, growers, importers, manufacturers, producers, refiners, etc.) are classified by commodity and service organization. Data on the relative size of each firm, its method of operation, lines handled, number of salesmen, and territory covered, are included.

U.S. Department of State. *Congressional Directory.* Washington, D.C.

American and foreign diplomatic and consular officers are listed in this directory.

U.S. Department of State. *Diplomatic List.* Bimonthly. Washington, D.C.

The names and addresses of foreign diplomatic representatives in Washington, D.C. are given.

U.S. Department of State. *Foreign Service List.* Quarterly. Washington, D.C.

The names and addresses of American diplomatic and consular officials abroad are given in this publication.

Journal of Commerce. Daily. New York, 63 Park Row, Journal of Commerce of New York.

This newspaper lists names and addresses of business visitors from foreign countries and indicates the purpose of their visits. Occasionally it names firms desiring distributorships abroad. News items on foreign trade, insurance, and shipping, and the advance sailing schedules of steamships are also included.

Trade Opportunities with Latin America. Fortnightly. New York, 111 Broadway, Council for Inter-American Cooperation.

The names and addresses of business visitors from Latin America, with information concerning the purpose of their visit, will be found here. A list of United States firms desiring distributorships abroad is also given.

MARKET SURVEYS AND SALES PROMOTION—SOURCES OF GEOGRAPHIC AND OTHER DATA

The references discussed so far in this chapter supply factual information in a highly condensed form. Individuals who desire more detailed facts on the political, cultural, and economic development of a particular country are advised to find out if it publishes a yearbook and consult the latest available issue. Several of them are described in Chapter 1, consequently they are not repeated here. Sources of general information about foreign countries—for example, encyclopedias—have not been included here either. They are also described in Chapter 1.

Rand McNally Commercial Atlas and Marketing Guide. 94th edition, 1963. Chicago, Rand McNally & Company.

Maps of all countries and data on their areas, population, climate, and so on, are provided. Special features include a descriptive index of each country's political divisions, leading products, exports, imports, and ports of principal foreign countries; information on the United States' communication and transportation systems; postal, air, and mail information; airline distances between forty-five leading cities of the world; steamship distances between twenty-five world ports; a world time table, general index of foreign towns, cities, and their physical features; and a flight map covering the North Pacific Ocean, North Atlantic Ocean, and Eurasia.

Chisholm's Handbook of Commercial Geography. Entirely rewritten by L. Dudley Stamp and S. Carter Gilman. 17th ed. London, Longmans, 1962.

This pioneer work has been brought completely up to the present by two competent geographers. The climates of the world and their relationship to man's activities occupy the first section. This is followed by descriptions of soil, labor, transport, instruments of exchange, and individual commodities on a world-wide basis. The economics and commerce of individual countries are dealt with in detail in the bulk of the book.

Jones, C. F. and Darkenwald, G. G. *Economic Geography.* Rev. ed. New York, Macmillan, 1954.

This text, by recognized authorities on the subject of economic geography, emphasizes the occupational approach. It discusses and analyzes the various economic activities and industries of man as they are influenced by the geographical characteristics of each region, and the stage of cultural development which has been obtained. The effects of World War II and reconstruction have been incorporated in the text and the maps and statistics brought up-to-date. The content consists of ten parts: I—The Field of Economic Geography; II—The Occupations of Hunting and Fishing; III—The Forest Industries; IV—The Grazing Industries; V—The Occupation of Farming; VI—The Occupation of Mining; VII—Manufacturing; VIII—The Chemical Industry; IX—Transportation Facilities and Trade; X—Basis of International Trade.

Smith, J. R. and Phillips, N. G. *Industrial and Commercial Geography.* 4th ed. New York, Holt, 1955.

After describing commodities, the authors discuss trade routes, methods of transportation and trading centers. Climate and energy sources are examined as they influence economic development, and this section is followed by the fundamentals of an industrial society, namely, supplies and location of coal, petroleum, iron ore, copper, etc., and the industries built upon these resources. Chapters follow on agriculture, the animal industries, fisheries, leather, rubber, and textiles. Trade and trade routes are treated with great detail. The concluding chapter discusses the effect of man on geography.

Wheeler, J. H. Jr., Kostbade, J. T. and Thoman, R. S. *Regional Geography of the World*. New York, Holt, 1955.

The economics and trade of the various trading regions are discussed in detail. These regions are: Europe, the Soviet Union, Middle East, the Orient, Pacific Islands and Australia, Africa, Latin America, and Anglo-America.

U.S. Department of Commerce. Bureau of International Commerce. *Overseas Business Reports*. Washington, D.C., Bureau of International Commerce. Irregular.

These reports replaced the *World Trade Information Service* in January of 1963. It is planned to publish up to 250 of them each year. They comment on economic conditions and trade opportunities in specific countries along with digests of currency and customs regulations. This service is designed to provide foreign traders with current data on international trade.

U.S. Department of Commerce. Bureau of Foreign Commerce. Investment in various countries. *Basic Information for United States Businessmen*. Washington, D.C., Bureau of Foreign Commerce, 1956–.

Up to 1961, seventeen of these handbooks had been published. A general outline of the possibilities for investment in the country is followed by chapters of factual background of the people, their history, government, natural resources, and national income. Government regulations, position of the country in the world economy, doing business in the country, labor, monetary and fiscal policies, industry and transportation, mining, agriculture, and forest products industries are dealt with in succeeding chapters. Each handbook contains excellent statistical tables and a short bibliography. These publications contain a large amount of information on the country covered. This information is kept current by the *Overseas Business Reports* and the weekly periodical, *International Commerce*.

South American Handbook. New York, H. W. Wilson Company, 1923–.

This guide to the countries of Latin America, including South and Central America, contains information and statistics on their foreign commerce and transportation facilities.

The following directory will also be useful to the foreign trader in search of obtaining information:

U.S. Department of Commerce. Bureau of Foreign Commerce. *Directory of Foreign Advertising Agencies and Marketing Research Organizations*. Washington, D.C., U.S. Bureau of Foreign Commerce, 1959.

IMPORT AND EXPORT STATISTICS—UNITED STATES AND FOREIGN

Statistics that have been tabulated over a long period give the importer and exporter some indication of trends in foreign commodities and markets. Current figures on foreign commerce, however, have an immediate value because they may indicate pending price changes or imminent revisions of government regulations, which affect foreign trade. Because the statistical sources which follow supplement the general sources mentioned in Chapter 5, references to pages 69–75 is also suggested.

Allen, R. G. D., and Ely, J. E. *International Trade Statistics.* New York, Wiley, 1953.
> The main body of this work is an analysis of international trade statistics. The regularly issued publications which carry statistics on foreign trade are listed in the appendix. Part III has a detailed account of the statistical reporting programs of foreign countries.

U.S. Bureau of the Census. *Catalog of U.S. Foreign Trade Publications.* Washington, D.C., U.S. Bureau of the Census.
> A listing of all statistical foreign trade publications.

U.S. Bureau of the Census. *Quarterly Summary of Foreign Commerce of the United States.* Quarterly. Washington, D.C., U.S. Bureau of the Census.
> Statistics showing the quantity and value of exports and imports are given by articles for each quarter. The data cumulates in each issue and annual figures appear in the fourth quarter.

United Nations. *Direction of International Trade* (Statistical Series T). Monthly with an annual issue. New York, United Nations.
> Dollar values of imports and exports of all countries and all areas of the world are given. Also trade statistics between specific countries are reported.

The following publications may be obtained from the Bureau of the Census, U. S. Department of Commerce, Washington, D.C.:

United States Airborne Exports of Domestic and Foreign Merchandise, Commodity by Country of Destination. Monthly, with issue for calendar year.

United States Trade with Puerto Rico and with U.S. Possessions. Monthly with annual cumulation.

United States Gold and Silver Movements. Monthly and annual cumulation.

United States Foreign Trade—Total Export Trade. Monthly.

United States Foreign Trade—Total Import Trade. Monthly.

United States Foreign Trade—Export Trade by Commodity. Monthly.

United States Foreign Trade—Import Trade by Commodity. Monthly.

United States Foreign Trade—Export Trade by Country. Monthly.

United States Foreign Trade—Import Trade by Country. Monthly.

United States Foreign Trade—Export Trade by Customs District. Monthly.

United States Exports of Domestic and Foreign Merchandise: Commodity by Country of Destination. Monthly and annual.

United States Imports of Merchandise for Consumption: Commodity by Country of Origin. Monthly and annual.

Customs Information

U.S. Treasury Department. Bureau of Customs. *Customs Regulations of the United States.* Washington, D.C., Government Printing Office, 1954 ed. reprinted 1962 with loose-leaf service.

U.S. Customs regulations on Marine Inspection and Navigation are also available in this reference. The regulations and statistics under which customs officers and employees perform services for other agencies are given in the appendix, plus general reference material.

U.S. Tariff Commission. *United States Import Duties, 1962.* Washington, D.C., U.S. Tariff Commission, 1963.

Schedules of articles subject to duty and those free of duty appear in this publication. The loose-leaf arrangement makes it easy to file changes.

U.S. Department of Commerce. Bureau of the Census. *Schedule A. Statistical Classification of Commodities Imported into the United States.* Available from the Superintendent of Documents, Washington, D.C.

The entry details required by Collectors of Customs for goods imported into the United States are given in this loose-leaf pamphlet.

U.S. Department of Commerce. Bureau of the Census. *Schedule B. Statistical Classification of Domestic and Foreign Commodities Exported from the United States, Including Numerically Arranged Classification of Exports and Alphabetic Indexed Code Classification of U.S. Customs Districts and Ports (Schedule C).*

Obtainable from the Superintendent of Documents, Washington, D.C. Loose-leaf. Here is provided the specific information necessary for accurate preparation of the Shippers' Export Declaration, as required by the United States Government for statistical purposes before shipments may leave this country.

U.S. Department of Commerce. Office of Export Control. *Summary of U.S. Export Control Regulations.* Washington, D.C., U.S. Department of Commerce, 1962.

We learn what may and may not be exported to Iron Curtain countries and regulations on commodities in short supply.

U.S. Department of Commerce. *Export Control.* Quarterly. Washington, D.C., U.S. Department of Commerce.

Security export controls and short supply export controls are explained. A table shows commodities controlled for export and U.S. exports to and imports from the countries of Eastern Europe and Asiatic Soviet Bloc. This quarterly keeps information on these regulations current.

U.S. State Department. *General Agreement on Tariffs and Trade Schedules of the United States of America. Annotated to Show Countries with which Concessions were Negotiated at Geneva in 1960-61.* (Commercial Policy Series 195.) Washington, D.C., U.S. State Department, 1962.

U.S. Department of Commerce. Bureau of the Census. United States *Import Duties*

Annotated . . . including Supplementary Material for an Indefinite Period. Washington, D.C., Government Printing Office, July, 1962 (latest). Obtainable from Superintendent of Documents Office.

U.S. Tariff Commission. *Special and Administrative Provisions of the Tariff Act of 1930 as Amended, as in Effect on Dec. 1, 1960.* Loose-leaf with current changes available on a subscription basis. Obtainable from Superintendent of Documents. This publication contains the text of Title III, Special Provisions and Title IV, Administrative Provisions.

Information on foreign import, export, and shipping regulations is now published on an individual country and current basis in:

U.S. Department of Commerce. Bureau of International Commerce. *Overseas Business Reports.* Washington, D.C., U.S. Department of Commerce. Irregular.

International Commerce. Weekly. Washington, D.C., U.S. Department of Commerce, Bureau of International Commerce.

Laws, Regulations, and Treaties

American Import and Export Bulletin. Monthly. New York, Import Publications, Inc.

For reports and news items about the regulations, administrative rulings and opinions of the Bureau of Customs, Bureau of Internal Revenue, Department of Agriculture, and Department of Commerce, as they affect import and export activities, this publication is indispensable. It also has sections on import activities, foreign trade activities, special articles, and notes issued by the Department of State, steamship notes, decisions of the United States Customs Court, reports and articles by the United States Tariff Commission, and world-wide changes.

U.S. Department of Commerce. Bureau of Foreign Commerce. *Comprehensive Export Schedules.* Annual. Obtainable from the Superintendent of Documents.

This loose-leaf publication covers export control regulations and policies, with instructions, interpretations, and explanatory material. It is kept up-to-date by the supplementary *Current Export Bulletin.*

U.S. Tariff Commission. *Trade Agreement Manual; a Summary of Selected Data Relating to Trade Agreements Negotiated by the United States since 1934.* Rev. 1959. Washington, D.C., U.S. Tariff Commission, 1959.

This publication shows the number of rates reduced and bound, the volume of imports subject to reduced rates, type of commodities on which rates have been reduced, and the extent of reduction in rates of duty. A list of agreements made to date is given.

U.S. Department of State. *Treaties and Other International Acts Series.* Obtainable from the Superintendent of Documents, Washington, D.C.

This series of pamphlets contains the texts of individual treaties and agreements. They are later replaced by *Treaties and Other International Agreements Series* in bound form.

Foreign Laws, Regulations

World Trade Law Journal. Quarterly. Chicago, Ill., Commerce Clearing House, Inc.
Recent foreign legislation, interpretations of foreign rules and regulations, and other pertinent data are reported in this journal which also includes signed articles on foreign law topics.

Information concerning industrial property and its protection in foreign countries may be obtained in published form for more than thirty nations as Part 2 of the *World Trade Information Service* under the heading "Patent and Trademark Regulations (name of the country)." The information is now carried in *Overseas Business Reports* issued by the United States Department of Commerce, Bureau of International Commerce. A summary of overseas patent laws appeared in *International Commerce,* November, 1962, pages 22–25.

Financial Aspects—Credit and Collections

Persons engaged in foreign trade have their operations complicated by fluctuations in value of the monetary units. They must keep abreast constantly of the value changes of those in which they buy and sell. They usually consult the foreign exchange department of their bank for the very latest quotations bearing on a specific transaction. The large metropolitan newspapers, the *Wall Street Journal,* and the *Journal of Commerce* also publish quotations daily. Foreign exchange quotations appear monthly in the *Federal Reserve Bulletin.* Various changes in the regulations which govern monetary exchanges are announced in current supplements of the *Exporters' Encyclopedia.*

Valuable suggestions on the financing of foreign shipments are presented both in the handbooks and basic texts which have been published. The *Exporters' Encyclopedia* published by Thomas Ashwell & Co., Inc., and the *Dictionary of Foreign Trade* by Frank Henius, mentioned earlier (p. 274), deal with this aspect of foreign trade in detail.

An exporter's credit policy can make or break his business just as it does in domestic business. Time and distance are also handicapping factors—he seldom does business across the desk from his customer. Good sources of credit information are, therefore, of paramount importance to the exporters. The most important single source of credit information is the *Foreign Report* service offered to American exporters by the Foreign Division of Dun & Bradstreet. This service prepares and maintains filed reports on practically all the leading foreign customers for American goods. The foreign reports on overseas concerns are written by credit specialists in export trade who have a well-rounded knowledge of the languages and trade conditions in the countries upon which they report. Thorough, on-the-spot investigations are made of local exporters, importers, and numerous interested enterprises.

The *Latin American Sales Index,* described on page 275 and *Trade Lists,* mentioned on p. 277, also contain information useful for determining the credit risk of a prospective buyer abroad.

The National Association of Credit Management, 44 East 23rd Street, New York 10, N.Y., has a Foreign Credit Interchange Bureau to assist its members in the whole field of export trade. Their Foreign Credit Executive Department seeks to promote sound credit techniques abroad, and the Foreign Credit Interchange Bureau, under an Administrative Committee of its own members, holds monthly conferences on foreign finance, credit, collection, and exchange problems which are of great value to the members. The Foreign Department also provides members with individual credit reports on foreign buyers

Overseas units of American Chambers of Commerce give information (upon request) regarding companies in the cities where they are located.

BASIC TEXTS

Horn, P. V. *International Trade Principles and Practices.* 3d ed. Englewood Cliffs, N.J., Prentice-Hall, 1958.

> The author analyzes and appraises fundamentals underlying foreign trade from the time of the Phoenicians to reciprocal trade agreements, the rise of the common market, and current American practices. Among the subjects discussed are: historical and economic background of international trade; international commercial policies; transportation and communication facilities; international finance and foreign exchange; world and United States trade surveys; and practical procedures in exporting and importing.

Enke, S. S. and Salera V. *International Economics.* 4th ed. Englewood Cliffs, N.J., Prentice-Hall, 1959.

> This work provides an up-to-date analysis of international trade, foreign commerce, and investment, in the light of today's theories and practices. The

authors stress the following phases: trade control by means of exchange control and quotes; balance of payment analysis; exchange stabilization through the International Monetary Fund (Bretton Woods); trade policies of the Great Powers; and the general equilibrium explanation of national specialization.

Kindelberger, C. P. *Foreign Trade and the National Economy*. New Haven, Conn., Yale University Press, 1962.

The author discusses questions of what determines the nature and amount of goods which a country buys and sells in international trade, and what is the impact of foreign trade on national economic life. All aspects of foreign trade are taken up: transportation cost; natural resources; capital; technology; capacity to transform raw materials; interference with private enterprise economies; international trade under socialism; effects of growth on trade; impact of growth on trade; and the effects of trade on the economic stability, social, and political life of a country.

U.S. Department of Commerce Bureau of Foreign Commerce. *Channels for Trading Abroad*. Washington, D.C., U.S. Department of Commerce, 1954.

A concise presentation of market analyses, organization of foreign trade, methods of importing and exporting, and sources of information are given in this publication

Day, C. *History of Commerce*. New York, Longmans, Green & Co., 1938.

This well-known, authoritative textbook traces the development of commercial activities and foreign trade in various countries from ancient times to the present. The following subjects are covered: material resources, machinery and manufacturers, modes of transportation, commercial policies, exports, imports, and the internal and foreign trade of the principal countries during the various periods of history.

FOREIGN TRADE PRACTICES

MacDonald, P. *Practical Exporting and Importing*. 2d ed. New York, Ronald, 1959.

Detailed information is given on methods of preparation of goods for export, different types of credit arrangements, packing and shipping, advertising and promotion of sales abroad, and the various governmental controls.

U.S. Department of Commerce. Bureau of International Business Operations. *What You Should Know About Exporting*. Washington, D.C., U.S. Department of Commerce, 1962.

A basic reference work designed to help the American businessman get started in exporting. This booklet will aid him in opening profitable overseas markets. There is a selected list of useful references.

OVERSEAS BRANCHES

The burgeoning of the Common European Market plus exchange restrictions and raising costs at home have induced many American firms to establish branches abroad. The following books are helpful in this area:

Fenn, D. H. Jr. ed. *Management Guide to Overseas Operations.* New York, McGraw-Hill, 1957.

Experienced overseas executives discuss the prospects and problems of operating overseas branches. These include proper management, dealing with labor and with foreign government officials, and restrictions on foreign operations. The profitable opportunities of foreign operations are also brought out.

Bryson, G. D. *American Management Abroad: A Handbook for the Business Executive Overseas.* New York, Harper, 1962.

The author draws on his fifteen years of experience abroad to supply many valuable suggestions to executives going abroad to operate a business. These suggestions are both how to operate the business and how to conduct themselves.

Cleveland, H. and Mangone, G. J. *The Art of Overseasmanship.* Syracuse, N.Y., Syracuse University Press, 1957.

This book offers much sound advice as to the selection of personnel for overseas branches. The strengths and weaknesses of Americans abroad are pointed up. The difficulties which arise from temperament and reactions to a foreign environment are discussed in the selection of personnel. The policies of handling and training Americans in foreign countries are indicated. There are many excellent suggestions both for the organizations sending people abroad and for the individual going abroad to work.

Barlow, E. R. *Management of Foreign Manufacturing Subsidiaries.* Boston, Mass., Division of Research, Graduate School of Business Administration, Harvard University, 1953.

A detailed study of the operations of subsidiaries of American companies operating in Mexico. There are practical suggestions as to the organization, operation, management, and staffing of foreign subsidiaries. This information is drawn from actual operations of foreign subsidiaries in this country. Sound advice is given on the selection and training of executives to man these subsidiaries and on their management relationship with the parent company.

PERIODICALS

U.S. Department of Commerce. Bureau of International Commerce. *International Commerce.* Weekly. Obtainable from the Superintendent of Documents, Washington, D.C.

This periodical replaces *Foreign Commerce Weekly* and is designed to bring to the attention of businessmen news on the broader aspects of international trade. Contents include a roundup of commercial developments around the world, trends in overseas commerce, trade opportunities, current news on tariff changes, and other important foreign trade information. Foreign visitors to the United States and the place and dates of trade fairs are noted.

American Exporter. Monthly. New York, Johnston Publishing Co.

Articles of interest to the exporter include those on foreign trade developments, new products, and sources of supply in the United States. The reports on overseas markets, the section on world trade news (including items of interest about export organizations), national shows, and international programs, is a regular feature. Another special section presents world trade opinions, including pertinent quotations from recent comments by leaders in business and government. The many advertisements of exporters provide a listing of suppliers of various products.

American Import and Export Bulletin. Monthly. New York, Import Publications, Inc.

The bulk of the information supplied by this publication is reports on tariff changes, on port facilities, foreign trade opportunities, and notes on persons engaged in foreign trade.

Board of Trade Journal. Weekly. London, Her Majesty's Stationery Office.

British overseas trade is reported in the periodical. This covers notes and statistics on British trade in general, imports and exports, tourist trade, and balance of payments. There are also sections on trade fairs, opportunities for British traders, and import restrictions in other countries.

Brazilian Business. Monthly. Rio de Janeiro, Brazil, The American Chambers of Commerce for Brazil.

Readable articles of a general nature about business and other activities of Americans in Brazil, plus summaries of business conditions in Brazil, comprise the material in this publication.

Business International. Weekly. New York, 17-22 Vanderbilt Avenue, Haynes Publishing Co., Inc.

Short up-to-the-minute articles on business and investment activities abroad appear in the journal. "Business Radar" describes new opportunities and unfavorable developments in foreign countries. The objective of the editors is to keep those Americans doing business abroad aware of developments. The very thorough indexing makes material readily available.

Economic Survey. Weekly. Buenos Aires, Argentina, Economic Survey.

News and statistics on all phases of the economy of Argentina are published by this nongovernmental source. Here is a publication which is a good source of information on commercial activities.

Economic Review of ———. London, The Economist Intelligent Unit. Irregular.

An excellent economic survey of specific countries, some of which appear quarterly and others at less regular intervals. The brief but good analyses of politico-economic conditions are well-supported by charts and tables. Countries covered are Austria, Belgium, Luxemburg and the Congo Republic (one publication), Brazil, Central America, Ceylon, Chili, Columbia and India.

The Export Buyer. Monthly. New York, Commodity Research Bureau, Inc.

General news and articles of interest to the exporter appear in each issue. The regular features include an analysis of commodity prices; an alphabetical list of commodities offered to the export trade with the names and addresses of the suppliers; a list of commodities wanted by export buyers, giving their names, scheduled arrival and length of stay in the United States, and the products in which they are interested.

Export Trade. Weekly. New York, Thomas Ashwell & Company.

The latest news on new plants and new businesses, activities abroad, and government regulations, is followed by articles on political activities affecting foreign trade. Other information carried is news of persons engaged in foreign trade, export opportunities, foreign exchange rates, and steamship lines serving the major ports.

Far Eastern Economic Review. Weekly. Hong Kong, Far Eastern Economic Review.

This publication supplies current accounts of activities in trade, industry, finance, transportation, and public affairs in East and South Asia. It provides valuable insights into developments in these areas along with economic indicators for each country.

Foreign Information Service. Monthly. New York, First National City Bank.

Current information is available in this publication on business, finance, and commerce in a large number of countries around the world.

Foreign Tax Law Weekly Bulletin. New York 7, 170 Broadway, Foreign Tax Law Association.

The Association translates the official gazettes in French, German, Spanish, Italian, and Portuguese into English. Digests of laws and decrees affecting changes in income and social tax laws are digested and published in the *Bulletin* along with interpretive articles on these actions. Miscellaneous information includes important changes in import duties, commercial laws, and other important information; concise articles discussing the effect of certain foreign taxes on the United States Federal Tax Code; and sections of tax, commercial, or social codes previously translated at the request of members. Complete translations of codes may be obtained from the Association.

Inter American Economic Affairs. Quarterly. Washington, D.C., Inter American Economic Affairs.

The news about business and other activities including governmental policies in North and South America, is covered by this publication.

International Management. Monthly. New York, McGraw-Hill Publishing Company.

Designed to keep the manager of foreign operations abreast of what is going on in his field, this journal carries a large number of short news articles. These articles are concerned with the activities of American firms abroad and of foreign companies, foreign markets for specific products, new products coming onto the market, and marketing methods abroad.

Latin American Highlights. Quarterly. New York, Chase Manhattan Bank.

This publication contains articles on general and commodity trends in Latin American countries. It also briefly discusses political activities affecting foreign commerce.

Foreign Trade Associations

Chamber of Commerce of the United States. Foreign Commerce Department. *American Chambers of Commerce in Foreign Countries.* Washington, D.C. List available on request.

American chambers of commerce abroad usually welcome inquiries from business houses in the United States. Detailed service, however, is ordinarily provided free only to members of a chamber of commerce. Some chambers have a set schedule of charges for services rendered to nonmembers. A booklet entitled "Activities of American Chambers of Commerce Abroad" is available upon request.

Chamber of Commerce of the United States. Foreign Commerce Department. *Foreign Chambers of Commerce in the United States.* Washington, D.C. List available on request.

These organizations are in a strategic position to furnish valuable information regarding the resources, industries, and trade of the countries they represent. All render services to nonmembers, either in the form of general information or data on a specific problem. Sometimes a nominal charge is made for service rendered, but generally, service is free, since their primary aim is to improve trade relations between the United States and the country they represent.

Chamber of Commerce of the United States. Foreign Commerce Department. *Foreign Trade Departments and/or Bureaus in Chambers of Commerce Throughout the United States.* Washington, D.C. List available on request.

Chambers of Commerce in the United States that maintain foreign trade bureaus, or render specific foreign trade service, are listed together with the names of individuals that supervise foreign trade matters.

Chamber of Commerce of United States. Foreign Commerce Department. *Foreign Trade Clubs in the United States.* Washington, D.C. List available on request.

Leading United States Associations for Foreign Trade

Association of International Advertising Agencies, 405 Lexington Avenue, New York 17, N.Y

This organization includes the leading advertising agencies engaged in promoting American products abroad. It provides an interchange of ideas among the members and strives to improve the methods of advertising abroad.

Bankers Association for Foreign Trade. First National Bank Building, Dallas, Texas.

United States banks are regular members of this association, although foreign banks may be elected to associate membership. The object of the organization is to exchange ideas and experiences in the banking and foreign trade field; to promote public interest in, and legislation on, these subjects; and to standardize foreign trade banking practices.

Chamber of Commerce of the United States, 1615 H Street, N.W., Washington 6, D.C.

Membership consists of more than 2,400 local chambers of commerce, trade associations and United States chambers of commerce abroad, with broad underlying membership of over 1,000,000 business enterprises. Its Foreign Commerce Department maintains close liaison with official agencies. The objectives of the organization are to keep chamber members informed as to developments in the field of foreign trade; to crystallize their views in the form of policy declarations; to promote foreign trade via publications and the sponsoring of National Foreign Trade Week. It issues a booklet of foreign commerce declarations representing views of American business. The organization is actively interested in international developments, political and social as well as economic, and in the work of the United Nations. At the annual meeting of the Chamber, the members discuss current foreign trade problems. Various other departments of the Chamber also have interests in matters of foreign commerce. The volume of correspondence on specific problems of foreign trade is large.

Local chambers of commerce in the larger cities usually maintain foreign trade bureaus which render useful services. American chambers in foreign countries, for which the National Chamber acts as a clearing house, likewise offer valuable export and import services to members and others.

There are export associations of the producers of commodities such as American Machine Tool Export, California Dried Fruit Export, etc., registered under the Webb-Pomerene Export Act. These organizations handle the mechanics of the export of their products and are also a source of information within their limited scope.

Commercial Museum, 34th Street below Spruce, Philadelphia, Pa.

This nonprofit institution, supported in part by public funds, is devoted to the promotion of international commerce of the United States. It performs a wide variety of services, including maintenance of exhibits of commercial products from all parts of the world, issuance of *Commercial America* (in English and Spanish), and other publications. The Museum also maintains credit information files and its Foreign Trade Bureau supplies information on all phases of exporting.

International Executives Association, 93 Worth Street, New York 13, N.Y.

Formerly the Export Managers Club, the membership of this national organization is confined to export executives. Its purpose is to facilitate the interchange of ideas and opinions on matters of international trade. Reports of its frequent meetings which are held for discussion of foreign trade policies and practices are published, and a questionnaire service is maintained for the benefit of members. The "Annual Get-Together" is a significant event. International Executives Associations of cities other than New York render similar services to their membership.

Foreign Credit Interchange Bureau, 44 East 23rd Street, New York 10, N.Y.

The foreign arm of the National Association of Credit Men, this bureau keeps current files on the capitalization and credit ratings of firms all over the world.

National Association of Manufacturers, 2 East 48th Street, New York 17, N.Y.

All classes of manufacturers belong to NAM. The association's Committee on International Economic Relations is concerned with major economic matters such as problems and proposals considered by the Economic and Social Council of the United Nations, the International Trade Organization, and all the international economic conferences and special economic committees which may be set up by the United Nations.

National Council of American Importers, 111 Fifth Avenue, New York 3, N.Y.

This specialized organization of importers renders a variety of services to members, especially assistance on regulatory matters. It issues a *Members' Service Bulletin* and *Current Information Bulletin.*

16

A BASIC BOOKSHELF

Business publications, like machines and methods, are subject to obsolescence. In building up either a personal library or a business one for ready reference, it is advisable to select only those titles which provide basic facts. These can be supplemented by the information that is published in business magazines and pamphlets. The works suggested in the following list do give essential coverage and they should prove valuable to a great number and variety of businesses. However, since the suggested grouping will not remain useful unless it is kept up to date, methods for so doing are also described.

This list has been assembled with three assumptions in mind: first, that the user subscribes to his local newspaper; second, that he receives regularly the trade publications on his particular type of business; and third, that, as he becomes better informed on his particular field of activity, he will read and/or buy books on the subject.

Because words are used so loosely and inaccurately today, the first purchase should be a good dictionary. It is unnecessary to be burdened with the bulk and expense of an unabridged dictionary—the abridged versions of either *Webster's New International Dictionary* or *Funk & Wagnall's New Standard Dictionary* will suffice. The collegiate abridgments are the most satisfactory as they contain more words than do some of the others. Although the choice is largely a matter of the one to which the user has become accustomed, the following work is recommended by the author.

Funk & Wagnall's College Standard Dictionary of the English Language. New York, Funk & Wagnalls Company, 1953.

In addition to the spelling, pronunciation, and definition of words, this dictionary contains a gazeteer which gives population figures of the United States, foreign countries, and ranking cities. Definitions of foreign phrases commonly used in English are another useful feature.

Because the need for a variety of miscellaneous facts and statistics arises every day in business, this work is also essential:

New York World-Telegram. *The World Almanac and Book of Facts.* New York, New York World-Telegram. Annually.

Tables of statistics on all types of human activity, résumés of new laws, a chronology of events, and other information make this publication a time-saver.

Since statistics are a vital tool of business, some standard sources should be on hand at all times.

U.S. Bureau of the Census. *Statistical Abstract of the United States.* Washington, D.C., Government Printing Office. Annually.

The cumulation of a large proportion of the statistics prepared by the federal government can be found in this volume. Most of them extend over a long period of years.

National Industrial Conference Board. *The Economic Almanac.* New York, Newsweek, Inc. Annually.

Information and statistics which are not found in the *Statistical Abstract* often can be located in this publication. Statistics and indices are, in some instances more up to date. The "Glossary of Selected Terms" defines terms in current use.

Survey of Current Business. Monthly. Washington, D.C., U.S. Superintendent of Documents, Government Printing Office.

The *Survey* analyzes current business conditions and supplies current statistics which supplement contents of the two works above.

Many business practices are commonly referred to and accepted by businessmen as a matter of course. However, when it comes to knowing the correct practice for a board of directors to observe, the type of insurance to carry, or the proper collection methods to use it is often difficult to locate exact information on approved procedures. A general handbook has been prepared to meet these situations.

Brown, Stanley M. and Doris, Lillian, eds. *Business Executive's Handbook*. 4th ed. New York, Prentice-Hall, 1953.
> Written clearly and with a minimum of technical detail, this handbook provides the answers to many perplexing questions. Particularly good material can be found on correspondence and sales letters. The presentation is so easily understood that even the office boy can refer to this book with profit.

A person using the books mentioned in this chapter cannot expect to become an expert in the many specialized fields of business activity. Nevertheless, from time to time he will be called upon to know something about procedures beyond the range of his own particular job. The following handbooks will enable him to gain sufficient knowledge (with the minimum expenditure of time and effort) to understand these operations in a general way. Because the works have been described in detail earlier, and because the titles are self-explanatory, they will merely be listed here.

Aspley, J. C., ed. *The Salesmanagers' Handbook*. 8th ed. Chicago, Dartnell Corporation, 1959.

Bogen, J. I., and others, ed. *The Financial Handbook*. 3d rev. ed. New York, Ronald, 1957.

Carson, G. B., ed. *Production Handbook*. 2d ed. New York, Ronald, 1958.

Lasser, J. K., ed. *Business Management Handbook*. 2d ed. New York, McGraw-Hill, 1960.

Wixon, R., ed. *Accountant's Handbook*. 4th ed. New York, Ronald, 1956.

Yoder, D., and others. *Handbook of Personnel and Labor Relations*. New York, McGraw-Hill, 1958.

Business and business conditions change so rapidly that subscription to some of the business magazines is essential in order to keep up to date on trends and new developments. *The Survey of Current Business* has already been cited for its statistical content and articles on general business conditions. The two periodicals mentioned below also provide broad coverage of the business world.

Business Week. Weekly. New York, 330 W. 42d Street, McGraw-Hill Publishing Company.
> Discussions of broader aspects of business plus accounts of various industries, firms, and business personalities are featured in each issue. A page of business indicators mirror business trends. The magazine is a valuable source of timely information on what is doing in the world of business.

Barron's. Weekly. New York, 40 New Street, Barron's Publishing Co., Inc.

Financial news bulks largest in this magazine, but the analysis of current economic situations is splendid. It is a good source for the past week's New York Exchange stock and bond quotations.

The field of labor has become so important that every businessman should keep posted on its activities and trends. This can be done best by regular reading of the following monthly:

Monthly Labor Review. Washington 25, D.C., U.S. Bureau of Labor Statistics. (Send subscriptions to U.S. Superintendent of Documents, Government Printing Office, Washington 25, D.C.)
The best sources of labor news, cost-of-living statistics, and check lists of articles and books on labor are found in this periodical.

A useful periodical for keeping up with new publications in all fields of business is prepared and issued by the Newark, New Jersey, Public Library

Business Literature. Monthly. Newark, N.J., Public Library of Newark, N.J., Business Branch, 34 Commerce Street.
The short annotations indicate quite adequately the content of the books, pamphlets, and magazines listed.

The immensely valuable publications of the federal government can be located by using the *U.S. Government Publications Monthly Catalog,* U.S. Superintendent of Documents, Government Printing Office, Washington 25, D.C.

The U.S. Superintendent of Documents' *Price Lists* are another short cut for locating the issuer of federal government documents. These lists are issued at least annually and contain a description of all federal government publications that are in stock. The list most useful for businessmen is *Commerce and Manufactures, Price List 62,* Washington, D.C., U.S. Superintendent of Documents, Government Printing Office. It is issued annually and is free.

THE BASIC BOOKSHELF

Aspley, J. C., ed. *The Salesmanager's Handbook.* 8th ed. Chicago, Dartnell Corporation, 1959.
Bogen, J. I. et al, eds. *The Financial Handbook.* 3d rev. ed. New York, Ronald, 1957.
Brown, S. M. and Doris, Lillian eds. *Business Executives' Handbook.* 4th rev. ed. Englewood Cliffs, N.J., Prentice-Hall, 1953.

Carson, G. B., ed. *Production Handbook.* 2d ed. New York, Ronald, 1958.
Funk & Wagnalls' College Standard Dictionary of the English Language. New York, Funk & Wagnalls Company, 1953.
Lasser, J. K., ed. *Business Management Handbook.* 2d ed. New York, McGraw-Hill, 1960.
*National Industrial Conference Board. The Economic Almanac. New York, The National Industrial Conference Board. Annually.
*New York World-Telegram. *The World Almanac and Book of Facts.* New York, New York World-Telegram. Annually.
*U.S. Bureau of the Census. *Statistical Abstract of the United States.* Washington, D.C., Government Printing Office. Annually.
*U.S. Superintendent of Documents. *Commerce and Manufactures, Price List 62.* Washington, D.C., U.S. Superintendent of Documents. Annually.
Wixon, R. ed. *Accountant's Handbook.* 4th ed. New York, Ronald, 1956.
Yoder, D. and others. *Handbook of Personnel and Labor Relations.* New York, McGraw-Hill, 1958.

Magazines

Barron's. Weekly. New York, 40 New Street, Barron's Publishing Co., Inc.
Business Literature. Monthly. Newark, N.J., 34 Commerce Street, Public Library of Newark, N.J., Business Branch.
Business Week. Weekly, New York, 330 W. 42d Street, McGraw-Hill Publishing Company.
Monthly Labor Review. U.S. Bureau of Labor Statistics. Washington 25, D.C. (Send subscriptions to U.S. Superintendent of Documents, Government Printing Office, Washington, D.C.)
Survey of Current Business. Monthly. Washington, D.C., U.S. Superintendent of Documents, Government Printing Office.
U.S. Government Publications Monthly Catalog. Washington, D.C., U.S. Superintendent of Documents, Government Printing Office.

Book reviews should be consulted, of course, to keep your basic bookshelf current and to know what is published in various business fields. Many trade magazines review new business literature that is within the scope of their particular field. The best approach to this problem is to use the publications which present numerous reviews from a variety of periodicals. The two compilations that follow are especially helpful for businessmen.

The Book Review Digest. Monthly with semi-annual and annual cumulations. N.Y., H. W. Wilson Company, 1905-.

---

* Annual purchase or subscription

Short digest of reviews which appear in seventy-nine scholarly, technical, and general interest publications are presented in this work. Such well known reviewing periodicals as the *Saturday Review of Literature* and the *New York Times Book Review* are included as a matter of course. Usually more than one review is digested for each book, and whether the review is favorable or unfavorable is indicated. The coverage is very broad and does not always include highly technical new books.

Technical Book Review Index. Monthly. New York, 31 East 10th Street, Special Libraries Association.

Digests of book reviews of scientific, technical, and business books are published without comment. This is a good place to get an evaluation of the more technical books. It is too specialized to carry many reviews of general business books.

Two journals are notable for the quality of their book reviews on social science topics, especially in the fields of economics and political science. Reviews from both of them appear in the *Book Review Digest*, but is is often worthwhile to read the complete reviews. Recognized authorities on given subjects prepare the longer reviews.

American Economic Review. Five times per year. Evanston, Ill., American Economic Association, Northwestern University.

Although the books reviewed tend to be concerned with the theoretical side of economics and business, nevertheless many are included that have a direct bearing on business. The lists of new titles and articles in periodicals are also very useful.

The Annals of the American Academy of Political and Social Science. Bimonthly. Philadelphia, Pa., 3457 Walnut Street, American Academy of Political and Social Science.

The reviews are shorter and concerned with books of a more general nature than those reviewed in the work above. Because the publication is issued more frequently, the reviews are available sooner than those in the *American Economic Review*.

Periodicals that contain numerous, more critical reviews in specific fields are as follows:

ACCOUNTING

The Accounting Review. Quarterly. Menasha, Wis., American Accountancy Association.

Journal of Accountancy. Monthly. New York, 13 East 41st Street, American Institute Publishing Company.

Advertising and Selling

Printers' Ink. Weekly. New York, 205 East 42d Street, Printers' Ink Publishing Company, Inc.
Sales Management. Semimonthly. New York, 630 Third Avenue, Sales Management, Inc.

Of these two, *Sales Management* is usually the most regular and best source of book reviews.

Labor

Monthly Labor Review. Washington, D.C., U.S. Bureau of Labor Statistics.

Management

Advanced Management. Quarterly. New York, 84 William Street, The Society for the Advancement of Management.
The Management Review. Monthly. New York, 330 West 42d Street, American Management Association.

Marketing

The Journal of Marketing. Menasha, Wis., American Marketing Association.
Sales Management. Semimonthly. New York, 630 Third Avenue, Sales Management, Inc.

Personnel and Industrial Relations

Personnel. Bimonthly. New York, 330 West 42d Street, American Management Association.

Other trade publications carry book reviews, but the majority of them are so brief that they are little more than book notices.

The *Basic Bookshelf* represents the minimum equipment for an individual or a very small business firm. After a period of usage there comes the realization that these informational resources must be expanded.

Frequently, the first step is to have a secretary route the incoming magazines to various members of the firm. This service can be expanded and the time of executives saved if periodicals are first scanned and articles of interest to a particular executive immediately brought to his attention. Books, magazines, and pamphlets tend to become lost within the organization unless some provision is made for recording them and controlling their use. Too often valuable information is buried in a corner of some department and additional copies of an expensive, technical work are bought by several departments each acting independently of the other.

To utilize effectively all sources of information, all reference materials should be arranged in a central, convenient place and one person made responsible for their care. Some simple arrangement whereby the material can be easily located, perhaps a simple alphabetical system by author and title, may be sufficient. Each time a book or magazine is removed, a notation should be made of the item borrowed and the borrower.

It is wise to work out some scheme of classification when the collection is still rather small. This has two advantages: it makes the material more readily accessible, and it is easier and cheaper to classify the collection when it is small.

When the collection begins to assume the proportions of a library the services of a trained librarian are practically imperative. A trained librarian can increase significantly the usefulness of a library. Adequate cataloging and indexing of the library's resources obviously speeds up the location of a needed source. The training and knowledge of where and how to locate information makes the librarian of an immense assistance to busy executives. Furthermore, the alert librarian anticipates their needs by calling their attention to pertinent articles and acquiring information and books in advance.

A trained librarian responsible for the informational and research resources in a firm's library can result in a dollars-and-cents saving to that firm. The services performed: immediate routing of material to the executive who most needs it; issuance of bulletins and abstracts of important articles and their prompt circulation among the staff; and the automatic supplying of each executive with current material in his particular field—all represent a very substantial saving of valuable executive time. The time saved multiplied by the salaries of the executives concerned represents a significant saving. This does not take into account, either, the additional saving to the concern that may result because of information provided by the librarian.

To summarize, the steps in setting up a company library are as follows:

1. Collect all books, magazines, and pamphlets in one central place.
2. Place someone, preferably a trained librarian in charge. This person should be made responsible for the circulation of the material.

3. Classify and arrange the material so that it may be located and used easily.

4. Work out a routing system so that each executive will receive current material in his field.

5. Use bulletins and abstracts of important articles to acquaint the company's staff with the resources of the collection.

This represents the minimum and very mechanical set-up of a company library. In the hands of a trained librarian, the value and usefulness to the firm of the materials in the collection will be multiplied many times over.

Since writing the above suggestions for the establishment of a company library, there has come to hand a publication of the Special Association which has issued a brochure on the planning and equipping the library. This publication is C. M. Lewis, Ed., *Special Libraries: How To Plan And Equip Them,* (SLA Monograph No. 2), Special Libraries Association, 1963. Planning procedures and structural and space requirements are discussed followed by information on the utilization of confined space, the flow process chart, wood and metal furniture, and copying and microphotographic equipment. There are chapters on how to move the library and how to establish a small technical library. Ten case histories of special libraries complete with lay-outs and illustrations make the previous chapters more intelligible. The annotated bibliography compiled by Gertrude Schutze, Chief Librarian of Union Carbide Research Institute, brings together citations on all aspects of the building which are useful to librarians. The directory of manufacturers and suppliers along with their addresses is another most helpful feature of this work.

INDEX

322   INDEX

Pigors, P., co-author, *Personnel Administra-
tion*, 184, 200
Pit and Quarry, 247
Pit and Quarry Handbook, 247
Pitcher, Robert M., *Practical Accounting for
Oil Producers*, 148
*Plant and Equipment Expenditures of United
States Business*, 99
Plant Location (annual), 168, 174
Plant Location, by Yaseen, 168, 174
Plant Purchasing Directory, 39, 46
Plasterers and Cement Mason, The, 247
Plowman, E. G., co-author, *Business Organ-
ization and Management*, 164–165, 172
Plum, L. N., *Investing in American In-
dustry*, 92–93, 107
Political Science, United States Government
Price List, 18
Polk's Bankers Encyclopedia, 86, 105, 109
Polk's Bankers Information Bulletin, 86, 109
Polk's Bankers Information Service, 86, 109
*Polk's Directory of the Chemical and Oil
Industries*, 250
Poor's Register of Directors and Executives,
43, 45, 47
    Geographical Section, 43, 47
*Popular Guide to Government Publications,
A*, 21, 32
Population Index, 55, 58
Potter, N., co-author, *Trends in Natural
Resource Commodities*, 236
Potts, James E., *Bank Accounting and Audit
Control*, 146
Practical Accounting for Oil Producers, 148
Practical Builder, 245
Practical Business Statistics, 64, 79
Practical Exporting and Importing, 285
Practical Financial Statement Analysis, 93,
105, 107
Practical Public Relations, 231, 235
Practice of Management, 166, 173
Practice of Unionism, The, 188, 199
Praeger, Frederick A., *The Yearbook of
World Affairs*, 5
Prasow, P., *The Management of Personnel
and Labor Relations*, 184–185, 200
*Prentice-Hall Accountants Weekly News
Letter*, 142, 149

Prentice-Hall Capital Adjustments Service,
105
*Prentice-Hall Employee Relations Guide and
Arbitration*, 193, 200
Prentice-Hall Federal Bank Service, 84
Prentice-Hall Federal Tax Course, 142, 149
Prentice-Hall Federal Tax Guide, 142, 149,
150
Prentice-Hall History of Money and Credit,
83, 108
*Prentice-Hall Installment and Conditional
Sales Service*, 84
Prentice-Hall Labor Course, 192, 200
Prentice-Hall Labor Guide, 192, 200
Prentice-Hall Labor Service, 193, 201
Prentice-Hall Payroll Service, 143, 149,
150
*Prentice-Hall Pension and Profit Sharing Serv-
ice*, 194, 201
*Prentice-Hall Personnel Policies and Prac-
tices*, 191–192, 201
Prentice-Hall Real Estate Service, 118, 131
Prentice-Hall Sales Tax Service, 144, 149,
150
Prentice-Hall Securities Regulation Service,
104
Prentice-Hall Social Security Tax Service,
149, 150
Prentice-Hall State and Local Tax Service,
143–144, 150
*Prentice-Hall Trade Regulation Edition of
the Labor Guide*, 217, 225
*Prentice-Hall Union Contracts and Collective
Bargaining Service*, 194, 201
*Prentice-Hall Wills, Trusts and Estates
Service*, 84–85
Preparing for Collective Bargaining, 189–190,
198
Present Day Banking, 82, 108
Price List 36—Government Periodicals, 22,
32
Price Lists, 18, 30, 33, 180
Price Lists of Government Publications, 19,
33
Princeton University, Industrial Relations
Section, publications, 177–178, 197
*Principles of Accounting—Intermediate, Ad-
vanced*, 137, 146